SAGE was founded in 1965 by Sara Miller McCune to support the dissemination of usable knowledge by publishing innovative and high-quality research and teaching content. Today, we publish over 900 journals, including those of more than 400 learned societies, more than 800 new books per year, and a growing range of library products including archives, data, case studies, reports, and video. SAGE remains majority-owned by our founder, and after Sara's lifetime will become owned by a charitable trust that secures our continued independence.

Los Angeles | London | New Delhi | Singapore | Washington DC | Melbourne

ADVANCE PRAISE

Globalization is about sourcing capital and other resources from where it is cheapest; sourcing talent from where the best is available; producing where it is most efficient; and selling where the markets are, without being constrained by national boundaries. To be a successful manager and to be a successful corporation it is necessary to be global in mindset, strategizing and actions. *Smartonomics* prepares a manager who wants to succeed in this globalized world. It is a must-read book.

N.R. Narayana Murthy, Founder – Infosys Limited

Economics isn't everyone's cup of tea. But Smartonomics should certainly be. This book is a must read to understand how organizations can navigate their way in the uncertain times that we are all besieged by. The tools provided are simple, yet profound. It's an excellent mind opener!

Rajiv Gupta, VP – Marketing & Strategy, Honda Cars India and alumnus, Harvard Business School

Maital and Seshadri bring together unique insights by combining contrarian logic and challenging the status quo with fact-based analyses and unique but simple to use tools. A must-read and a must-use.

Rajendra Srivastava, Dean – Indian School of Business

Sure, Management is an art ... but, Art also requires tools! A must-read book to help managers with 8 handy tools in a VUCA world.

Peeyush Gupta, Vice President – Steel (Marketing & Sales), Tata Steel

This exceptionally well written and informative book provides deep insight about global market place and associated risks. It provides powerful tools to global managers to handle risk and uncertainty. Must-read for every manager.

Janat Shah, Director – IIM Udaipur

SMARTONOMICS

SMARTONOMICS

Simple, Powerful Macroeconomic Tools For Success in an Uncertain World

Shlomo Maital
D.V.R. Seshadri

Los Angeles | London | New Delhi
Singapore | Washington DC | Melbourne

Copyright © Shlomo Maital and D.V.R. Seshadri, 2017

All rights reserved. No part of this book may be reproduced or utilized in any form or by any means, electronic or mechanical, including photocopying, recording, or by any information storage or retrieval system, without permission in writing from the publisher.

First published in 2017 by

SAGE Publications India Pvt Ltd
B1/I-1 Mohan Cooperative Industrial Area
Mathura Road, New Delhi 110 044, India
www.sagepub.in

SAGE Publications Inc
2455 Teller Road
Thousand Oaks, California 91320, USA

SAGE Publications Ltd
1 Oliver's Yard, 55 City Road
London EC1Y 1SP, United Kingdom

SAGE Publications Asia-Pacific Pte Ltd
3 Church Street
#10-04 Samsung Hub
Singapore 049483

Published by Vivek Mehra for SAGE Publications India Pvt Ltd, typeset in 11/13 pt ITC New Baskerville by Zaza Eunice, Hosur, Tamil Nadu, India and printed at Saurabh Printers Pvt Ltd, Greater Noida.

Library of Congress Cataloging-in-Publication Data Available

ISBN: 978-93-860-6236-9 (PB)

SAGE Team: Sachin Sharma, Sudeshna Nandy and Shobana Paul

*For the next generation of global managers,
who will serve humanity*
— Shlomo Maital

*To our granddaughters, Yamini, Eshani and Akshara, and all
children of the world of their generation, who represent the hope of
the future to make the world a better place!*
— D.V.R. Seshadri

Thank you for choosing a SAGE product!
If you have any comment, observation or feedback,
I would like to personally hear from you.

Please write to me at **contactceo@sagepub.in**

Vivek Mehra, Managing Director and CEO, SAGE India.

Bulk Sales

SAGE India offers special discounts
for purchase of books in bulk.
We also make available special imprints
and excerpts from our books on demand.

For orders and enquiries, write to us at

Marketing Department
SAGE Publications India Pvt Ltd
B1/I-1, Mohan Cooperative Industrial Area
Mathura Road, Post Bag 7
New Delhi 110044, India

E-mail us at **marketing@sagepub.in**

Get to know more about SAGE

Be invited to SAGE events, get on our mailing list.
Write today to **marketing@sagepub.in**

This book is also available as an e-book.

CONTENTS

LIST OF TABLES	ix
LIST OF FIGURES	xi
LIST OF BOXES	xiii
ACKNOWLEDGMENTS	xv
INTRODUCTION	xvii
1. A COUNTRY IS A BUSINESS	1
2. ANTS AND GRASSHOPPERS: ANALYZING NATIONAL SAVING	24
3. 'FLATION: IT'S LIKE CHOLESTEROL (GOOD AND BAD)	56
4. MONEY: WHAT IT IS, WHAT IT DOES	86
5. BOOMS AND BUSTS: WHAT COMES NEXT?	114

6. TORRENTS OF CAPITAL — 140
7. THE GAP — 171
8. MINING FOR OPPORTUNITIES — 195

EPILOGUE — 221

INDEX — 229

ABOUT THE AUTHORS — 233

LIST OF TABLES

1.1	GDP and Components: US 2015, 4th Quarter, Annual Rate $ Billion (Inflation Adjusted at Constant 2009 Prices)	15
1.2	GDP: The World's 10 Largest Economies, 2014 ($ Billion) and Their Contribution to World GDP (%)	17
1.3	World GDP Growth (%), 2006–15	18
2.1	Historical Gross Savings Rates, 10 Countries, as a Percentage of GNP: Pre- and Post-World War II	32
2.2	Gross Capital Formation and Gross Domestic Saving as a Percentage of GDP, Israel and Selected Nations, 2013	36
2.3	Gross and Net Investment as a Percentage of GDP, 2004 and 2005 ($ Million)	41
2.4	Net Investment, Net Saving, and Foreign Borrowing: US, China, 2005	44
2.5	30 Globally Competitive Nations with Highest GDP Per Capita: GDP Per Capita, Domestic Saving/GDP, Gross Capital Formation/GDP, GDP Growth	46
3.1	Consumer Price Inflation: Selected Countries, May or June 2016 (Annual %)	59

3.2	Two Inflationary Forces	80
4.1	Money Supply, Velocity, Price Index and Real GDP: Economic Momentum, 2008–14	104
4.2	Percent Change in M, V, P, and Q, 2008–14	105
5.1	Number and Duration of Business Cycles, US, 1854–2007	130
8.1	India: Velocity of Money (M1), 2006–14 (Billions of Rupees)	209

LIST OF FIGURES

I.1	TOWS Matrix	xxxi
1.1	The Economic Center of Gravity of the Earth, AD 1 to AD 2025	6
1.2	World Economic Forum: Global Risk Landscape 2016	8
1.3	IMF World Growth Forecasts, 2011–16	19
2.1	US Net Savings as a Percentage of GDP (Gross National Income), 1947–2010	43
2.2	GDP Per Capita as a Function of Domestic Saving/GDP, 30 Nations	48
2.3	Global Wealth, 1980–2006	49
3.1	Demand-side and Supply-side Inflation	67
3.2	Dow Jones 30-Industrial Stock Average, 1930–2010: Unadjusted for Inflation	77
3.3	Dow Jones Industrial Average, Divided by the CPI: 1950–2012	78
4.1	Snapshot Data for Each of the Three Definitions of "Money" for the US, as of December 31, 2015	89
4.2	Economic Momentum: Money Times Velocity	97
4.3	The Impact of the Decline in Velocity: 4th Quarter 2008	98

4.4	Velocity of Money (V), US, 1960–2014	107
4.5	Federal Reserve Short-term Interest Rates, United States, 1953–2009	108
5.1	US Trade Deficit and Budget Deficit, 1980–2006	137
6.1	US Money Supply, 2006–16	143
6.2	World GDP Growth, 2010–15, and Sources of Growth	145
6.3	Short-term Interest Rates in the US, UK, Eurozone, and Japan, 1990–2015	147
6.4	Crude Oil Prices, 2006–15	151
6.5	Big Mac Index: Percent Currencies are Overvalued (+) or Undervalued (–) Relative to the US Dollar, January 2016	158
7.1	Share of Global Wealth: Top 1 Percent and Bottom 99 Percent	175
7.2	Global Wealth, 1980–2006	176
7.3	National Capital as a Percentage of National Income, Europe, 1870–2010	178
7.4	Cumulative Distribution of Income from Capital (Lorentz Curve), 1979 and 2007	179
7.5	Global Total Private Wealth, $ Trillion (2012–19) (Annual Growth Rates in Circles)	186
8.1	India Annual GDP Growth Rate, 2012–16	207
8.2	India: Balance of Trade (Exports Minus Imports), 2012–16	207
8.3	India: Government Budget Deficit as a Percentage of GDP 2006–16	208
8.4	India: Government Debt as Percentage of GDP 2006–14	208
8.5	India: Interest Rates 2012–16	210
8.6	India: Ease of Doing Business: Rank	210
8.7	India: Global Competitiveness Ranking	211
8.8	India: Corruption Perception Ranking	211
8.9	India: Rupees Per US Dollar: Official Exchange Rate	212

LIST OF BOXES

I.1	BREXIT: Britain's Exit from the European Union	xxiii
1.1	The Checklist Manifesto	3
1.2	Global Trends Roadmap 2015	9
1.3	How GDP was Invented	20
2.1	How Much Do *You* Save	27
2.2	The Tragedy of Greece	29
2.3	The Impending Meltdown: Eight Causes	34
3.1	Understanding Cholesterol—and 'Flation	57
3.2	The Dow Jones Industrial Average (DJIA)	76
4.1	FOMC	91
4.2	The Crucial Role of Velocity and Momentum	96
5.1	"We Won't Do It Again"	117
5.2	Consumer Sentiment	128
6.1	How Economists Got It Wrong—Again!	152
6.2	$9 Billion Loss	166
7.1	Reverse Innovations: From the Bottom to the Top	183
7.2	Internet of Everything	190
8.1	Survival	198

LIST OF BOXES

1.1	BREXIT: Britain Exits from the European Union	xxiii
1.2	The Chuckles Mongers	2
1.3	Global Invoice Failure Dollars	6
1.4	How GDP was Lost	9
2.1	How Much Inequality?	22
2.2	The Tragedy to Society	24
2.3	The Importance of a Clean Right Curve	21
3.1	Understanding the Two-Legend Charts	27
3.2	The Dow Jones Industrial Average (DJI)	30
4.1	FOMC	41
4.2	The Central Role of Markets and Economies	46
5.1	"We Won't Do It Again"	117
5.2	Consumer Confidence	128
6.1	How Economies Start Growing Again	142
6.2	\$9 Billion Loss	160
7.1	Reserve Innovations from the Bottom Line Up	163
	Journal of Everything	170
8.1	Survival	198

ACKNOWLEDGMENTS

I would like to thank my friend, philosopher, guide and co-author, Prof. Shlomo Maital of Israel. Our friendship has blossomed over the last fifteen years and withstood the distances of time and space. Gratitude to Prema, my better half, who has endured my idiosyncrasies for three and a half decades and still continues to bet on me through her unflinching love! And to our daughters, Divya and Nitya, our sons-in-law Narayana and Aditya, and our three grandchildren, who have given immense meaning to our lives. I would like to offer my profound gratitude to Prof. Mithileshwar Jha, who put me on the academic track some sixteen years ago, when I was going through several basic existential issues. I would also like to thank several friends at IIM Bangalore, as well as Prof. Rishi Krishnan (IIM Indore) and Prof. Janat Shah (IIM Udaipur), who have encouraged me along the academic path. And finally, I offer my sincere gratitude to my new academic home, Indian School of Business, Hyderabad, India; its Dean, Prof. Raj Srivastava; and Senior Associate Dean, Prof. Sridhar Seshadri, as well as to my wonderful colleagues at ISB for believing in me and giving me space to grow.

D.V.R. Seshadri

A chance meeting, and an instant 'click,' began years of fruitful collaboration with Seshadri, who brought his deep spirituality and moral compass to our work together. I am grateful to my university, Technion–Israel Institute of Technology, whose president granted me early retirement, enabling me to focus on writing books, and to the S. Neaman Institute for National Policy Research, which offers me a stimulating environment to write. Thanks to our talented and creative editor, Sachin Sharma, who first suggested the title for our book and guided its direction with sure hands. I would also like to thank Fran Orford for the cartoon illustrations in this book (www.francartoons.com). And as always, I am thankful to my country Israel, where creative ideas and innovation thrive.

Shlomo Maital

INTRODUCTION

Smartonomics: [*smart-uh-noh´-mics*]—*the insightful use of simple, powerful macroeconomic tools, to identify and capture global business opportunities for creating value in a chaotic uncertain world.*

Smart managers create opportunities from risks that clever managers avoid and flee from.

—Folk saying

What is Smartonomics? Why is it so crucial in these turbulent and uncertain times? Why does every global manager need to understand the basic ideas of Smartonomics and how to use them daily?

In today's global village, every manager is a global manager. Even if your business is putatively "local," with no sales abroad, you still probably face various sorts of competition from competitors in other countries. John Donne's famous poem written in 1624 warns that "no man is unto himself an island"—nor is any business, however local. Even if you own and run a hair salon, and haircuts cannot be imported, tomorrow a competitor may open on the opposite side of the street with a winning business concept imported from abroad. No hair salon is an island.

Paris-based Hommage has been setting up high-end men's grooming stations in existing salons such as Paul Labrecque's Men's Grooming Salon in New York and the Trump Hotel spas in Chicago and Las Vegas. And now the company is spending $9 million to roll out three Hommage-branded salons, the first in New York's renovated Plaza Hotel. The company's platinum and steel razor (with sheath and lacquered box) sells for $30,000.[1]

Will Hommage compete with your hair salon tomorrow? If it does, how will you respond? A global mindset asks those questions. As the proverb says, forewarned is forearmed.

Today, markets for labor, capital, goods and services, information, and management skills are all global. Even services, which comprise the bulk of developed nations' output, are globally competitive, because while many services are personal and not exportable, the business models that generate them are definitely "spreadable" globally. Hence, we argue that everyone who studies management and/or practices it is also, by definition, a global manager.

If so, then, what are the key skills or "core competencies" that global managers need to succeed in today's business world, as well as in tomorrow's?

Foremost, is the ability to assess and manage global macroeconomic risk. MIT professor Lester Thurow, the prophet of globalization, defined the term as the ability to buy or sell anything, anywhere, to anyone, any time. In today's challenging global climate, where macro "shocks" (unanticipated events that impact the world economy strongly) occur regularly, every global manager must become his or her own chief risk officer (CRO). Our book provides global managers with a simple, powerful set of macroeconomic tools, many of which have been until now rather opaque for noneconomists, that empower global managers to think independently, swim against the tide (when warranted), and at times enter markets when everyone else is abandoning them. Smartonomics is a set of simple tools that together give global managers a systemic, holistic picture of the global marketplace and the systemic risks it conceals.

Contrarian Thinking

Swimming against the tide—moving opposite to prevailing sentiment—is sometimes labelled "contrarian" thinking. The problem is that at times the majority "herd" opinion is right. And sometimes it is wrong. Besides, even if the majority is wrong, if enough people act on a wrong thinking, it actually becomes right. For instance, when enough shareholders dump shares of a company that is fundamentally sound, the stock price collapses, justified or not.

How can you tell when the majority is wrong? How can you, a global manager, see things that others do not? Assuming the majority is wrong always is a recipe for disaster. Assuming the majority is *never* wrong is equally disastrous. Telling the difference (when market opinion is right and when it is wrong) requires the sensitive, intelligent use of macroeconomic tools. In this book, we provide 10 of them, combining basic theory, applications, and case studies along with action-learning exercises.

Together, we believe that these tools comprise the armory of Smartonomics. Learn them, understand them, and use them daily and, we are convinced, you will, at least, become a global manager with a global mindset and, at best, leverage Smartonomics to achieve outstanding business success. For those who practice Smartonomics, transforming risk into opportunity is an operational skill, not an empty slogan.

Throughout this book, readers will find numerous case studies, illustrating how smart global managers transform risk into opportunity, as well as numerous action-learning exercises, to help readers test whether they understand the 10 tools well enough to employ them and, through them, achieve important insights.

To make our case from the outset, here is a brief case study about how smart global managers practicing their own brand of Smartonomics have done extremely well.

Case Study: Investing in Africa

Africa is a huge continent, with a fifth of the world's land area and a sixth of its population, or 1.1 billion people. Partly because colonial powers carved up Africa with borders that ignored or confronted tribal and ethnic boundaries, African nations today face a wide number of social and political challenges, including civil wars, brutal dictatorships, corruption, poverty, disease, and rebellions. These challenges are amplified by persistent press reports and new broadcasts describing the Ebola plague, terrorist massacres, civil wars, and other unrests.

As a consequence, a widely held assumption was, mine Africa for its oil and commodities, if you can, and avoid the rest. But several smart specialist private equity funds have dispelled this myth, tapping into the "strong demand for all manner of products and services among an expanding middle class." The *Financial Times* reports, "[P]rivate equity funds investing in fast-growing African economies are significantly outperforming established markets and achieving returns on exit comparable to China and Latin America."[2] Hurley Doddy, co-CEO of Emerging Capital Partners, made 56 investments in Africa in a broad range of sectors, including rubber and sugar, restaurant chains, utilities, financial services, and telecoms. In Tunisia, this group invested in a Tunisian personal care company that returned 1.6 times its original investment (in dollars). It will be recalled that the so-called "African spring" (spontaneous democratic protests that sprang up in Mideast nations) began in Tunisia on December 18, 2010, frightening away many investors. Runa Alam, CEO of a London-based private equity firm that specializes in Africa, describes how difficult (and rewarding) it is to invest smartly as a global manager. "We looked at 510 deals to do nine investments," she notes. She estimates that private equity firms now manage $25 billion in assets in Africa.[3]

How do smart global managers analyze nations and businesses within them, to find opportunities others miss? What macroeconomic tools can be helpful? How do Runa Alam, Hurley Doddy, and those who invest like they do achieve their insights? We do not, of course, know precisely how they do their analysis. But we do know how we would advise global managers to systematically apply simple basic economic concepts and frameworks, should they choose to emulate these successful, independent-thinking managers.

Learning Objectives of this Book

Before one sets out on a long journey, it is good to know your planned destination. What are the learning objectives our readers can attain in reading this book and in tackling the action-learning exercises?

- To understand what it means to think and to act as a global manager, with a true global perspective.
- To adopt a holistic approach to global risk, in which "systemic risk" (the risk inherent in an ecosystem, stemming from how its pieces interact) plays a key role.
- To acquire a new toolbox of eight simple macroeconomic ideas and concepts, and to learn to use them

effectively, daily, to gain insights and communicate them clearly to others.
- To learn how to acquire macroeconomic data, and how to organize, visualize, and process the data to find hidden meaning and insights.
- To gain facility and confidence in global management skills in the context of an increasingly uncertain, volatile, and unstable world economy and marketplace.

An Uncertain World

It is said that an ancient Chinese curse is: "May you live in interesting times." Sometimes curses may become blessings. In the 21st century, in just a decade and a half, there have been these events, all of which have impacted the global economy:

- The dot.com bubble, which peaked on March 10, 2000 with the NASDAQ stock exchange (where many technology stocks were listed) reaching 5,123.5 points, then quickly losing about three-quarters of its value.
- The 9/11 (September 11, 2001) attacks on the World Trade Center and the Pentagon, and the ensuing war in Afghanistan.
- The US invasion of Iraq, which was launched on March 20, 2003.
- The 2007/08 global financial crisis, whose true beginning is often marked by the collapse of Lehman Brothers investment bank on September 15, 2008.
- The euro crisis, which began in October 2009, when Greece reveals a "black hole" in its budget showing deficits much larger than previously known.
- The outbreak of the Arab Spring on December 18, 2010.
- The outbreak of the Syrian Civil War on January 26, 2011, which began with peaceful protests in Damascus.

Introduction xxiii

- The outbreak of the Ebola epidemic in West Africa in December 2013, when a two-year-old boy died in the village of Meliandou, Guinea, and the 2015 outbreak of Middle East respiratory syndrome coronavirus (MERS) virus in South Korea.
- The massive flow of refugees from Syria, Iraq, and Eritrea toward Europe in the summer of 2015; 60 million refugees in 2014 alone, the highest number ever recorded, fled their homelands for other nations.[4]
- Greece nearly defaulted on its debt in July 2015, plunging Europe and the euro into crisis; a last-minute bailout package is provided, with austerity measures approved by the Greek Parliament.
- China's stock market plunged 30 percent in June and July 2015, after rising 75 percent since the previous October.
- The price of oil declined sharply in 2015/16, falling to below $30 per barrel before recovering somewhat. Many countries' economies were hurt, especially those relying principally on oil revenues, including Russia, Saudi Arabia, and Venezuela.
- The human wave of migrants from Syria, Libya, Iraq, Pakistan, Afghanistan, and other countries desperately seeking to reach safety and safe haven in Europe created an immense European Union (EU) crisis, with EU countries differing on how to deal with the problem.
- On June 23, 2016, in a referendum, Britain voted narrowly to leave the EU. The wave of migrants flowing into Britain was a contributing factor (see Box I.1).

Box I.1: BREXIT: Britain's Exit from the European Union

On Thursday June 23, 2016, some 33,577,342 voters in England, Wales, Northern Ireland, Scotland, and

Gibraltar cast "yes" or "no" ballots on, "Should the United Kingdom remain a member of the European Union (EU) or leave the European Union?" Some 51.89 percent, or 16,141,241 voters, said "yes." The turnout, 72.2 percent, was the highest since the 1992 elections. This surprising result caught the experts by surprise—it was widely believed the result would be to remain in the EU—and touched off a wave of repercussions, like a huge rock tossed into a quiet pond. Experts say that leaving the EU will cost Britain between 1.1 and 3.1 percent of its gross domestic product (GDP). But no one knows for certain, because the terms of Britain's EU exit remain to be negotiated, and those terms can be either favorable to Britain (retaining free trade with the EU) or vindictive and punitive (slashing Britain's economic ties with the EU). The Brexit crisis comes at a bad time for Britain. In January–March, the economic growth lost momentum, slowing to only 0.4 percent, as both housing and manufacturing slumped. Britain's economy slowed sharply in the first three months of 2016 as factors unrelated to the looming in/out EU referendum put a brake on growth. There were big repercussions in financial markets. Stock exchanges in Tokyo, Frankfurt, and the US, all fell by between 4 and 8 percent on June 24, while gold (a thermometer for global illness) rose by nearly 5 percent. Financial losses totaled some $2 trillion worldwide.

Source: https://en.wikipedia.org/wiki/United_Kingdom_European_Union_membership_referendum,_2016

This is only a small part of a very long list. Each of these events strongly impacted global financial markets and economies. None were highly predictable.

The question is, in a world in which uncertainty is increasing, how should global managers manage their businesses? Some respond that the heavy fog in which world markets are wrapped makes planning and risk management impossible. But other wiser persons argue that strategic global management becomes far more important when uncertainty grows. And, they add, each of the 14 crises listed earlier created major opportunities for creating value and changing the world. Alacritous companies have invested in developing an Ebola virus, backed by heavy public investments. Some have gained from the sharp fall in the euro–dollar exchange rate, from only about 67 US cents per euro (in 2011) to 90 cents (2015). Others sold dubious dot.com companies short well before the bubble burst.

The Need for Agility

Global uncertainty makes strategic decision-making even more vital. But it also requires that such decision-making should be "agile" and rapid. Strategy guru Professor Yves Doz, together with his colleague Mikko Kosonen, who heads the Finnish innovation fund SITRA (suomen itsenäisyyden juhlarahasto), have defined the three key elements of rapid, agile strategy.[5] They are:

- Strategic sensitivity (the ability to spot changes in trends quickly);
- Leadership consensus (the ability to unite key senior managers around a common view); and
- Resource fluidity (the ability to shift resources—labor, capital, and knowledge—among various branches, business units, and endeavors, quickly and smoothly, to capitalize on perceived opportunities).

Action Learning: Rate Your Strategic Agility

On a scale of 1 to 10 (1 is lowest, 10 is highest): Rate your organization's competency, (or an organization with which you are familiar) at these three vital components of strategic agility:

1. *Strategic Sensitivity* 1 _____ 10
2. *Leadership Consensus* 1 _____ 10
3. *Resource Fluidity* 1 _____ 10

If you were CEO, what changes would you implement in order to strengthen weaknesses and improve speed and agility?

> Our Smartonomics tools can strengthen all three components. They can improve resource fluidity by constantly generating a stream of business opportunity ideas that offer strong returns (in the face of high, but well-assessed risks). They contribute to leadership consensus by providing a common *language and logic* for those who make key strategic decisions. And, above all, they strengthen strategic sensitivity by showing global managers how to constantly and consistently track global trends, reading the data without resorting to the assessments of "expert" economists, often influenced by the views of other economists more than by the data themselves.

The Vital Importance of Simplicity

The author Shlomo Maital taught a course based on an early version of this book in the MIT Sloan School of Management's Management of Technology MSc program—a kind of MBA degree tailored for research and development (R&D) engineers. His initial effort in 1984 was nearly catastrophic.

The students were R&D engineers from many nations, employed by global high-tech multinationals. Toward the end of one lecture, in which the instructor filled the board with equations and mathematics, a frustrated student, who was a senior manager from IBM, stood up. She asked, politely but very bluntly, "[W]hy do we need to know this?"

The instructor was dumbfounded. He thought the answer was obvious. One needed to know this because, well, it was a macroeconomics course and this is what macroeconomics is, according to us economists. But clearly, this was an inappropriate answer. R&D engineers do not need to become economists. They do need tools that will help understand the global economy.

These talented R&D engineers, many of whom had won scholarships for a year of study at MIT because of their excellent work in developing new products and services, were studying not to learn economics *but to be better R&D engineers and to become capable global managers.* They needed *tools*, not theories. And they were not in the least impressed by the equations the instructor plied.

So the right answer to this blunt, provocative question, he finally understood much later, was:

> You need to know this, because, these are macroeconomic tools, concepts and frameworks that you will need, perhaps desperately, in order to be successful global managers, in a highly unstable, volatile and rapidly-changing world; and in my course, I will show you why these tools are beautiful, simple, logical and above all powerful, and help you practice putting them to use. If you work hard and invest time and effort in learning to use these tools, I think you will find I am right.

In 1985, Maital began this new direction in the course. And thanks to his students, it was far more successful.

There is a very well-kept secret in economics. Macroeconomics, the study of national economies, can be highly complex, with math as complex as that used in particle physics or electrical engineering. But the basic ideas of macroeconomics are extremely simple, at their core. You do not have to be a PhD economist to use and understand them. In our book, we choose to present the eight tools in a simple manner, mostly visual, to make them accessible to all.

The reason simplicity is so important is that global managers need to build a team to implement their ideas; and in order to do so, global managers must persuade others their ideas (often, seemingly risky ones) are right and explain them very lucidly. And to explain and convince others, ideas must be simplified. All too often, complexity serves as cover-up for misguided wrongheaded and confused ideas. To achieve the leadership consensus that is such a vital part of strategic agility, simplicity must be maximized and given high priority.

We seek to do this in our book, in each of the eight tools.[6] None of the tools are beyond the understanding of first-year freshman economics. Comprehending them is quite simple. The hard part is in applying them successfully to making vital decisions about where, and how, to do business, whom to sell to, and why it is a good idea.

 **Action Learning: A Memo from the CEO**

Here is a preliminary exercise to help set the stage for our journey through the eight tools.

The following memo from your company's CEO has just landed in your email inbox:

Greetings! I've decided to open a new frontier for our company in [choose one or more countries from the list below]. Perhaps we can sell our low-end products there, or do some component outsourcing; perhaps, build an assembly operation, or site some of our R&D there, especially for local-market adaptation. Or even, develop new "reverse innovation" products there (low-cost products suitable for emerging markets and sellable in developed nations). I expect opposition from the Board and need lots of "ammunition." Write me a terse report, no more than 10 pages, about the country's economy and our business prospects there, and analyze the risks and opportunities. Could we find a market there? A new outsourcer? Investment opportunities? Talent? I need a big picture analysis.

Choose one or more of these relatively high-risk countries: Ukraine; Bangladesh; Argentina; Iran; Brazil; Russia; Kazakhstan; Indonesia; Vietnam; Nigeria.

Where do you start? Where do you seek data? How will you organize your report?

When you complete the last page of Chapter 8 and the Epilogue, you, dear reader, will have a well-stocked toolbox to help you meet this challenge. When you've finished

> reading our book, perhaps you will choose to return to this exercise, tackle it, and see how much better equipped you are to perform with speed, skill, and insight, the crucial task assigned to you by your CEO—find opportunities where others see only risk.

SWOT: AN ORGANIZING FRAMEWORK

Nearly all students of management learn to conduct a strategic analysis by zooming in, diagnosing an organization (or business unit), and identifying its strengths and weaknesses then zooming out and analyzing the threats and opportunities that exist in the organization's global business environment. This is known as SWOT analysis, an acronym that stands for Strengths, Weaknesses, Opportunities and Threats.

We choose to use a variant of SWOT, known as TOWS.[7]

In our variation of this simple method, global managers study a nation, or region, and identify its major strengths (skills, resources, and competencies that can potentially generate business opportunities) and weaknesses (constraints, problems, and deficiencies that hinder business opportunities). This is an internal analysis, and there are sources of data that are very helpful in doing so.[8]

Next, global managers scan the world and identify the main business threats and opportunities relevant for the nation under study. This is an external analysis of the prevailing business environment. Threats are trends or events that actually or potentially cause economic harm to a nation (e.g., sharp fall in the price of oil or commodities, for an oil-producing or commodity-producing nation). Opportunities are trends or events that actually or potentially, create major business opportunities for a nation.

The TOWS analysis is summarized in Figure I.1. Strengths and weakness (only the main ones) are listed in the matrix columns. Opportunities and threats are listed in the matrix rows.

Figure I.1 TOWS Matrix

	S	W
O	SO	WO
T	ST	WT

Source: Authors.

Business opportunities are one of four kinds: SO (leveraging a strength to seize an opportunity); ST (leveraging a strength to overcome a weakness); WO (correcting, eliminating or improving a weakness in order to seize a business opportunity); and WT (correcting a weakness in order to meet an external threat). It is obvious that SO and ST are far more obvious, in general, than WO and WT; but, precisely for this reason, the latter two cells of the matrix are often most ignored.

Action Learning: Your Own Personal TOWS Matrix

- Conduct a TOWS analysis of you yourself. What are your (internal) strengths? Your weaknesses? List the main ones as the matrix columns.
- Now, examine, externally, what are the main opportunities you face? What are the main threats you personally face, to your career as a manager and to your savings and assets?

Can you identify one or more of these four interactions, SO, ST, WO, WT, to create a major business or management career opportunity for yourself?

TOWS Case Studies

"SO": In the 1990s, after the fall of the Berlin Wall, Asian "tiger" nations—mainly China, India, and Korea—identified a major global opportunity: The desire and need on the part of Western multinational corporations to lower their manufacturing costs and, thus, raise their profit margins, by outsourcing production from high-cost sites in the West to low-cost sites in the East. They leveraged their own internal strengths—low-cost modern factories built with capital generated by a high-saving population; low-wage productive labor force with nearly infinitely elastic supply; and cheap undervalued currencies. China achieved double-digit GDP growth for two decades in this way; India came to dominate IT, call center, and business process outsourcing. The Taiwanese company Foxconn (formally, Hon Hai Precision Industry Co.), a global manufacturing company, in particular, managed to achieve enormous growth by building plants in mainland China, even though officially Taiwan had banned investment in the mainland. Foxconn has over a million employees and annual revenues of over $132 billion, all built on a base of contract manufacturing of electronics and electronic components.

"WT": Switzerland's currency, the Swiss franc, is traditionally a "strong" one, owing to the inflow of foreign capital to Swiss banks as tax havens, thus, making Swiss goods very expensive. This is an internal weakness. Switzerland faced the threat of losing its export markets to fierce competition from efficient, lower cost manufactures in Asia. It overcame this WT challenge by focusing on high-quality brand-name products, which are price insensitive, by strengthening the Swiss brand image, and by cleverly attaining EU membership with regard to trade while avoiding the trap of embracing the unstable euro currency, thus, gaining vital access to the 27 EU member nations. Switzerland exports over $300 billion annually and has an export surplus, despite the very expensive cost of Swiss goods owing in part to the very strong Swiss franc.

THE EIGHT TOOLS

Here, in order, are the eight Smartonomics tools that global managers can use to successfully carry out the action-learning exercise described previously, and to achieve profit and success in their global endeavors. Each chapter explains a single tool, illustrates its use with a case study or examples, and provides an action-learning exercise to help readers practice its implementation.

Chapter 1. *A Country Is a Business.* This chapter shows why global managers, expert in Smartonomics, are good at both "zoom in" (microscopic analysis of opportunities) and "zoom out" (global telescopic holistic analysis of the world's markets). It shows how to map global risk, understand the concept of GDP and its components, and learn key facts about a country by analyzing GDP data. In this chapter, we define "due diligence" for analyzing a country and show how the national accounts (the system for measuring the strength and growth of a country's economy) can reveal important insights.

Chapter 2. *Ants and Grasshoppers: Analyzing National Saving.* In a famous Aesop's fable, an ant industriously prepares for winter by gathering and storing food, while a happy-go-lucky grasshopper fiddles and enjoys life in the balmy autumn days. This chapter reveals the link between the resources a nation saves and the resources it invests in capital formation.

The featured tool, net saving and investment, is derived directly and simply from the previous chapter's tool, GDP. We explain how to tell whether a country is an "ant" (a country that saves and invests for the future), or a "grasshopper" (a country that uses most of its resources for enjoying present consumption). We discuss the prevailing global anomaly, in which the wealthy nations of the West borrow large sums from the poorer nations of the East, a situation that is unsustainable and that requires "rebalancing." We also show how enormous amounts of wealth have been created globally in the past two decades and why that wealth is very inequitably distributed in favor of the very rich.

Chapter 3. *'Flation: It's Like Cholesterol (Good and Bad)*. Inflation can be a puzzling phenomenon for global managers. For example, for decades, federal reserve chairpersons lost sleep over excessively rising prices (inflation) and fought to prevent or mitigate them. Today, Federal Reserve Chair, Janet Yellen, worries about the opposite: Too *little* inflation, and promises to find a remedy. This chapter explains why too little inflation is worse than too much, shows how inflation is measured, and explicates the two "drivers" or engines or inflation—supply forces and demand forces—and how they differ. We show how inflation can distort the meaning of stock prices and how to correct for this; and explain clearly the difference between good and bad inflation, and how they impact equity prices. Finally, we explain to global managers how to develop an independent view on global inflation, which may differ from those of the media and the experts.

Chapter 4. *Money: What It Is, What It Does*. Among the key subjects global managers need to understand thoroughly, money is foremost—where it comes from, who creates it and how it impacts the economies of nations and the world. In this chapter we ask and answer a series of questions: What is money? How has the nature of money changed in the US (and elsewhere in the world) and why? How does money affect output, income, growth, and employment? What is economic momentum, and why is the velocity of money a crucial—and often overlooked—variable? How do central banks control the supply of money and the rate of interest? How are money, interest, and inflation related? Why are interest rates today the most important single macro variable in the US, Europe, and many other countries? How can managers track interest rates globally? Why should they? How do interest rates affect the economy? How do central banks influence interest rates? Which rates can they determine? What is the fatal flaw in the current "dollar standard" global financial system? The tool we provide in this chapter is that of economic momentum, a 250-year-old theory that fell into disuse but, we believe, is exceedingly powerful and insightful for Smartonomics practitioners.

Chapter 5. *Booms and Busts: What Comes Next?* Economic cycles—periods of alternating boom and growth, and bust and stagnation—have existed for hundreds of years. But why? Why is economic activity cyclical? This chapter helps readers understand the main economic theories that explain business cycles and choose one or more that they personally favor. We will help readers understand in what ways business cycles are similar, and in what ways each is unique; know how trade deficits and budget deficits impact the real economy, and how are these two deficits interrelated; and know what "animal spirits" are and how they drive the global economy. At any point in time, if the global economy is not already contracting, then we know for sure a contraction is on the way. But when? How? Where? This chapter provides a tool that helps Smartonomics adherents find useful answers. It helps answer the crucial question: In global markets—what comes next?

Chapter 6. *Torrents of Capital.* This chapter focuses on the vast amounts of money created by US, EU and Chinese central banks, how this money and credit are being transformed into capital, and how this is impacting global markets. Readers will learn why the world has become virtually addicted to zero interest rates and understand why falling crude oil prices have depressed global markets and economies, rather than revived and energized them. In this chapter, we will explain why the US, EU, and China cannot control exchange rates, even when they collaborate and work together. We will explain how to calculate whether a nation's foreign exchange rate (the rate at which its currency exchanges for other currencies) is too expensive, too cheap or just right? And, we will explain why the global dominance of the dollar may be ending.

A basic flaw exists in today's global markets—the chronic problem created in July 1944 and never truly resolved, now haunting the world: The dual role of the dollar, as America's currency and also as the world's currency. Smartonomics believers are keenly aware of this flaw and plan their strategies accordingly.

The chapter's tool is an unusual one: It uses the fast food chain McDonald's and the Big Mac hamburger to show how to judge whether a country's currency is too expensive (in terms of dollars) or too cheap.

Chapter 7. *The Gap.* When we hear or read about "the gap," it has become crystal clear to which gap people refer. It is the huge and growing gap between the rich and poor, between those with wealth and those who lack any. One consequence of globalization—the rise of global markets, trade, and capital flows among nations—has been to greatly increase the inequality in the distribution of wealth and income, both within and among nations. Only 62 very wealthy billionaires now own and control half the world's total wealth, more than the combined wealth of the poorest 3.5 billion people.

This chapter shows how and why wealth is increasingly concentrated between and within nations; examines the geopolitical impact of the rich–poor gap; and shows why the mostly ignored poorest half of the world, known as the "bottom of the pyramid," offers promising and rewarding business opportunities. Readers will learn about what solutions and palliatives have been proposed, and how to distinguish between those that are viable and those that are not.

Chapter 8. *Mining for Opportunities.* In this chapter, we return to our starting point—how to do "due diligence" for the global economy and for a country's economy. We learn how to conduct such due diligence, how to combine macroeconomic analysis with microeconomic "opportunity mining," and how to become proficient in employing a checklist—a framework that integrates the previous seven essential tools and adds to them noneconomic factors related to culture, politics, and ethics. We explain why major paradigm shifts (transforming changes in the way we perceive reality) occur in global markets and key industries, and how and why such shifts can create exceptionally attractive, new business opportunities. This chapter integrates the previous seven chapters and helps those who practice Smartonomics to understand how to build a "global narrative"—a story that describes your view of how events will unfold in global markets in the coming 3–5 years and reveals the opportunities hidden in unfolding crises and uncertainty.

Epilogue. In this brief afterword, we outline and highlight a few of the most important sources of the myriad of potential uncertainties in the world today. Our purpose in presenting these is to sensitize you, global manager, to the fact that there are many factors outside the realm of rational economics that can derail the most well-intentioned plans. As a manager, you will have to keep your antennae well-tuned to catch these signals and factor them into your planning. It is our fondest desire that the eight tools provided by our book will prove useful to you, your families and friends, and to the organizations small and large that you serve and lead.

FINDING DATA

There are numerous comprehensive databases that provide free of charge economic time series data for a large number of countries. The largest and most comprehensive is that of the World Bank.[9] This database, known as World Development Indicators, has data for 249 countries and some 1,343 economic time series, dating back to 1960. (For some countries, a great deal of data is missing). Unfortunately, this database, while huge, is also exceptionally unfriendly. For example, the concept of GDP (the first of the 10 tools in this book, explained in Chapter 1) has at least four different measures (in constant local currency, current local currency, current dollars, dollars—purchasing power parity (PPP)—all of these will be explained later). Matching the right components of GDP to the right measure of GDP is itself challenging. These data, it should be understood, are compiled by the countries themselves, not by the World Bank; for some countries, especially very poor ones, the dataset is nearly empty.

There are other databases that provide GDP data, for instance, and at times the data are conflicting and inconsistent. For instance, the CIA World Factbook[10] and the International Monetary Fund's World Economic Outlook database.[11] For data on the US economy, see the economist report of the President.[12]

So, in consequence, we have chosen to use primarily a single database in this book, the World Competitiveness Yearbook, compiled and updated yearly by the Swiss business school, IMD, based in Lausanne.[13] This Yearbook ranks some 60 countries in terms of the overall global competitiveness, based on four key dimensions: Economic performance (84 variables), government efficiency (71 variables), business efficiency (74 variables), and infrastructure (116 variables). From time to time, we will mention additional data sources which are, regrettably, far less friendly, though many are provided free of charge. The source we often used is the website of Trading Economics,[14] which provides user-friendly graphs for many countries and a great many economic variables at no charge.

Dear Reader: After reading this book, we hope you will be able to say with a high degree of credibility that you are indeed a global manager, with a key core competency—your ability to marshal the tools used by economists to understand what is going on in the world—and, at times of great uncertainty and instability, to understand what in the world is going on, well enough to endure and to prevail!

To paraphrase Rudyard Kipling's famous poem, "If":

> "If you can keep your head when all about you are losing theirs....If you can trust yourself when all men doubt you, If you can think [independently]—and not make thoughts [but action] your aim; If you can make one heap of all your winnings and risk it on one turn of pitch-and-toss, and lose, and start again at your beginnings and never breathe a word about your loss; If you can fill the unforgiving minute with sixty seconds' worth of distance run, yours is the Earth and everything that's in it..." and you'll be a global Smartonomics manager with a true global mindset.

NOTES

1 http://www.forbes.com/2008/08/26/mens-luxurious-barber-shops-forbeslife-cx_kb_0826style.html, accessed September 22, 2016.
2 William Wallis, "African investors discover routes to riches beyond commodities," *Financial Times*, October 5, 2014; http://www.ft.com/cms/s/0/3712e17c-1e4f-11e4-ab52–00144feabdc0.html#ixzz3PopEDdTp, accessed January 25, 2015.
3 William Wallis, "African Investors Discover Routes to Riches Beyond Commodities," *Financial Times*, October 5, 2014; http://www.ft.com/cms/s/0/3712e17c-1e4f-11e4-ab52-00144feabdc0.html#axzz4Kx-vEV3B0, accessed September 14, 2015.
4 *Economist*, "Daily Chart: The Dispossessed," *The Economist*, June 18, 2015.
5 Yves Doz and Mikko Kosonen, "How Agile Is Your Strategy Process?," *Strategy Magazine*, no. 15, March 2008, 6–10.

6 See John Maeda, *The Laws of Simplicity* (Cambridge, MA: MIT Press, 2013). Maeda's book is under 100 pages, and includes 10 laws for simple design and how to implement them.
7 See Heinz Weihrich, "The TOWS Matrix—A Tool for Situational Analysis." *Long Range Planning*, 15 no. 2 (1982): 54–66.
8 See, for instance, the World Competitiveness Yearbook (IMD Lausanne, yearly) which shows each of 60 or so globally competitive nations what their main strengths and weaknesses are, and quantifies them.
9 http://databank.worldbank.org/data/reports.aspx?source=world-development-indicators, accessed September 22, 2016.
10 https://www.cia.gov/library/publications/the-world-factbook, accessed September 22, 2016.
11 https://www.imf.org/external/ns/cs.aspx?id=28, accessed September 22, 2016.
12 https://www.whitehouse.gov/administration/eop/cea/economic-report-of-the-President/2015, accessed September 22, 2016.
13 The 2016 World Competitiveness Yearbook, published in June, is very expensive: 1,400 Swiss francs (or about $749) for academic institutions and nonprofits and 2,200 Swiss francs for companies (a Swiss franc is about one dollar). Parts of the database can be bought for much lower fees.
14 www.tradingeconomics.com, accessed September 22, 2016.

A Country Is a Business

 **Tool 1: Gross Domestic Product and Components**

Learning Objectives

- Know why global managers expert in Smartonomics are good at both "zoom in" and "zoom out"
- Understand how to analyze, and visually map, global risk
- Know how gross domestic product (GDP) (national accounting) originated
- Grasp the fundamental meaning of GDP and its components
- Know how to analyze GDP and its components to learn key facts about a country and its economy

GLOBAL DUE DILIGENCE

How do wise global managers who practice Smartonomics track global markets and trends? How do they do global "due diligence"?

"Due diligence" is a legal term meaning "an investigation of a business or person prior to signing a contract." It usually refers to the in-depth X-ray analysis performed inside a company before it is acquired by another company. Those who have been subjects of due diligence, or who have engaged in it, know how thorough and painstaking the process is. Due diligence literally means that those entrusted by the shareholders to investigate a potential deal have been thorough (diligent) and invested in the process all the attention, hard work, and effort that is the acquiring shareholders' due.

Global due diligence is the investigation of global risks and opportunities. Rather than investigate a single business, or even country, global due diligence analyzes the global financial and economic ecosystem—risks, challenges, opportunities, fragilities, crises-in-the-making, hidden and visible trends.

Global managers are constantly zooming out, tracking global markets. Their due diligence is done daily. We believe that global managers often follow their own versions of a simple model, which we call as ZiZoZi, or "Zoom in/Zoom out/zoom in."[1]

- Zoom in on your own specific business function, product, market, or responsibility. Grasp the smallest of details—one of them may be crucial.
- Zoom out on global markets and map them as a dynamic ecosystem. Identify key trends. Gather insights and knowledge.
- Then zoom in again on your own business responsibility to apply your zoom-out insights and to help your organization grow and prosper, and better serve its clients.

This constant zoom-in/zoom-out process ensures that while one eagle eye focuses on your business responsibility, microscopically, another sharp eye constantly scans the global horizon looking for risks and opportunities (which often are one and the same thing) that impact your business and offer ways

A Country Is a Business 3

to build and grow it or, in times of crisis, save it from unexpected disaster.

In this chapter, we provide some examples of zoom-out analysis of the global financial and economic ecosystem and show how to zoom in on national economies by using our first tool, known as GDP. We begin by arguing that skilled Smartonomics practitioners should implement a systematic process, which airline pilots know as "checklists," and which doctors call "procedure protocols."

Systematic Systemic Risk Management: The Protocol Approach

In the Greek language, *protocollon* was a leaf of paper glued to a manuscript volume, which described its contents. Today protocol has come to mean a *clearly-defined specific set of rules or procedures that guide a process*. Airline pilots have a protocol or checklist which they follow with great discipline before the airplane takes off. In general, processes and procedures that involve risk are best guided by systematic protocols that minimize human error. Similarly, global managers can construct a protocol for analyzing global risk and opportunity before they send their organizations into perilous global markets.

Box 1.1: The Checklist Manifesto

Dr Atul Gawande is a Harvard Medical School professor, practicing surgeon, *New Yorker* staff writer and brilliant author. His book is called *The Checklist Manifesto* (Metropolitan Books: 2009). As one reviewer wrote: "The book's main point is simple: no matter how expert you may be, *well-designed check lists can improve outcomes (even for Gawande's own surgical team)."* The best-known use of checklists is by airplane pilots. Among the many interesting stories in the book is how this dedication to checklists arose among pilots.

Author Malcolm Gladwell (author of *The Tipping Point* and *Blink*) writes: "Gawande begins by making a distinction between errors of ignorance (mistakes we make because we do not know enough) and errors of ineptitude (mistakes we made because we do not make proper use of what we know). Failure in the modern world, Gawande writes, is really about the second of these errors, and he walks us through a series of examples from medicine showing how the routine tasks of surgeons have now become so incredibly complicated that mistakes of one kind or another are virtually inevitable: it's just too easy for an otherwise competent doctor to miss a step, or forget to ask a key question or, in the stress and pressure of the moment, to fail to plan properly for every eventuality. Gawande then visits with pilots and the people who build skyscrapers and comes back with a solution."

Experts need checklists—written guides that walk them through the key steps in any complex procedure. In the last section of the book, Gawande shows how his research team has taken this idea, developed a safe surgery checklist, and applied it around the world, with staggering success.

Management educators teach that business success requires three essential disciplines: innovativeness, operational excellence, and customer intimacy. They stress that these disciplines are closely related. Innovation succeeds only when combined with operational skill. Operational skill, in turn, may require adherence to a checklist, as Gawande suggests. The trick is, how to combine the chaotic rule-defying creativity with the rule-adhering Prussian discipline of checklists. *Great innovators succeed.*

In this chapter we provide you, our reader, with a suggested Smartonomics protocol, or checklist, in two parts. The first part is a Global Risk Protocol, to help global managers analyze and manage the enormous uncertainties now prevalent in global markets. The second part is a Country Risk Protocol, to help global managers analyze and manage specific country risk.

The Global Risk Protocol

We begin with a big-picture zoom out, covering the world and 2,000 years of economic history.

The Center of the World

Later in this chapter we will provide a detailed definition of "GDP." For now it is sufficient to understand that GDP is a measure of the total amount of goods and services produced within a country's borders, usually during a year's time.

The global consulting firm McKinsey has used GDP cleverly to provide a 2,000-year, birds-eye view of economic history.

Let a country's GDP (measured in dollars) represent that country's weight. Use that weight to calculate the precise center of economic gravity of the nations of the world (see Figure 1.1). Technically, the center of gravity is the point at which, if you placed a pencil under it, the system would be in perfect balance. So the economic center of gravity is literally the economic center of the world. It is the point at which the world as a tabletop would balance, if each country's GDP were instead its weight, in kilograms.

For over 1,500 years, from AD 1 through AD 1,500, China was essentially the center of the earth. It had the world's most advanced technology, science, and the largest economy (see Figure 1.1).

Then, the Emperor, in around AD 1,500, decided to close China to the world and burn its fleet, fearing the instability

Figure 1.1 The Economic Center of Gravity of the Earth, AD 1 to AD 2025

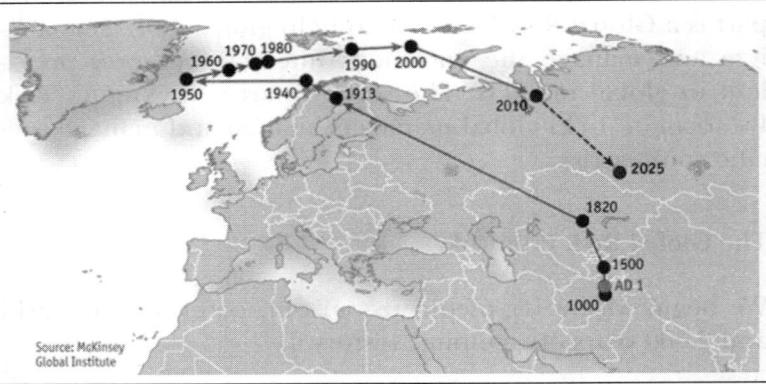

Source: The Economist; McKinsey Global Institute.

that trade and contact with the outside world would bring. Meanwhile, the First and Second Industrial Revolutions occurred in Europe and later in the US, while China missed them. Rapidly, the economic center of gravity migrated westward.

The First Industrial Revolution began in around 1760 in Great Britain and spread quickly to the US and Western Europe. It evolved into the Second Industrial Revolution, between 1840 and 1870. The industrial revolutions were driven by use of machines, rather than hand production, use of water power and steam power and later electricity, and the use of machine tools. The key product was textiles. Basically, it was steam that transformed GDP from stagnant to growing. China was not part of the revolution.

This isolation rapidly began to reverse itself after Deng Xiao Ping introduced market economy reforms to China, and its economy began a remarkable period of double-digit growth for more than two decades. If this rapid growth continues, by the year 2025 the global center of gravity will have returned almost to its starting point in AD 1500.

This is a remarkable achievement, but it is not 100 percent certain it will occur. Much depends on China's ability to move up the value chain, to create innovative products invented in China rather than produce goods and services designed elsewhere.

Zoom Out Global "Due Diligence"

Global managers practicing Smartonomics need unusual vision. One eye has microscopic vision, able to zoom in on the smallest details of the manager's business and function. The second eye should have telescopic vision, capable of zooming out, to embrace the entire global village—global financial markets, product and service markets, information markets, labor markets, technology markets—while tracking global trends, geopolitical instability and social change, all this with a broad historical understanding of the dynamics that got the world to where it is today.

There is a very useful "roadmap" tool available to global managers, useful as part of the zoom out due diligence that summarizes the experts' view of global risks and trends: IMD's Global Roadmap.

The World Economic Forum Global Roadmap

It provides a birds-eye view, updated annually, of the main global risks, divided into categories: technological, economic, geopolitical, environmental, and societal. The 2016 version is shown in Figure 1.2.

Figure 1.2 maps each of the global risks in (X,Y) space, where the X axis represents the probability that the risk will occur, from low to high, and the Y axis shows the aggregate impact of the risk, if it happens, measured in billions of dollars. The most serious risks, in both likelihood and impact, are failure to deal with climate change and migration flows, and the water scarcity.

Figure 1.2 World Economic Forum: Global Risk Landscape 2016

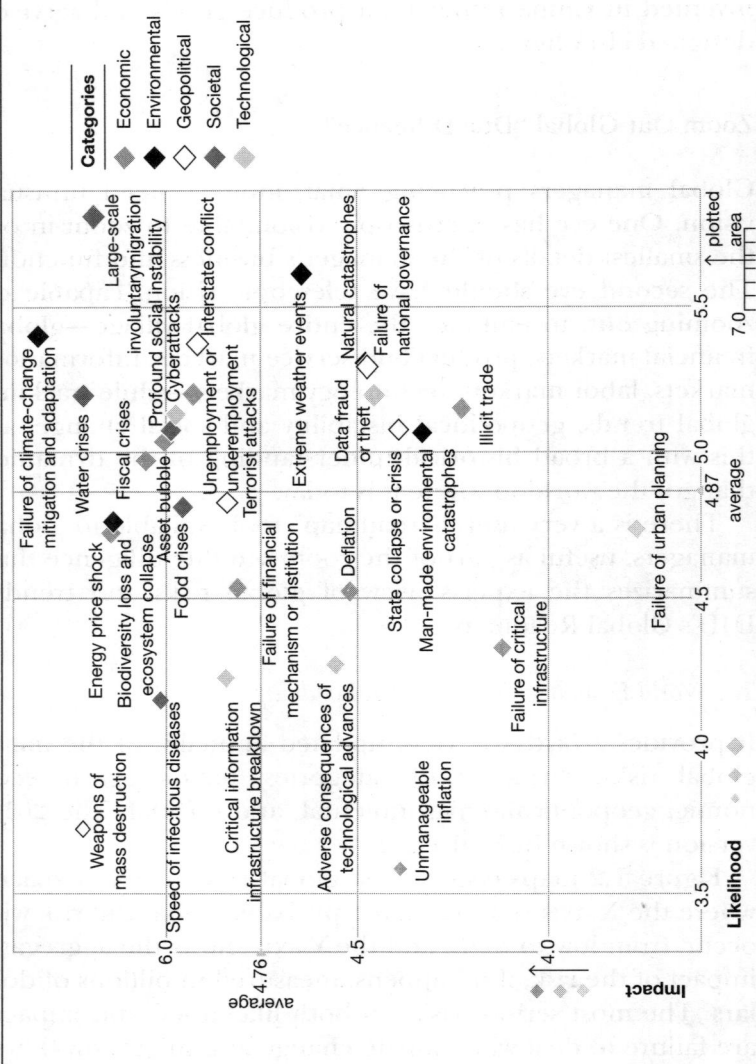

 **Action Learning**

Smartonomics readers are urged to copy the global risk map and mark it up. Analyze each of the colored diamonds. Are the experts right? Is the risk's impact larger, or smaller, than the map shows? Is its probability higher or lower? How does each risk impact your organization and your own business function? The country in which you live? In which you work?

Another version of the global risk map, the Swiss business school IMD's Global Risk map, also identifies 13 key global risk trends.[2] Box 1.2 shows those trends that global managers should be keenly aware of because they comprise and contribute to global risks and opportunities.

Box 1.2: Global Trends Roadmap 2015

1. Economic power: More than half of global growth will come from the US and China. By 2030, the global middle class will triple—from 1 billion to 3 billion—with most of the growth in Asia.
2. Fracturing social fabric: Social unrest is rising, owing to austerity, high unemployment, and aging societies that burden health and pension systems.
3. Geopolitics and security: Conflicts in the Mideast, Ukraine/Russia, and Asia grow, leading to north-south migration, record defense spending, and concerns over nuclear security.

4. Growing stakeholder demands: Declining public trust in businesses and their leaders continues, leading to greater shareholder activism.
5. Capital landscape: Global asset values rise, as does price volatility. Global financial risk is increasing.
6. Knowledge landscape: Information, and knowledge, will soon all exist in the cloud.
7. Labor landscape: Economic recession has affected a generation of workers. New skills will become key—virtual collaboration, computational thinking, cross-cultural competency, and transdisciplinarity.
8. Pressure on resources: By 2025, 1.8 billion people will live in areas plagued by water scarcity; energy demand will rise by one third by 2035.
9. Technology landscape: The Internet of Everything as well as the new economy, will impact health care, transportation, energy, and retail services.
10. Consumer landscape: Global online spending is booming; global smartphone traffic will rise eightfold by 2020.
11. Industry landscape: Competition for talent is heating up; technology forces are reshaping competition in all industries.
12. Shifting market landscape: By 2025 a new global consuming class will emerge and the majority of consumption will take place in developing countries, driven by online and mobile payment systems.
13. Triple bottom line: Corporations will face pressure to measure, and report on, their social and environmental performance as well as their financial performance.

Action Learning: Analyze the 13 Trends

As part of your own global due diligence: Analyze each of the 13 global trends in terms of its impact on your own organization or business function. Which are most important? Which are less relevant? What action items emerge, when you analyze the three key trends and examine how to leverage them as global business opportunities?

Action Learning: Build a Smartonomics Global Risk Protocol

Here is a start at a global risk protocol checklist.

On separate pages, write these headings: Economics, Geopolitics, Society, Environment, Technology.

For each of these key areas: How do you regularly track trends, risks, events, and opportunities in each? Is your "telescope" sufficiently wide-angle?

For each of the five key areas: Visit the area regularly, keeping in mind one key question for each:

- Economics: Is the world economy likely to grow faster in the near term, the same, or will it slow? Why?
- Technology: What are the major new technologies, especially disruptive ones, that are emerging, and that are creating new businesses and products?

- **Society:** What are the major trends in society, in the way people work, learn, marry, have children, communicate, and argue, in small and large groups?
- **Geopolitics:** What are the major changes in the ever-changing relationships among countries and regions?
- **Environment:** What changes are occurring in the air, water, land, and energy of the world and how are they impacting the quality of life?
- **Overall:** What do wise global managers read regularly, to track key changes in these five areas?

Now, it is time to build a tool for zoom in: country analysis. Our tool will be the concept of GDP. Just as businesses have accounting systems that track their financial results, so do countries have national accounting systems.

A COUNTRY IS A BUSINESS

When it comes to analyzing national economies, managers have a major advantage over even the most experienced economists.

Economists read numbers. Managers, in contrast, "read" and analyze businesses. A country is, among other things, a business, or a vast collection of small and large businesses; and a country's government too is like a business, in that it has revenue, expenditure, clients and strategic goals. A country, like a business, makes and sells goods and services, employs people, invents things, and seeks to grow. Because managers know how to analyze businesses—their own and those of others—they can apply some of the same principles to analyzing countries.

Not everyone agrees. Nobel laureate Paul Krugman, a *New York Times* columnist, once wrote, "[A] country is not a big corporation....The U.S. economy is the ultimate

A Country Is a Business 13

conglomerate, with tens of thousands of distinct lines of business.... A successful business leader is no more likely to be an expert on economics than on military strategy."³

Krugman does not think Smartonomics skills necessarily relate to being smart. He writes that the 100 top US business executives are far smarter than the 100 leading economists.⁴ It has to do with mindset.

But even if a country is not precisely a business, it still should be run like one. "Run a country like a business, or it will go bankrupt," is the advice of a leading blogger named Frank Li.⁵ Perhaps Greece in 2015 is a good example. Greece's public debt in 2014 was 177 percent of its national product. In July 2015, Greece found itself unable to pay back money it owed to creditors and faced bankruptcy.

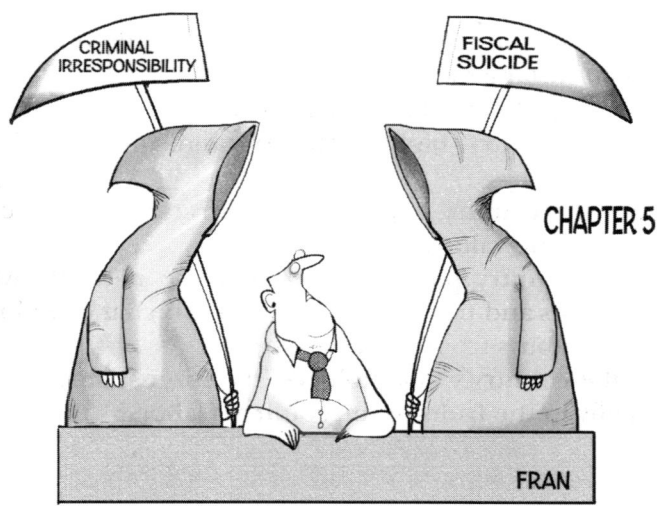

CHAPTER 5

Suppose that payment of interest and principal on this debt is, say, 10 percent of the debt annually. That means that 18 percent of Greece's national product goes to servicing its public debt. This is not sustainable, for a country or for a business. Greece Inc. was excessively "leveraged" (indebted). It was a badly run business.

Action Learning: Build a Smartonomics Country Risk Protocol

Here is a start at a *country risk protocol*.

Choose a country—one of the 249 countries for which the World Bank supplies macroeconomic data. Add "Inc." (incorporated) or "Ltd." (limited liability) or private limited company (PVT) to its name. Analyze it as if it were a business.

- Does the country have a competitive advantage? Can you describe it in one sentence? How strong or unique is it?
- Does the country have a competitive strategy? What is it? Is it sustainable?
- Is the country successful at growing, or is it stagnant?
- Is the country highly efficient and productive, or backward?
- Does the country have a stable currency, or is its currency losing value rapidly?
- Is the country part of a strong value network, with neighbors and trading partners with which it gets along well and buys from (and sells to)?
- Do the country's stakeholders (its citizens) share fairly equally in the fruits of the country's labors?

Many of the tools presented in this chapter and the following ones are designed to help provide answers to these questions, sometimes by showing where to find data and understanding how to read them once found.

A Country Is a Business   15

INTRODUCING GROSS DOMESTIC PRODUCT

All businesses have a profit-and-loss (P&L) statement and a balance sheet. The P&L statement shows the revenues the business earns and what it does with the money (buy components and raw materials, pay rent, pay wages and salaries, pay interest, and pay dividends to the shareholders). The balance sheet shows the value of what the company owns (assets) and what it owes (liabilities), and the difference between the two (shareholders' equity).

Countries have a financial statement not unlike the P&L. It is known as GDP and components. The six numbers that comprise the statement of GDP and its components are highly revealing for managers who want to analyze a country as a business. The numbers can tell you a lot of new things even about the country in which you have lived all your life.

For the US, in the 4th quarter of 2015, for instance:
One way to interpret GDP data, and Table 1.1, is to observe that the left-hand-side, GDP, is the supply of goods and services, and the right-hand-side comprises the demand for those goods and services, from families, government, businesses, and foreigners.

Table 1.1   GDP and Components: US 2015, 4th Quarter, Annual Rate $ Billion (Inflation Adjusted at Constant 2009 Prices)

GDP =	Personal + Consumption	Public + Consumption	Gross + Capital Formation	Exports – Imports	
$16,442	$11,323	$2,875	$2,842	$2,108	$ 2,674

Source: Economic Report of the President, 2016 (Table B-2, p. 408). The sum of the components of GDP differ slightly from the GDP figure owing to rounding error.

Action Learning: Six Things You Can Learn about the United States from GDP Data

- How does the size of the US market compare with the other nine leading nations' GDP? (See Table 1.2)
- How important is personal consumption as a component of GDP?
- How large is the part of GDP that goes toward goods and services supplied by state, local and federal governments in the US (public consumption)? Is public consumption relatively large or small?
- How large is gross capital formation? Do you think America's investment in building new physical capital is sufficient?
- How important are exports for the US economy? How large are imports?
- How does the gap between imports and exports affect the economy? Does this gap act to increase GDP or to decrease it? Why?

For any country of your choice, perhaps your own, find data for its GDP and the five components that comprise it, for consecutive years. Apply the "country protocol" to learn six things about the country. If the country you chose is your own: Did you learn anything new?

GDP can help us compare the size of leading economies. Table 1.2 shows, for example, that when measured in dollars, and using current actual exchange rates, the United States

Table 1.2 GDP: The World's 10 Largest Economies, 2014 ($ Billion) and Their Contribution to World GDP (%)

US	China	Japan	Germany	UK	France	Brazil	Italy	India	Russia
$17,419	$10,360	$4,608	$3,853	$2,948	$2,843	$2,346	$2,144	$2,073	$1,861
22.5%	13.4%	6%	5%	3.8%	0.7%	3.0%	2.8%	2.7%	2.4%

Source: IMD World Competitiveness Yearbook, 2015, 287–88.

Table 1.3 World GDP Growth (%), 2006–15

	2006	2007	2008	2009	2010	2011	2012	2013	2014	2015
World	5.6	5.7	5.7	3.0	5.4	4.1	3.4	3.3	3.3	3.5
Advanced Economies:	3.1	2.8	0.1	–3.4	3.1	1.7	1.2	1.3	1.8	2.4
US	2.7	1.8	–0.3	–2.8	2.5	1.6	2.3	2.2	2.4	3.6
Emerging Economies:	8.2	8.6	5.8	3.1	7.5	6.2	5.1	4.7	4.4	4.3
China	12.7	14.2	9.6	9.2	10.4	9.3	7.7	7.8	7.4	6.8
India	9.3	9.8	3.9	8.5	10.3	6.6	4.7	5.0	5.8	6.3

Source: U.S. Economic Report of the President, 2015. Table B-4.

accounts for close to a fourth of the world's economic activity, followed by China (about 13.4 percent). The world's five largest economies comprise half of world GDP. So by tracking these Big Five, a global manager can gain a good perspective on the world economy and its overall growth rate.

Together, in 2014, the 10 biggest economies in the world produced GDP worth $50,455 billion, out of total world GDP of $77,315 billion, at market prices, or two-thirds of all global GDP. China and the US together produced more than one of every three dollars' worth of goods and services made in the world.

Table 1.3 shows the annual year-to-year rate of change in world GDP, going back to 2006. It is clear that the global financial crash of 2008 took a large bite out of global growth, slashing economic growth in the advanced economies to almost zero and cutting growth in emerging markets sharply as well. The world still has not managed to restore the pre-crisis growth rates of GDP, and a major question now facing economists and global managers is: Will the world be able to return to the high growth rates that preceded the 2008 crash, or is the current relatively

Figure 1.3 IMF World Growth Forecasts, 2011–16

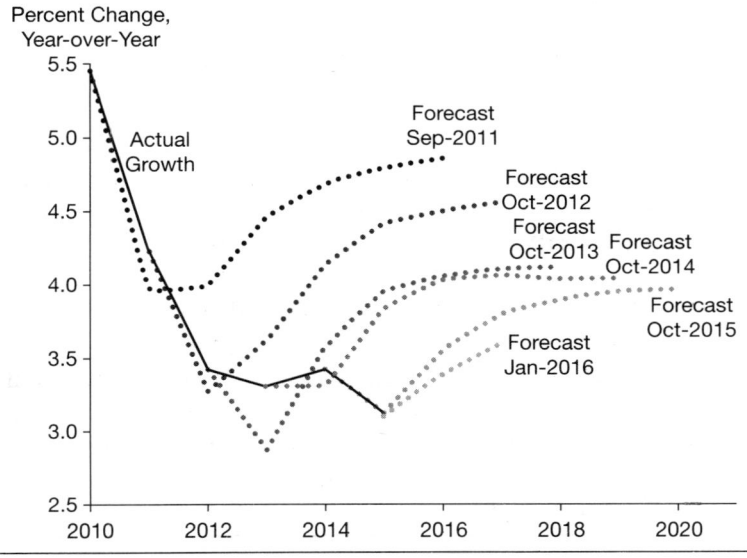

Source: Economic Report of the President, 2016, p. 121.

slow 3.5 percent annual growth in GDP likely to be more or less permanent?

Figure 1.3 shows a rather bleak picture of global economic growth rates, from 2010, declining rapidly, with the International Monetary Fund (IMF) consistently predicting recoveries and upturns, and constantly adjusting these optimistic predictions downward.

Figure 1.3 is a powerful advocate for Smartonomics. If the top forecasters in the world, at the IMF, who have access to both published and unpublished data, have difficulty in accurately "reading" the global economy, perhaps independent-minded Smartonomics practitioners can do no worse, and perhaps even a bit better?

Action Learning: Questions for Reflection

- Refer to Table 1.2. Can you discover how China managed to maintain its rapid GDP growth, when Western nations' GDP growth was negative, in 2009? Do the components of GDP tell the story?
- Why has India's GDP growth slowed, from the torrid pace almost equal to that of China in 2009–10?
- Will world GDP growth return to its 5.6–5.7 percent annual growth in 2006–07, or will it remain permanently at the current 3.3–3.5 percent level? What is your own view?
- Why is the US economy expanding more rapidly than the economies of Europe?

Box 1.3:   How GDP Was Invented

The statistical measurement of GDP is relatively new. It began with a team led by the eminent British economist John Maynard Keynes, including Richard Stone and James Meade, who in 1939–40 were faced with a very practical question: What is the size of the resources that Britain can muster in order to prosecute the newly declared war against Nazi Germany? Until Keynes and his team did their calculations, there was surprisingly no clear answer to this key question.

The team first calculated the size of the annual output of goods and services that Britain could produce. This is now known as GDP.

Next, they deducted the minimal amounts of resources necessary to feed, clothe, and house the people of Britain, during the war. This is known now as personal consumption.

Next they deducted the minimal amounts of resources necessary to provide for public services, such as law and order, education, and so on. This is public consumption.

Next, they deducted the minimal amounts of resources necessary to maintain the national capital infrastructure—to keep it adequate, but no more.

Next, they deducted the resources needed to produce goods and services for exports in order to generate sufficient foreign exchange to purchase imports (including arms).

Finally, they added the maximum amount of resources available for purchase from other countries (imports), using the maximum amount of foreign exchange available and credit that other nations would extend.

What remained was defense—the largest amount of goods and services available to prosecute the war, by producing planes, ships, tanks, ammunition, and other war material.

The formula was a variant of that in Table 1.1:

Defense Consumption = GDP − Personal Consumption
+ Civilian Public Consumption
+ Gross Capital Formation + Exports − Imports

This measurement system has evolved into what is now known as the national accounts, or national accounting. Keynes used the numbers in his proposed plan for mustering the resources needed for the war, published as a small book in 1940.[6] His basic GDP measurement for Britain was (millions of pound sterling):

GDP = Personal Consumption + Public Consumption
+ Capital Formation + Net Imports
$5,940 = 4,380 + 850 + 370 + 340$

> In 1952, British economists published a UN White Paper, *UN System of National Accounts*, that became the standard method for measuring national GDP and its components. It was based on the 1941 British White Paper prepared by Keynes and his team. Stone and Meade both won Nobel Prizes in economics. J.M. Keynes passed away before the economics Nobel was launched.

CONCLUSION

Practitioners of Smartonomics use both a microscope and a telescope. With a microscope, they zoom in on every small and large detail related to their organization, business, product, and professional discipline. With their telescope, they zoom out on the dynamic global economic and financial ecosystem, constantly tracking changing trends, preferences, and developments, within the framework of a global risk map that shows both impact and likelihood of a variety of risks. They then zoom back in, bringing their new hard-won insights to bear on their organization, always with a view to exploring new opportunities and avoiding potential crises and pitfalls.

A systematic checklist or protocol can be very helpful, just as the pilot and co-pilot of an Airbus A320 airliner run down a checklist of dozens of items even before they start their engines (parking brake, throttle, fuel flow, gear lever, panel light, and so on). Smartonomics proposes a basic global risk checklist and a country risk protocol. Country risk begins, but, of course, does not end, by gathering the six numbers that comprise GDP and its five components. These numbers alone tell global managers how large the country's market is and how the country uses its resources for achieving a variety of goals.

We began by claiming that in many ways, a country is a business. As we observe how poorly many countries' economies are managed by political leaders, and how often countries get into deep hot water over deficits, debt, wasteful spending, and mismanagement, we cannot help but ponder wistfully what the world might look like if countries were indeed run like businesses, to the benefit of their stakeholders, the citizens.

NOTES

1 See A. Ruttenberg and S. Maital, *Cracking the Creativity Code* (New Delhi: SAGE Publications, 2014).
2 http://www.imd.org/uupload/imd.website/wcc/Road%20Map_2015.pdf, accessed September 22, 2016.
3 Paul Krugman, "A Country is Not a Company," *Harvard Business Review*, January–February 1996, 4, 6 and 11.
4 Paul Krugman, "A Country is Not a Company," 4.
5 http://econintersect.com/b2evolution/blog2.php/2011/09/23/a-country-must-be-run-like-a-business, accessed June 29, 2015.
6 John Maynard Keynes, *How to Pay for the War: A Radical Plan for the Chancellor of the Exchequer* (New York: Harcourt, Brace, 1940).

Ants and Grasshoppers: Analyzing National Saving

Tool 2: Net Investment and Saving

Learning Objectives

- *Understand the link between national saving and investment.*
- *Know how to tell "ants" from "grasshoppers" and why it matters*
- *Learn the difference between domestic saving and foreign saving*
- *Know how to calculate net investment and capital consumption*
- *Understand why the current global flow of capital needs rebalancing*
- *Learn why vast amounts of wealth have been created and why they are held mainly by the super-rich*
- *Understand why the current global savings anomaly (rich nations overspend and borrow from poor nations) is unsustainable*

INTRODUCTION

Apart from their simplicity, one of the main advantages of the eight Smartonomics macroeconomic tools is their versatility. For instance, take Tool 1, that is, GDP.

In Chapter 1, we provided an accounting definition, comprising the annual production of goods and services made in the country, as well as imports (supply) and allocated as demand among the four different purchasers—the government, families, businesses, and foreigners. The focus was on the demand for goods and services and its relative proportions among the four sets of buyers:

$$[1] \quad GDP = Personal\ Consumption + Public\ Consumption + Gross\ Capital\ Formation + Exports - Imports$$

With a little sleight of hand, like a skillful magician, we can transform the GDP identity into something completely different, yet equally revealing—the savings and investment statement, that shows the extent to which a nation is growing its stock of physical capital and how that capital formation is being financed (through the savings of the people, government and businesses, or through borrowing from savers abroad, in foreign countries). Tool 2 is the Saving and Investment Statement, discussed in this chapter.

The first version of it is found by isolating gross capital formation on the left-hand-side:

$$[2] \quad Gross\ Capital\ Formation = [GDP - Personal\ Consumption - Public\ Consumption] + [Imports - Exports]$$

OR

$$Gross\ Capital\ Formation = [Gross\ Domestic\ Saving] + [Foreign\ Borrowings]$$

where:

(a) Gross Domestic Saving is GDP less Personal Consumption less Public Consumption, and (b) Foreign Borrowing is Imports – Exports.

For comparisons across countries, it is convenient to express capital formation and saving as a proportion of GDP:

[2'] *Gross Capital Formation/GDP = Gross Domestic Saving/GDP + Foreign Borrowing/GDP*

The right-hand-side of [2] and [2'] requires explanation. Saving, for economists, is simply the act of refraining from consuming. Hence, domestic saving is simply GDP, (which, as Chapter 1 explained, is also gross national income) minus the two components of consumption, public and personal. It is the part of GDP which is not consumed. Therefore, GDP minus public and personal consumption is defined as gross domestic saving. It is "gross" because, as we will explain in greater depth, it includes resources needed for capital consumption—the capital that is used up, through obsolescence, wear and tear, and accidents. Since Tool 2 includes "net saving," we will have to find a way to calculate this capital consumption component, as we will later in this chapter.

It is not obvious why the second right-hand-side component of [2], [Imports – Exports], has suddenly been transformed into "Foreign Borrowing." Here is the explanation:

> When an *individual* spends more than he or she earns, it is necessary to borrow to fill the gap. When a *country* buys more abroad than it sells (i.e., imports exceed exports), it must also borrow to make this possible. So the gap between imports and exports can be seen as the opposite side of the coin, as the amount of borrowing required to make the import surplus possible. What if exports exceed imports? Then "foreign borrowing" is negative, i.e., it becomes "foreign lending."[1] Foreign borrowing is positive for the US and negative for China.

The information conveyed by Tool 2 is vital, because (a) the ability of a nation to compete in global markets is crucial for its growth and well-being, and (b) the pace at which a nation's economy grows and prospers, and becomes and remains globally competitive, depends in large part on the proportion of resources the nation sets aside for building its future stock of factories, machinery, schools, communication and transportation infrastructure, ports, and computers and software.

It emerges that the global financial crisis that began in 2008 (and to some extent, is still unfolding) can be understood in part by applying Tool 2 to the US economy, and indeed every economy. Economies that plunge into debt, without using the borrowed capital wisely, become like businesses that are overburdened with debt—ultimately, they collapse. So while Tool 1 focuses on spending and demand, Tool 2 reverses the coin and looks closely at the other side—refraining from spending, or saving.

All of us know people who are strong savers, and others who delight in spending all their income. The quality of saving for the future, or spending for present enjoyment, is also a key aspect of the culture of nations (see Box 2.1).

Box 2.1: How Much Do *You* Save

One of the authors taught summer courses at MIT Sloan School of Management for many years, to a group of R&D engineers from many countries. Once he asked the class what fraction of their income each student saved. An engineer from Taiwan replied, 40 percent. The American students were astonished. Their savings rate was 5 percent or even less. The Taiwanese engineer explained simply that Taiwan had no real social safety net; hence, if he fell ill or became unemployed, he could only rely on his own saved assets. In the US, the social security system, indexed to the cost of living, was seen by many as a reliable safety net, though less so today as the population ages and the Social Security fund is depleting.

Source: Author (S. Maital).

To highlight national saving (an important aspect of national culture), in this chapter, we will distinguish nations of the world according to whether they are "ants" (those who save for a rainy day) or "grasshoppers" (those who primarily consume and ignore the need to save and invest). Thus, we begin with a 2,600-year-old venerable Aesop's fable where this metaphor originated.

The Ant and the Grasshopper

Aesop is believed to have been a slave, and a magical storyteller, who lived in ancient Greece about 2,600 years ago, between 620 and 560 BCE. His collection of fables, known as the Aesopica, has enjoyed immense popularity over the centuries. Apollonius, a 1st century. CE philosopher, said about Aesop: "he made use of humble incidents to teach great truths…he told the truth by the very fact that he did not claim to be relating real events." Paradoxically, Aesop spoke the truth by inventing fiction.

Here is one of his wonderful stories:

In a field, one summer's day, a Grasshopper was hopping about, chirping and singing to its heart's content. An Ant walked by, grunting as he carried a plump kernel of corn.

"Where are you off to with that heavy thing?" asked the Grasshopper.

Without stopping, the Ant replied, "To our ant hill. This is the third kernel I've delivered today."

"Why not come and sing with me," said the Grasshopper, "instead of working so hard?" "I am helping to store food for the winter," said the Ant, "and think you should do the same."

> "Why bother about winter?" said the Grasshopper; "we have plenty of food right now." But the Ant went on its way and continued its work.
>
> The weather soon turned cold. All the food lying in the field was covered with a thick white blanket of snow that even the Grasshopper could not dig through. Soon the Grasshopper found itself dying of hunger.
>
> He staggered to the ants' hill and saw them handing out corn from the stores they had collected in the summer.
>
> Then the Grasshopper knew: It is best to prepare for the days of necessity.

It is best to prepare for the days of necessity, Aesop teaches. This is a wise and simple notion—but a large part of the world has ignored it for decades, causing great damage. Smartonomics practitioners discern, from the outset, whether the country on which they are performing due diligence is an ant or a grasshopper. Eventually, over time, grasshopper countries that pile up debt run into trouble. Greece is an example (see Box 2.2).

Box 2.2: The Tragedy of Greece

Two trucks speed toward each other on a deserted highway. They are 50 km apart. Each drives at 100 km/hr. They have 15 minutes before they meet. Plenty of time to slow down, stop, turn off the road.

Yet they still collide head on, with massive damage. Then, the experts debate why this happened.

Greece joined the European Union (EU) in 1981. It joined the eurozone in 2000, in time to implement paper euros and coins when all of Europe did in January 2002.

Here is what former European Central Bank (ECB) Chief Economist Otmar Issing said in March 2011:

> Greece was only able to join the euro through deception [its budget deficit was far above permissible levels] and the currency bloc's leaders have been "too polite" ever since to deploy adequate sanctions that could have averted the region's debt crisis. When I worked for the ECB, I suffered every time countries didn't meet the criteria...Greece cheated to get in, and it's difficult to know how we should deal with cheaters.... Greece will probably be unable to honor its debts as it grapples with insolvency. The country's repayment ability remains questionable even after the government endorsed an accelerated asset-sale plan and a package of budget cuts necessary to draw a fifth tranche of its bailout.

With cheap credit easily available, the Greek government borrowed massively. The money was not used to build capital or future assets, but instead paid for pensions and welfare. It was obvious in 2011, four years ago, that Greece could not pay back all that it had borrowed. Today its public debt is an unsustainable

> 177 percent of its GDP. The debt burden is increasing, and so-called "bailout" plans simply allocate funds to pay back urgent debts, rather than rebuild the ruined Greek economy. It is obvious—much of the debt cannot be repaid by Greece. Yet its EU debtors refuse to acknowledge this. And the people of Greece and the economy of Greece continue to suffer.
>
> *Source:* Wienberg (2011).[2]

Ability and Willingness to Defer Gratification

> Temptation is when you want to do what you don't want to do.
>
> —*Caroline, age 12*

> The problem with immediate gratification is that it takes too long.
>
> —*Carrie Fisher, Postcards from the Edge*

Some 40 years ago, Shlomo Maital and his wife, a psychologist, published a research paper with a rather unusual argument: The key drivers of financial markets and of saving behavior, they argued, are psychological and cultural in nature and are driven by an important psychological variable widely used to characterize personality—the ability and willingness to defer gratification.[3] We argued that economic inequality is driven by this component of personality—the ability to refrain from spending and build assets, or the lack of it. Those who save, grow wealthy. Those who spend everything, do not. At the time, in 1978, behavioral economics (the application of psychology to the understanding of economic choice behavior) was not yet embraced by mainstream economists.

Later, in 1994, we drew attention to a rapid and worrisome decline in national saving in the developed nations during the 1970s and 1980s, driven by the fact that the psychological rate of interest (the premium people attach to present consumption in favor of future consumption) is much higher than the cost of borrowing. People constrain themselves from excessive debt by a variety of self-imposed constraints. But deregulation and a vast sophisticated financial services industry designed to encourage rising borrowing and debt have overcome these constraints.[4]

In our article, we offered historical data for national savings rates (Table 2.1).

Germany and Japan both had rapid post-World War II recoveries, driven in part by high capital formation and relatively high saving, and admittedly assisted by generous US Marshall Plan aid. In contrast, the US saving rate has been relatively low, perhaps in part because the US has been regarded as a safe haven for capital and, hence, has been able to attract large amounts of foreign capital—a topic we will

Table 2.1 Historical Gross Savings Rates, 10 Countries, as a Percentage of GNP: Pre- and Post-World War II

	Pre-World War II		Post-World War II	
			1950–59	1960–84
United States	18.7%	(1869–1938)	18.4%	18.0%
Australia	12.4%	(1861–1938)	26.2%	22.7%
Canada	14.0%	(1870–1930)	22.4%	21.2%
Japan	11.7%	(1887–1936)	30.2%	32.5%
Denmark	10.1%	(1870–1930)	18.9%	19.6%
Germany	20.0%	(1851–1928)	26.8%	23.7%
Italy	12.0%	(1861–1930)	19.8%	21.0%
Norway	11.5%	(1865–1934)	27.5%	27.1%
Sweden	12.1%	(1861–1940)	21.4%	21.4%
United Kingdom	12.3%	(1860–1929)	16.2%	18.1%

Source: Maital and Maital, 1994, p. 26.

return to later. But first, it is important to understand the causes and nature of the global financial crisis.

Sub-prime mortgage crisis: It can be argued that the US sub-prime mortgage crisis, the root cause of the global financial crisis that began in 2008, emerged precisely as a result of an under-regulated industry that urged Americans to take out mortgages, acquire debt, and buy homes, even when they could not afford to pay the monthly payments—a case of a greedy industry exploiting and feeding the human desire for immediate gratification. As the housing boom sent housing prices soaring, Americans felt that their newfound wealth (in home equity) made saving unnecessary. When housing prices collapsed, their savings disappeared.

Credit-card debt, too, added fuel to the fire.

Credit cards as personal banks: The legal right to issue currency is held only by a nation's central bank, or monetary authority. The right to lend money is allocated to banks and financial services companies, usually regulated by the central bank. But, increasingly, individuals and families have become their own bankers. They can lend themselves money by using their credit card (up to the debt limit) and then paying only the minimum monthly sum.

Save, then spend: A subtle change has occurred in Western countries, and increasingly in Asia. Once, the sequence was: Save then spend. One saved sufficient funds to make a purchase, and then made the purchase. Today, the sequence can be reversed—spend, then save to pay off the resulting debt. The end result may be the same, but the impact on society and the economy is not.

The expansion of credit card use has encouraged a "spend, then save" mentality. Today, credit cards mean that, unlike in the past, one need not have sufficient funds to enable a purchase; overdrafts will take care of it. In Israel exorbitant interest rates on overdrafts are highly profitable for credit card companies.

In the past, the logical sequence was "save, then spend." Individuals and families saved and, when they had accumulated sufficient resources, used them to make the desired purchase (house, car, or education).

In short, in the developed economies of the West, people once were ants, because they had to be—they had to save, and only then spend. Then they were persuaded to become grasshoppers, using debt and credit. The result was a massive mountain of debt that ultimately led to financial collapse in 2008. And it could happen again. This is why Tool 2 is so vital, and why global managers need to track saving behavior within countries and globally as well—because it is the underlying driver of debt and leverage. Some experts believe that the 2008 global financial meltdown, which began in the US, could occur again, though in entirely different shapes and forms. Is another global meltdown taking shape? (See Box 2.3.)

Box 2.3: The Impending Meltdown: Eight Causes

Professor Arturo Bris, a scholar at IMD, a leading business school based in Lausanne, Switzerland, offers eight reasons why another financial and economic meltdown like that of 2008 is likely. He may be wrong—it could occur in 2017 or later—but we should all be aware of the underlying danger signals. Forewarned is forearmed, or, as the Boy Scouts say, "be prepared."

1. Stock market bubble: Equities rose 18 percent between June 2013 and June 2014. Economics Nobel laureate Robert Shiller (Yale) says that the gap between stock prices and corporate earnings is larger than it was in the crisis periods of 2000 and 2007. Why the bubble? Because there is just so much money; those who hold it are desperate to put it SOMEwhere…no matter what.

2. Chinese banking system: Need more be said? China's stock market fell by more than 30 percent in July 2015.
3. Energy crisis: If the US Congress allows energy exports, it could crash the price for oil and sink Russia and other oil-reliant countries. This could lead to violence.
4. New real estate bubble: The housing bubble is back—low interest rates, rising real estate prices in many markets.
5. Corporate failures: Corporate debt is now rated, on average, BBB. This means that, in the next 5 years, about 16 companies in the S&P 500 will go bankrupt. This could have a major impact.
6. Geopolitical crisis: The world is a huge mess, with civil wars raging in the Mideast and elsewhere.
7. Poverty crisis: The number of people in the world living in abject poverty grows. This is dangerous; because desperate people may do desperate things.
8. Cash crisis: There is simply too much money out there. Central banks have printed enormous amounts of cash and it is floating around the world. Some banks and some companies are so rich they could buy entire companies. Right now that money is just sitting. If it starts to move, if its velocity rises, we may get huge problems.

It is possible to prevent a meltdown, if (a) politicians are aware it could happen and (b) begin taking action NOW. But both (a) and (b) are highly unlikely. Global managers should, therefore, be aware of the meltdown danger, and begin planning their own steps to protect their families and their businesses.

Source: http://www.imd.org/research/challenges/TC060–14-meltdown-2015-arturo-bris.cfm

COMPARING COUNTRIES' SAVING AND INVESTMENT

Before proceeding, we must clarify a semantic point. In everyday speech, we use the term "investment" to refer to a large range of financial transactions, many of which involve, say, converting cash into stocks or bonds, or vice versa. But when economists speak of investment, they mean economic investment or capital formation—something that results in creation of a new, real tangible asset (such as a building, machine, truck, road, fiberoptic network, or school). When performing due diligence on a country, global managers are keenly aware of this semantic point.

Table 2.2 provides data for capital formation and savings, as proportions of GDP, for selected countries, 2013.

Gross domestic saving provides resources for (a) domestic investment and (b) foreign investment. The data for the US are remarkable. America saves relatively little (even less than the table indicates, when net capital formation is calculated, discussed later) and saves much less even than the resources it needs for its minimal capital formation. Hence, the United States is dependent on foreign borrowing to make up the difference. The paradox of relatively poor nations (e.g., China,

Table 2.2 Gross Capital Formation and Gross Domestic Saving as a Percentage of GDP, Israel and Selected Nations, 2013

	2013	
Country	Gross Capital Formation (as Percent of GDP)	Gross Domestic Savings (as Percent of GDP)
China	46.6	49.5
Korea	29.7	34.0
India	28.5	30.7
Canada	23.7	24.0
Israel	19.7	20.9
United States	18.9	16.5

Source: IMD World Competitiveness Yearbook 2014 (Lausanne, Switzerland).

Taiwan, Korea) lending to rich (but highly indebted) ones (on a massive scale) is virtually unprecedented in history, and is only one of many pieces of data that reveal global imbalances and sources of instability.

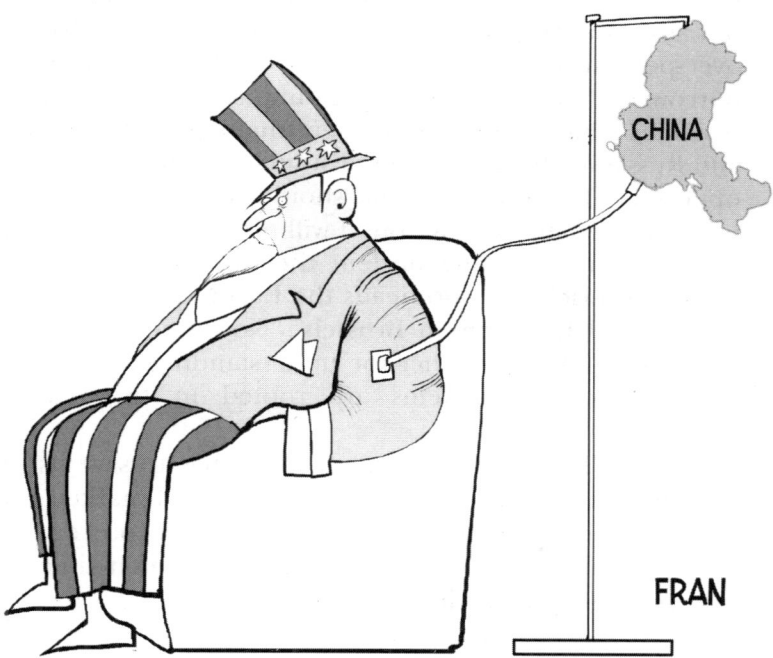

Benchmarking Two "Ant" Countries: We can learn much from two small, wise countries: Estonia and Norway. Each diligently insists on remaining "ants" while many around them become "grasshoppers." Norway has oil and gas resources and is wealthy; Estonia does not, but still refrains from debt.

Estonia: How to Avoid Debt

Not all countries have become excessively debt-ridden (highly leveraged).

Estonia has refrained from issuing government bonds, since 2002. Instead, the Estonian government took loans from the European Development Bank, which lends ONLY for infrastructure and approved investment, not to finance current government spending (or overspending). Maris Lauri says, "[W]e can't afford to borrow to finance current spending; such borrowing becomes a habit and we saw where that landed Greece and Russia in 1997/08." Some Estonian economists are opposed. They think Estonia should leap at the low interest rates and borrow. But it will not happen.

"Estonia is a strange bird in the Euro zone," says Frederick Erickson, who heads the European Institute for Political Economy in Brussels. "No other country has such a strong instinct for understanding the way macroeconomic problems are rooted in the real economy."

Estonia's Prime Minister says Estonia has to save its borrowing capacity and access to Euro capital markets, for the time when Estonia's GDP reaches 75 percent of the Euro average (it is now 73%), at which time European aid money dries up.

Norway: Prototypical "Ant"

Norway exports 87 percent of its oil and gas. But every dollar of state revenue from its energy resources is locked into a sovereign wealth fund set aside for future generations and mostly invested abroad (to avoid creating inflationary pressures in Norway, take advantage of good investment opportunities and spread overall risk). With wise investments, Norway's fund is today the largest in the world, surpassing that of Abu

> Dhabi last year and worth (in 2012) $656 billion, or nearly two-and-one-half times Norway's GDP (measured in exchange rates that reflect purchasing power). Both the people of Norway and its governments seem perfectly happy to set aside every oil and gas dollar for the future.

GROSS AND NET CAPITAL FORMATION

So far, we have referred solely to gross capital formation. It is gross because it includes resources used to replace capital that is worn out or obsolete technologically. This is why the adjective "gross" appears in GDP, and also in the term gross domestic saving.

This is highly misleading. It causes us to note, for instance, America's capital formation as 19 percent of GDP, nearly one dollar in every five, and believe that this is adequate, if not outstanding.

But what truly matters is net capital formation, which is gross capital formation minus capital consumption:

[3]
$$\textit{Net Capital Formation} = \textit{Gross Capital Formation} - \textit{Capital Consumption}$$

Here is a useful rule of thumb for calculating capital consumption.

- Assume a capital-output ratio of three to one; that is, it takes about three dollars of capital to generate an additional dollar of GDP. This ratio is widely accepted.
- Assume also an average lifetime of capital of 20 years. This implies a depreciation/obsolescence rate of 5 percent annually, (1/20 of the capital depreciates annually, or 5 percent).

- Hence, 5 percent of capital needs replacement yearly, or as a proportion of GDP, 5% × the capital-output ratio, Capital /GDP = 5% × 3 = 15%.

Therefore:

[4] $$\text{Net Capital Formation} = \text{Gross Capital Formation} - 0.15 \text{ times GDP}$$

Thus, fully 15 percent of the US 18.9 percent capital formation/GDP ratio is simply replacing obsolete and worn-out capital. Less than 4 percent is left as the net increase in capital stock, when capital consumption is deducted. This is far from sufficient. And it can be tested by observation. Smartonomics readers who travel to the United States will observe roads with potholes, badly crowded airports, poor or nonexistent public transportation, and, in general, shabby infrastructure.

Table 2.3 shows both gross and net investment, or net capital formation, for seven key nations. This is Tool 2, in real numbers. What appears at first to be a rather dull, confusing jumble of numbers turns out to be a startling revelation of fundamental structural weakness in the world's largest economy, the US, years before the US and global economic crisis began in 2008.

What we learn at once from this table is the extreme American (and to a degree, the British) version of the parable of the ant and the grasshopper, discussed in Chapter 4. Is it a coincidence that both the US and the UK, severe under-savers, had severe housing bubbles? America, one of the world's wealthiest countries, once was an ant, with relatively high levels of domestic saving, which it used for domestic capital formation and foreign investment.

At some stage, in the early 1980s, almost three decades ago, America switched from being an ant to being a grasshopper. This required America, a wealthy nation, to borrow from poorer countries, as imports exceeded exports. The poorer

Table 2.3 Gross and Net Investment as a Percentage of GDP, 2004 and 2005 ($ Million)

		GDP	Gross Cap. F.	As % of GDP	Net Inv.	As % of GDP
US	2004	10651700	2058200	19.32	460445	4.32
	2005	10995800	2152200	19.57	502830	4.57
India	2004	589668	170527	28.92	82077	13.92
	2005	644107	202667	31.46	106051	16.46
Brazil	2004	717346	107288	14.96	−314	−0.04
	2005	738166	111145	15.06	420	0.06
Russia	2004	328809	70093	21.32	20771	6.32
	2005	349853	75139	21.48	22662	6.48
China	2004	1715000	700930	40.87	443680	25.87
	2005	1893360	782240	41.31	498236	26.31
Japan	2004	4885068	1133619	23.21	400858	8.21
	2005	4978244	1155540	23.21	408803	8.21
UK	2004	1597273	284201	17.79	44610	2.79
	2005	1628133	290173	17.82	45953	2.82

Source: World Bank, World Development Indicators 2008. Net investment is calculated using the 0.15×GDP rule of thumb to compute capital consumption as previously discussed.

countries were largely the high-saving thrifty nations of Asia (though Japan, not a poor country, also lent to America). These nations saved a remarkably high fraction of their GDP, using a part of it to maintain high levels of domestic investment and a part of it to acquire the debt and equities of America. The phenomenon of poorer countries lending massively and willingly to wealthy ones is unprecedented in history, and is a clear signal of high and growing global risk. The reason Asia lent to America is clear. By buying American dollar assets, Asian nations kept their own currencies from appreciating relative to the dollar. Increased demand for US dollars kept the value of the dollar relative to Asian currencies (yen, yuan) high. This in turn kept Asian export goods prices competitive (in dollars). Their lending was not altruistic. It was in support of these nations' fundamental business model.

Country Risk for Borrowers and Lenders

> [N]either a borrower nor a lender be; for loan oft loses both itself and friend, and borrowing dulls the edge of husbandry.
>
> —Polonius, in Shakespeare's Hamlet

These words were written by Shakespeare in 1603, four centuries ago. Yet no better description of global risk during 1980–2007 has ever been written. And they are a good summation of what Tool 2, used to analyze, for instance, America's investment and saving data, seems to be telling us.

America has been borrowing and living beyond its means for decades. After the 2008 crisis, US national saving actually became zero (see Figure 2.1). The result has been to create growing country risk—rising leverage and debt among the government, businesses and individuals. Such borrowing dulled America's edge of husbandry. This trend was evident for at least a decade or more before the American financial crisis began in July 2007. Many people assumed that, since this situation had continued already for so long (interrupted by not infrequent downturns, which fairly quickly reverted to normal growth), it could probably continue forever. But, of course, no business, individual, family, organization, or even country can continue to increase its indebtedness forever, even America. The 2008 collapse was inevitable and possibly, using Tool 2, predictable.

A different kind of country risk exists for the high-saving nations, especially in Asia. Their business design is built on delayed gratification—very high levels of domestic saving to support higher domestic investment as well as a strong

Figure 2.1 US Net Savings as a Percentage of GDP (Gross National Income), 1947–2010

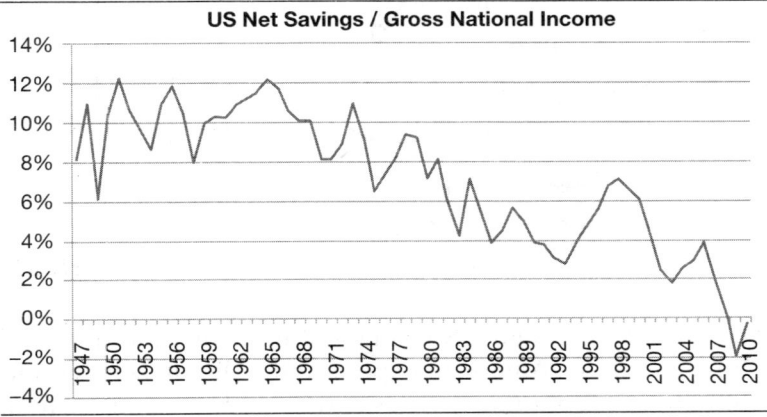

Source: Tverberg (2011).[5]

export surplus, implying foreign investment. This means that while GDP grows rapidly, living standards do not, because much of the added GDP dividend is set aside for future purposes. At some stage, younger generations begin to become impatient, asking that their hard work and effort be translated into present, rather than future, gratification. This can lead to rising wages and lower savings, which may endanger the nation's business design and create political instability. Asia's loans may not have lost themselves, in Polonius' words, but they do not seem to have made many friends in America, even though it is difficult to understand where America will find the lenders it still desperately needs, other than in Asia. Both high-debt and high-saving nations face country risk. Both require high levels of political wisdom and leadership.

Comparing China and the United States

Tool 2 can be used to x-ray China and the US for the year 2005, a year of prosperity and global growth, just three years before the global crisis began.

The contrast between US saving and investment and that of China is striking. American experts and policymakers tend to vilify China's economic policies and its undemocratic system. Yet the data in Table 2.4 for 2005 (close to the peak of the 2003–07 boom) reveal that even though China's GDP is about one-sixth that of the US, the absolute value of China's net investment matches that of America! Moreover, China's enormous domestic savings are sufficient to fund China's high level of investment and at the same time lend massive resources to other countries, in particular America, not only to fund America's investment but also to fund its present-oriented personal consumption.

Based on these data for 2005 alone, which country would, in the judgment of independent experts, comprise greater country risk? The answer is self-evident.

Table 2.4 Net Investment, Net Saving, and Foreign Borrowing: US, China, 2005

	Net Investment	Domestic Saving	Foreign Borrowing (+) or	Foreign Lending (−)
United States	$504 b.	−$116 b.	+$619 b.	
China	$498 b.	+$ 697 b.		−$ 199 b.

Source: World Bank, World Bank Development Indicators 2009. Available at www.worldbank.org, accessed September 20, 2016.

LACK OF SAVINGS, LACK OF CAPITAL, LOW PRODUCTIVITY: CAUSE AND EFFECT

In Chapter 1, we observed that the eight Smartonomics tools provide answers to key questions, but each, always, raises even more crucial questions. A "deep dive" into Tool 2 and the country "due diligence" it supports reveal the following: The world's largest economy, the US, and much of the Western world have for decades been under-saving and under-investing. The result has been to create inadequate, crumbling infrastructure of all kinds (transportation, communication, and education) and low and stagnating labor productivity. Beneath the smoldering embers of global financial crisis lie three burning inter-related structural challenges: inadequate domestic saving and capital formation, causing (in part) low and stagnating productivity, in turn partly owing to shoddy aging infrastructure for transportation, communication, and education.

There is a clear causal link between the growth rate of GDP and the rate at which a nation's capital stock grows. An analysis of the average GDP growth, public investment rate, and public capital growth during 1960–2000 for all countries in their sample (48 advanced and developing countries) shows that "cross-country differences in public capital growth explain much of the difference in long-term GDP growth during this period."[6]

When these IMF researchers plotted the average GDP growth, public investment rate, and public capital stock for advanced and developing economies from 1960 to 2000, they found that the public investment rate has been on a downward trend since the early 1970s in advanced economies. In contrast, the public investment rate increased significantly in developing countries in the 1970s, although it returned to its earlier levels in the 1980s. Public capital stock, as a percent of GDP, peaked for advanced economies in 1983 and for developing economies in 1985. (There is a close correlation between public capital stock and national capital stock.) The peak levels were 60 percent of GDP for advanced economies and 61 percent of GDP for developing economies. There was a downward shift in real growth of almost one percentage point on average around the time capital stock peaked.

We then examined the 30 globally competitive nations with the highest GDP per capita.[7] We gathered data on domestic savings, capital formation, GDP per capita, and GDP growth (see Table 2.5). Using data from the World Competitiveness Yearbook (IMD, Lausanne, 2014), we fitted a least-squares regression line to the data, with GDP per capita as a function of domestic saving as a percent of GDP. The results are shown in Figure 2.2.

The results indicate clearly that for a nation to increase its per capita GDP from the bottom of the pack, $30,000, to, say, $40,000, or 33 percent, it would need to raise its savings ratio by some 10-percentage points, from about 21 percent to around 31 percent. (Each one percent of saving/GDP adds $1,000 to GDP per capita). All five of the wealthiest nations in the world are "ants" (i.e., they save 30 percent or more of their GDP).

Our analysis shows that two-thirds of the variance in GDP per capita (across the sample of 30 wealthy countries) is

Table 2.5 30 Globally Competitive Nations with Highest GDP Per Capita: GDP Per Capita, Domestic Saving/GDP, Gross Capital Formation/GDP, GDP Growth

Country	GDP per cap PPP US $	Saving/ GDP %	Gross Cap/ GDP %	Real GDP% %	Ant
Qatar	99,371	73.2	29.2	6.5	1
Luxembourg	90,360	53.2	18.5	2.1	1
Norway	65,360	37.1	22.7	0.6	1
Singapore	62,276	51.3	23.1	4.1	1
Switzerland	53,769	31.4	20.1	2.0	1
China Hong Kong	52,340	24.6	23.7	2.9	0

(*Continued*)

(*Continued*)

Country	GDP per cap PPP US $	Saving/ GDP %	Gross Cap/ GDP %	Real GDP% %	Ant
USA	52,311	16.5	18.9	1.9	0
United Arab Emirates	44,205	42.5	21.9	4.8	1
Austria	44,092	26.2	21.1	0.4	1
Australia	43,710	27.0	27.7	2.4	1
Ireland	43,643	34.1	11.2	−0.3	1
Sweden	43,115	24.0	18.3	1.5	0
Netherlands	42,923	26.6	16.1	−0.8	1
Denmark	42,861	23.1	17.3	0.4	0
Germany	42,799	23.1	17.2	0.4	0
Canada	41,489	24.0	23.7	1.6	0
Belgium	40,752	21.7	19.7	0.2	0
Iceland	39,854	20.9	13.6	3.3	0
Taiwan	39,176	28.6	19.4	2.1	1
Finland	38,445	17.7	18.9	−1.4	0
France	38,027	19.7	19.5	0.2	0
Japan	36,259	18.2	21.7	1.6	0
UK	36,042	12.3	14	1.7	0
Italy	34,195	19.7	17.3	−1.9	0
NZ	33,406	22.3	20.5	2.5	0
Spain	31,764	20.7	17.7	−1.2	0
Israel	31,528	20.9	19.7	3.4	0
Korea	30,778	34.0	29.7	3.0	1
Average	45,008	28.28	20.08	1.40	0.433

Source: World Competitiveness Yearbook 2014, IMD: Lausanne.

Note: An "Ant" is defined as a country with domestic saving/GDP above the average (26 percent) for the 30 nations included in the IMD World Competitiveness Yearbook database, 2014. Forty-three percent of the 30 globally competitive nations have domestic savings exceeding 26 percent of GDP.

Figure 2.2 GDP Per Capita as a Function of Domestic Saving/GDP, 30 Nations

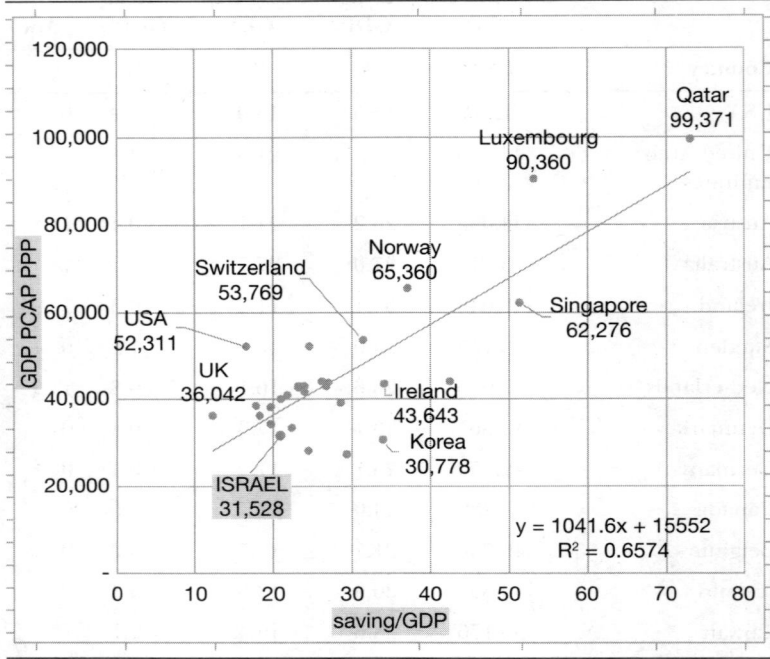

Source: World Competitiveness Yearbook 2014, IMD: Lausanne.

accounted for by domestic saving/GDP (which includes government saving, business saving and household saving) for the 30 globally competitive nations with the highest per capita GDP (PPP).

So, in a very real Smartonomics macroeconomic sense, Aesop was right. His truth, written 2,600 years ago, remains valid to this day. Ants grow faster. Grasshoppers often end up in debt.

The Astonishing Growth of Global Wealth

In the post-World War II period, there has been unprecedented growth in global wealth. Nations, businesses, and individuals have grown wealthy as economies grew and created

Ants and Grasshoppers: Analyzing National Saving   49

Figure 2.3   Global Wealth, 1980–2006

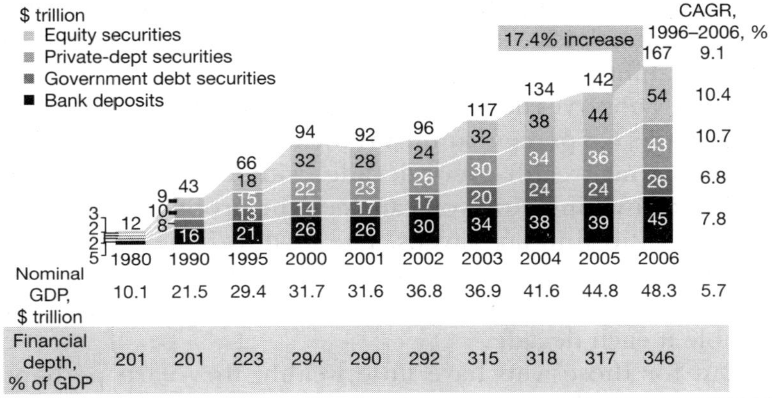

	1980	1990	1995	2000	2001	2002	2003	2004	2005	2006	CAGR, 1996–2006, %
Equity securities	3	9	43	66	32	28	24	30	34	36	43	167	9.1
Private-dept securities	2	10	15	94	92	96	117	134	142				
Government debt securities	2	8	13	22	23	26	32	38	44	54	10.4
Bank deposits	5	12	16	21	14	17			20	24	24	26	10.7
				26	26	30	34	38	39	45	6.8
											7.8
Nominal GDP, $ trillion	10.1	21.5	29.4	31.7	31.6	36.8	36.9	41.6	44.8	48.3	5.7
Financial depth, % of GDP	201	201	223	294	290	292	315	318	317	346	

17.4% increase

Source: McKinsey Global Institute (2009).[8]

a wide variety of assets, including equities, bonds, property, and bank deposits.

Figure 2.3 shows the remarkable growth in global wealth from 1980 to 2006, just before the global crisis. That crisis did see asset prices drop, but the result was to erase only a very small part of the growth in wealth from 1980.

Global wealth was 3.5 times global GDP in 2006, and it grew at a torried annual rate 17.6 percent. One cause of this newfound wealth was "monetization"—assets previously not traded in regular capital markets could not be captured in wealth data; once traded (as new stocks, new bonds, and new bank deposits), they became part of the wealth data.

This growth in wealth is in itself a good thing. The problem is, it violates the fertilizer principle—money, once quipped, is like fertilizer; in order to do good, it has to be spread around evenly. Global wealth is not.

THE DANGEROUS GROWING GAP BETWEEN RICH AND POOR

A recent bestselling book by Thomas Piketty uses official income-tax data to reveal how and why the gap between rich and poor is large and growing.[9] It emerges that there is indeed one group in the world whose savings are growing rapidly, effortlessly—the super-rich. The result is a threat to world stability.

Piketty observes that if you have great wealth, you can earn, on average, 6.8 percent annual return (above inflation). This doubles your wealth every decade, without your having to really do anything. And you can keep the profits, because the wealthy easily find tax havens. The wealthy benefit from low interest rates, borrowing at low rates that ordinary people have no access to. By leveraging their wealth, they more than double it each decade.

But for those who have little wealth, they earn perhaps 1 percent on their savings, or less, and often that is taxed. When the wealthy double their wealth every decade, in 30 years, it is eight times what it was at the start. When those saving for retirement earn get low returns, their saved assets are inadequate to sustain a dignified standard of living after retirement. Moreover, insurance companies take pension contributions and charge a whole range of fees that enrich the top managers but cut into the final pension substantially. It is said that invested pensions would be 40 percent higher without the fees. And with the insurance industry the pensioner has no way of knowing whether the company will still be around when retirement time arrives.

New data show that 80 billionaires hold more wealth than the poorest half of the world's population, and the wealthiest one percent of the world's population will hold fully half the world's wealth.

Where is the danger in this? For the super-rich, wealth grows much faster than their incomes. Hence, wealth concentrates in fewer and fewer hands, because the greater one's wealth, the greater the rate of return one can attain. And the final piece in the puzzle is this: Wealth corrupts democracy. With elections in the West growing more and more costly, politicians are increasingly tempted to trade favors for the wealthy in return for their political contributions, without which gaining re-election is very difficult.

Many have scorned Karl Marx's (and Friedrich Engel's) nearly-unreadable book, *Capital*, first published in German in 1867. But Thomas Piketty confirms at least some of Marx's predictions, that under capitalism wealth would become increasingly concentrated in fewer and fewer hands.

Global risk maps often cite growing wealth inequality as a source of risk and instability. The Arab Spring uprisings, beginning in Tunisia and spreading through the Mideast, can be interpreted as arising from corruption and unequal wealth distribution. (We will further explore the implications of this worrisome gap in Chapter 7.)

USING TOOL 2: A PERSONAL LOOK INWARD

We close this chapter with a rather difficult action-learning exercise, building on Tool 2. But first, some preliminary observations.

It is becoming increasingly clear that in the next 50 years, the world economy (and probably, the economy in which *you* live and work) will grow more slowly than in the past. A great many financial institutions have a keen interest in restoring a mood of optimism, to encourage borrowing. But it is becoming increasingly clear, that what was perceived as a temporary correction, due to the global financial crash of 2008, is now becoming a chronic slow growth, despite frequent upbeat reports that renewed growth is just around the corner.

Why?

A study by McKinsey Global Research, "Global Growth: Can Productivity Save the Day in an Aging World" (available from McKinsey's website) notes that "GDP growth was exceptionally brisk over the past 50 years, fueled by rapid growth in the number of workers and in their productivity."[10] But now, employment growth, which averaged 1.7 percent yearly between 1964 and 2014, is set to drop to just 0.3 percent a year.[11]

And productivity growth is slowing too. "Even if productivity were to grow at the (rapid) 1.8 percent annual rate of the past 50 years, GDP growth would decline by 40 percent in the next 50 years—slower than the past five years of recovery from recession." But productivity growth has declined and does not look like it will recover much.

A systems analysis of the world economy suggests that high-saving Asian nations are transforming their economies from export-driven to consumption-driven. They do this, because export markets in the US and Europe have been disappointing, owing to slow growth there. Maintaining high growth is essential for the Chinese economy, for instance, and, indirectly, for Asian nations that are part of the Chinese economic ecosystem. But as spending shifts from exports and capital formation toward consumption, productivity growth will decline, and already has, because productivity is driven by capital formation (investment in technology, new machines, software, infrastructure, and so on).

What can be done? "Catching up to best practice," says McKinsey. In other words, if we all benchmarked the world and defined and captured "best practice," productivity growth could nearly make up for the declining growth in workers.

Action Learning: A Challenge for Global Managers: Smartonomics in a Slow-growth World

Here are McKinsey's 10 key "enablers of growth." Can each Smartonomics global manager look at this list closely, and figure out, what is my role? How can I become really skilled, expert, at one or more of these enablers? If McKinsey is right, and if you can, you will be in great demand—and create value for the world.

Here is the list. Which of these suits you? What must you do in order to become a true enabler of growth in an increasingly slow-growth world?

(a) Remove barriers to competition in service sectors. (b) Focus on public and regulated sector efficiency. (c) Invest in physical and digital infrastructure. (d) Foster R&D demand and investment. (e) Exploit data to identify transformational improvement opportunities. (f) Improve education and skill matching and labor market flexibility. (g) Open up economies to cross-border economic flows. (h) Boost labor force participation among women, young people, and older people. (i) Harness the power of new actors through digital platforms and open data. (j) Craft regulatory environment, incentivizing productivity and innovation.

INFLATION, DEFLATION, AND SMARTONOMICS

On September 15, 2008, the bankruptcy of the once-venerable investment bank, Lehman Brothers, signaled a deepening global financial crisis. One result of that crisis was serious deflation in the West. Prices in Europe, Japan, and elsewhere have actually declined. During deflation, debt burdens become very heavy. In times of inflation, debt is paid back with inflated currency, which is easy to acquire. In times of deflation, debt is repaid with currency that is sometimes worth more at present than when the money was initially borrowed. This can increase the burden (cost) of repayment substantially. So, in times of deflation, companies, individuals, and governments seek to "deleverage," that is, reduce their debt burdens. The problem is, it is not logically possible for everyone, globally, to reduce their debt burden, because to do so, someone has to agree to hold or buy the debt, the opposite of deleveraging. If no one is willing or able to do so, simultaneous deleveraging is impossible.

Faced with stagnating economies, growing unemployment and excessive public debt, governments everywhere have sought to cut their budget deficits. This has further weakened economic growth. In response, central banks have acted aggressively, even uncharacteristically, to expand the money supply, with policies known euphemistically as "quantitative easing," initially done by the US Federal Reserve and lately by the ECB, which had been a bastion of conservative policy. Quantitative easing (QE) is simply the massive expansion of the money supply through purchase of bonds, which puts high-powered money into the hands of commercial banks and facilitates expanded lending.

Money supply in the US, Europe, Japan, and China has grown enormously. This bulge of money has inevitably brought down bond yields and interest rates and reduced the return on the invested pension funds. Many experts believe that this "solution" to the global deflation could itself sow the seeds for the next financial crisis, caused by the aggressive and perhaps excessive increase in money and credit—further fueling the speculative tendencies of human greed.

The moral of this story is simple. Debt in itself is not a problem, provided the debt is used to finance creation of real assets whose productive yield makes it possible to pay off the debt when it matures. But much of the huge expansion in debt, especially public debt, was used to finance public and private consumption, leaving no real assets available to pay off the debt.

Central banks in the West and East have now begun the delicate, crucial process of shifting from reducing interest rates to raising them. They do this, as the world gradually shifts from "deflation" (falling prices) to "inflation" (rising prices). Many younger global managers do not recall a time when prices rose and inflation prevailed. That is why it is so important to understand the nature and causes of both inflation and deflation, and the two types of each, bad and good—just like cholesterol.

This is the subject of Chapter 3, and Tool 3.

NOTES

1. Astute readers may ask: Since the dollar is the key global currency, and since America can create dollars by actions of the Federal Reserve (see Chapter 6), can America not import more than it exports simply by creating money (dollars), and paying for imports with them? This is true—but when foreigners hold dollars, the dollar itself is a kind of I.O.U. or obligation to pay, and, hence, represents US debt to foreigners. At some point foreigners who hold dollars can use them to acquire stocks, bonds or goods. China holds $4 trillion in dollar debt. When an individual spends less than she earns, the difference represents savings. When deposited in the bank, these savings are then loaned by the bank. Similarly, when a country's exports exceed imports, the resulting savings can be invested abroad in foreign countries in many ways: Purchase of bonds or equities, or property, or even acquisition of foreign companies.
2. Christian Wienberg, "Greece 'Cheated' to Join Euro, Former ECB Economist Issing Says," *Bloomberg*, May 27, 2011, http://www.bloomberg.com/news/articles/2011-05-26/greece-cheated-to-join-euro-sanctions-since-were-too-soft-issing-says, accessed September 22, 2016.
3. Sharone Maital and Shlomo Maital, "Time Preference, Delay of Gratification and the Intergenerational Transmission of Economic Inequality," in *Essays in Labor Market Analysis*, ed. Orley Ashenfelter and Wallace Oates (New York: Halsted Press/John Wiley & Sons, 1978), 179–99.
4. Shlomo Maital and Sharone L. Maital, "Is the Future What It Used to Be? A Behavioral Theory of the Decline of Saving in the West," *Journal of Socio-Economics*, 23 no. 1 (1994): 1–32.
5. Gail Tverberg, "Can We Invest Our Way Out of an Energy Shortfall?" based on U.S. Bureau of Economic Analysis Data (Table 5.1) (December 19, 2011).
6. S. Arslanalp, F. Bornhorst, and S. Gupta, "Investing in Growth," *Finance & Development*, 48 no. 1 (2011, March).
7. *World Competitiveness Yearbook 2014*. IMD: Lausanne, Switzerland. GDP is measured in U.S. dollars, using exchange rates that reflect true purchasing power (PPP).
8. McKinsey Global Institute, "Global Capital Markets: Entering a New Era," September 2009.
9. Thomas Piketty. *Capital in the Twenty-first Century* (Boston, MA: Harvard University Belknap Press, 2014).
10. http://www.mckinsey.com/insights/growth/can_long-term_global_growth_be_saved, accessed September 22, 2016.
11. http://www.mckinsey.com/global-themes/employment-and-growth/can-long-term-global-growth-be-saved, accessed September 22, 2016.

'Flation: It's Like Cholesterol (Good and Bad)

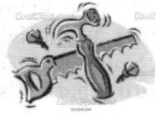

Tool 3: Inflation/Deflation: Good and/or Bad?

Learning Objectives

- *Understand why too little inflation is worse than too much*
- *Understand how inflation is measured*
- *Understand the two "drivers" of inflation, supply and demand, and how they differ*
- *Grasp the complexity of inflation, as different nations struggle with both inflation and deflation*
- *Know how inflation can distort the meaning of stock market data*
- *Learn why deflation is 100 times worse than inflation*
- *Develop an independent view on global inflation*
- *Know how good and bad inflation (and deflation) impact equity prices*

INTRODUCTION

Our book's subtitle makes an enormous promise—that after reading it, users may become wiser and richer. That is, they will derive both "light" (understanding, insight) and "fruit" (profit) from its macroeconomic tools. Libraries and bookstores are full of books that make unfulfilled promises. So, it is time we began to fulfill ours.

We cannot remember a time in the global economy when so much fog surrounded the major and minor economies of the world, both West and East. The US and European economies have failed to restore significant economic growth in the wake of the 2008–12 financial crisis. China's economy is slowing and Asia suffers as a result. Japan remains mired in deflation. South American economies face a variety of crises. Europe is stagnating and bidding farewell to Britain. Africa is hurt by commodity deflation. The Mideast oil producers face slumping oil prices.

What does the future hold? Can we help lift some of the fog, for our readers, using basic macroeconomics?

This chapter focuses on 'flation—inflation (rising prices) and deflation (falling prices), their causes, their impact, and, in particular, how to differentiate between two very different underlying causes of 'flation: those on the demand side, reflecting what people, government, and businesses wish to purchase, and those on the supply side, reflecting how well and how efficiently businesses product goods at low cost and high productivity. It turns out that the best way to understand 'flation is by an analogy, or metaphor—inflation and deflation are like cholesterol, there are good and bad kinds.

Box 3.1: Understanding Cholesterol—and 'Flation

Cholesterol is a molecule made by the bodies of all humans and animals, because it is vital for cell membrane health. It helps cells change shape and move.

> Cholesterol cannot dissolve in the blood. So it has to be carried, like trucks carry bread and milk, by carriers called lipoproteins, or "fat" proteins.
>
> There are two types of lipoproteins. One is low density (LDL) and the other is high-density (HDL). HDL and LDL make up most of our cholesterol count.
>
> HDL and LDL are very different. LDL is "bad." It contributes to plaque, a hard deposit on artery walls that makes them less flexible, causing atherosclerosis and possible heart attacks or strokes. HDL, in contrast, is good, because it acts as a garbage collector, carrying LDL away from the arteries to the liver, where it is broken down and discarded as waste.
>
> Inflation and deflation are like cholesterol. There is demand-side inflation (DSI) and supply-side inflation (SSI). There is demand-side deflation (DSD) and there is supply-side deflation (SSD). Like HDL and LDL, one type is good and the other, in general, bad. Knowing how to distinguish between them is an important first step in clearing away the fog that surrounds the global economy at this time. This is the theme of this chapter.
>
> *Source:* https://en.wikipedia.org/wiki/Cholesterol, accessed September 20, 2016.

Tool 3: 'Flation: Demand Side vs. Supply Side

Few macroeconomic topics are as baffling for global managers as inflation and deflation. In some countries, inflation is too high and officials struggle to reduce it. In others, inflation is too low and officials strive to increase it. Some types of inflation seem to have a positive impact on the well-being of a country's citizens. Other types of inflation have a highly negative effect. Efforts to forecast changes in inflation seem to be futile, with even central banks puzzled at times.

This chapter seeks to simplify this complex issue and clarify it. A good place to begin is with a Jules Verne' "Around the World" tour to understand just how central the issue of inflation is in the agenda of policy makers. During our tour, we will discover a series of "mysteries," worthy of Sherlock Holmes. After we complete our tour, we will resolve the mysteries using macroeconomics, perhaps in a manner almost worthy of the great Sherlock himself.[1]

To set the stage for our tour, Table 3.1 shows rates of price inflation for various countries in 2016. The inflation rates vary dramatically, from negative (deflation) to extremely high inflation. In some countries, inflation is too low. In others, far too high. The happy medium appears to be about

Table 3.1 Consumer Price Inflation: Selected Countries, May or June 2016 (Annual %)[2]

Italy	−0.4
France	0.2
Germany	0.3
UK	0.3
US	1.0
China (Mainland)	2.0
Japan	−0.40
India	5.8
South Africa	6.1
Russia	7.3
Venezuela	180.10
South Sudan	295

Source: http://www.tradingeconomics.com/country-list/inflation-rate, accessed September 20, 2016.

2 percent. But why? And if mainland China has 2 percent inflation, the only country with the "ideal" rate of inflation, like the three bears' porridge, not too hot and not too cold, why is China's economy said to be in crisis? And in countries like Italy and Japan, where consumer prices are falling, why are policymakers unhappy and want prices to stop falling and start rising?

These questions will, we hope, all find clear understandable answers in this chapter.

AROUND THE WORLD

United States: We begin our world tour of inflation and deflation in a rather unusual location—in Jackson Hole, a mountain resort in Wyoming, United States, where central bankers gather at the end of each summer to discuss the state of the world and how to improve it. We begin with the US, because it is still the world's largest economy (though barely) and because its monetary policies for the US dollar impact global interest rates and exchange rates.

It all begin in 1982, when the US Federal Reserve organized a central bank conference at a spot designed to attract the then-Fed Chair Paul Volcker, who loved trout fishing. In 2015, among the attractions at Jackson Hole are a Friday night barbecue and a line dance, with the world's central bankers donning cowboy hats and string ties. For the 2015 gathering, ECB Head, Mario Draghi declined to attend, as he was dealing with the ongoing euro crisis.

What did central bankers discuss at Jackson Hole in late August 2015?

A major topic was America's low inflation rate, well under 2 percent, at a time when the US Central Bank was trying to achieve its inflation target of at least 2 percent. (Too little inflation is as worrisome as too much, for central banks.)

America's inflation rate is crucial for the world, because the Fed's decision when to begin raising interest rates from near-zero levels depended crucially upon it. The Fed, under Federal Reserve Chair, Janet Yellen, was thought unlikely to begin raising its interest rates, a key signal for the world, until the US inflation rate reaches its desired level of 2 percent or higher. And interest rates elsewhere are crucially dependent on the Fed's interest rates. (See Chapter 4 for a detailed explanation.)

Federal Reserve Vice-Chair, Stanley Fisher, formerly deputy director of the International Monetary Fund and former governor of the Bank of Israel, told his fellow central bankers that America's low inflation rate is "transitory," driven by temporary factors. But some experts disagreed, saying that America's strong dollar, which cheapens imports, and low-commodity prices, which does the same, were less important for the inflation rate than long-term factors (i.e., consumer demand).

Sherlock Holmes mystery 1: Why is America's inflation rate lower than desired, despite massive amounts of credit and money created by the federal reserve since 2008?

Venezuela: Venezuela's inflation rate in 2014 was 62.2 percent. This is the official rate, and it was the highest in the world. But an expert disagrees with the official figures:

Professor Steve Hanke is director of the Troubled Currencies Project at the Cato Institute. He told *El Nuevo Herald*, "The economy is in a death spiral, moving from a bad situation to a worse situation." Hanke added, "The underlying inflation, which I'm figuring daily, is 615 percent. That's the real inflation of Venezuela."[3]

Sherlock Holmes mystery 2: How come Venezuela has price inflation that is apparently out of control?

South Africa: South Africa's 6 percent inflation rate occurs against a backdrop of ongoing "currency wars"—emerging market countries (including China) seek to lower the cost of their local currency, in terms of dollars and euros, to make their exports more attractive and stimulate their economies (see Chapter 8). Russian, Brazil, and Colombia all saw their currencies fall by more than 10 percent, relative to the dollar, from July to end of August 2015. South Africa, South Korea, Malaysia, Chile, and Thailand saw their currencies drop by between 4 and 6 percent. Clearly, if every country devalued its currency by, say, 10 percent, then relative to one another the exchange rate remains unchanged. This is why these "currency wars"—competitive devaluations—rarely help any country. It is not only emerging market currencies that have declined. The euro and the yen also have declined relative to the dollar, as has the Chinese currency, the renminbi.

South Africa's falling rand has made imports more expensive. As a commodity exporter, the decline in commodity prices have slowed its economy. China is largely responsible for this. China buys 57 percent of the world iron ore output, 51 percent of coal, 45 percent of aluminum, 41 percent of copper, 35 percent of gold, and 11 percent of oil. So when the Chinese economy slows, commodity prices fall (owing to reduced demand) and commodity-exporting nations suffer. Experts on South Africa claim that, "the effects of currency feed-through to consumer inflation can become very pronounced…leaving monetary authorities unable to contain inflation expectations."

'Flation: It's Like Cholesterol (Good and Bad)   63

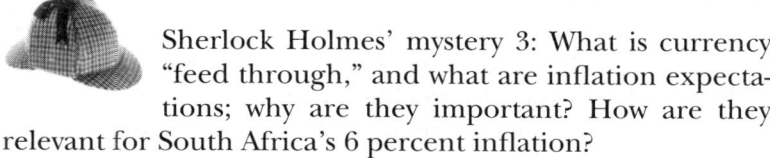   Sherlock Holmes' mystery 3: What is currency "feed through," and what are inflation expectations; why are they important? How are they relevant for South Africa's 6 percent inflation?

Russia: Facing economic sanctions over the Crimea/Ukraine conflict, Russia's economy is contracting. Russia's economy contracted by about 5 percent in the second quarter of 2015, after a 2.2 percent contraction in the first quarter. Yet, Russia's 2015 annual inflation rate is running at 15 percent, almost double that in 2014.

   Sherlock Holmes mystery 4: If Russia's GDP is declining, why then are prices rising rather than falling, as is common in a recession?

Japan: Japan has suffered from long-lasting mild deflation (falling prices) for 20 years, since the latter half of the 1990s.[4] Among the causes cited by experts are "decline in inflation expectations," "negative output gap," decline in import costs, and a strong yen-dollar exchange rate. They claim that there are "structural causes" for this deflation. During the deflation, Japan's economic growth has been weak or nonexistent. Japan's central bank has tried desperate measures to "re-inflate" the economy, without much success.

Sherlock Holmes mystery 5: What, in simple language, is Japan's deflation problem? And what is the solution? How can you have a 20-year deflation, when the central bank is aggressively increasing the money supply?

China: In the summer of 2015, China's stock prices fell by over 30 percent, (after a rapid rise from October to June of 65 percent). This sent shock waves throughout the world, as other stock markets also declined in response. China's economy has slowed, as China seeks to shift from an export-driven to a consumption-driven economy. China's currency, the renminbi, lost value relative to the dollar—perhaps 1 percent or so; relatively little, but enough to rattle global markets. China's official statistics show a 2 percent annual inflation, which many countries regard as ideal. Yet, despite this, China has major economic woes, and as the world's second largest economy those woes are affecting economies worldwide.

Sherlock Holmes mystery 6: How come China has "ideal" 2 percent inflation, but major economic problems?

India: India's inflation appears strongly related to the prices of food. And one indication of that is a perfect mystery for Sherlock: Theft of onions. Anand Naik, owner of a roadside stall in Mumbai, had 750 kg of onions snatched from underneath a tarpaulin in July. Why? The price of onions almost doubled in August compared to a month earlier. Supplies dropped by 70 percent in this period, owing to unseasonal rains, perhaps due to climate change. According to the Reserve Bank of India, households expect inflation to hit 10 percent, even though current inflation rates are around 6 percent. Half of the inflation is related to the price of food and onions are a key staple for Indians' diet. India's central bank wants inflation to fall to 4 percent, and, according to one expert, "needs credibility that it will act firmly against future inflationary threats." Meanwhile, Naik attributes theft of his onions to the price surge. "Otherwise who is going to try to steal these big [50 kg] bags?" he asks.

 Sherlock Holmes mystery 7: Why are thieves stealing onions? And why is India struggling to get inflation below 6 percent, to the desired target level of 4 percent?

European Union: The ECB, headed by Mario Draghi, is concerned about low inflation. Recently, it lowered its forecasts both for economic growth and for inflation, for the next two years. The ECB thinks inflation will remain "very low" for years to come. This could mean an expansion in the ECB's policy of "quantitative easing" (credit expansion and bond buying). Draghi said that since mid-August 2015, there is increased risk that the target of 2 percent inflation will not be attained. "Inflation could turn negative in the coming months," he noted. Fears of deflation led the ECB to initiate its credit expansion in March 2015, imitating the US Federal Reserve's policy initiated years ago. The ECB buys about 60 billion euros worth of bonds monthly, injecting cash into the banking system and presumably expanding credit and the money supply. However, in August, eurozone inflation was just 0.2 percent—far below the 2 percent target.

 Sherlock Holmes mystery 8: What in the world is going on in Europe? Why can't the ECB get inflation up to its target level of 2 percent?

How is Inflation Measured?

Before the world-famous private detective Sherlock Holmes can deal with the mystery of inflation, he needs to brief us on some basic definitions:

Sherlock says: "Inflation is generally defined as a rise in consumer prices. It is usually measured by the Consumer Price Index (CPI). In nearly all countries, the CPI is measured by a government statistical office, which first surveys consumers, to construct a typical, or average, basket of goods and services that the average family purchases. Then, each month, statisticians fan out into the economy, visit stores, supermarkets and markets, and gather data on the price of each item in the CPI 'basket.' They then calculate the cost of the typical basket. The percentage change in the cost of this basket then becomes the change in the consumer price index, widely used as an indicator of inflation (or, if prices fall, deflation). Essentially, the consumer price inflation number in each country simply tells us by how much the cost of a typical basket of consumer goods has changed during a given month."

"The CPI is like a two-headed coin—it has an opposite side. If you invert the CPI, that is, take 1/CPI, you get a measure of the purchasing power of the local currency. A rise in the CPI, thus, implies a fall in the purchasing power of the local money. Sometimes, the CPI is used as a 'deflator,' to convert economic data measured in current prices, to economic data in constant prices, or 'adjusted for inflation.' Sometimes, inflation-adjusted data are known as 'real,' as opposed to nominal, because they reflect real, quantitative changes in the underlying variable, rather than mix together changes due to both 'real' (quantities) and nominal (prices)."

Sherlock continues:
"I've convened this unusual meeting of all the world's experts—heads of central banks from Venezuela, China, Russia, India, Europe, United States, and South Africa—to try to resolve the massive confusion that apparently exists all over the world. And yes, I've chosen

my own home, 221B Baker Street, London, for this meeting. Thank you all for coming."

"Let's begin with some basic macroeconomics. Prices are determined by two forces: demand (what people want to buy, at various prices) and supply (what businesses want to sell, at various prices). Prices rise when people want to buy more at the given prices (demand) and/or when businesses want and need to supply less at the given prices (supply). Prices fall when people want to buy less at the given prices (demand), and/or when businesses want and can supply more at the given prices (supply). So, inflation (rising prices) and deflation (falling prices) are always driven by a combination of demand and supply forces.

"It is very important to know which is the predominant driving force. This is the key tool in solving our mysteries."

"I've prepared a simple diagram to explain the tool I used to solve all the mysteries you've posed for me" (see Figure 3.1).

There are two operative forces in markets. Together they are like blades of scissors that determine prices. And, like the blades of scissors, you need both.

Figure 3.1 Demand-side and Supply-side Inflation

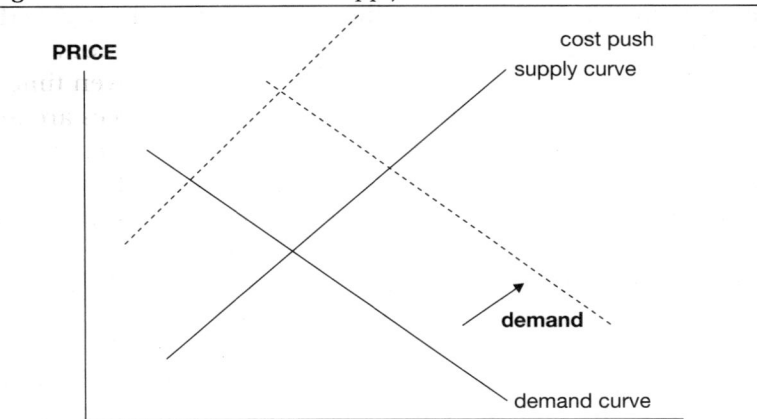

Source: Authors.

Demand-side inflation occurs when people and businesses want to buy more, at existing prices, perhaps because they are more optimistic, or richer, or simply fear things are getting more expensive. Higher demand implies both higher prices (inflation) and higher quantities of output, because suppliers are incentivized to produce more at the higher prices. This is a movement along a given supply curve. So, this type of demand-side inflation is a kind of mixed blessing. True, prices are higher, but output is also stimulated, and with it incomes and jobs. This is perhaps why 2 percent inflation is the target for Europe and America, rather than, say, zero. Perfect price stability would imply zero inflation. Yet, countries that have zero inflation (like Japan: as given further) are not doing well, and prefer 2 percent. So this type of inflation is in some ways "good."

Supply-side inflation occurs when productivity slumps, costs rise, wages rise, interest rates rise, taxes rise, and energy prices rise—in short, all the things that drive costs. In Figure 3.1, when the supply curve shifts upward and to the left, one can see that prices rise (inflation) but output shrinks, as the higher prices reduce the quantities that businesses and people want to buy. This type of inflation is "bad," because it is an unmitigated "minus"—higher prices and lower output, incomes and employment. It is sometimes called "stagflation"—inflation along with economic stagnation.

Note [Sherlock explains patiently] that at any given time, in any given country, both supply and demand forces are at work to influence prices. So, a wise economic detective, a wise global manager using the Smartonomics tools, will try very hard, with "pincers" [he removes some from his pocket] to separate these two forces and determine which of the two is the most important, at a given moment. This is the key to solving all the "around the world" mysteries!

What about deflation? Well, the picture is similar, but, logically, not exactly the obverse. You see, demand-side deflation means that the demand curve has shifted downward and to the left. This is purely bad. Because while prices have fallen, so have output, income, and employment. This is what happened in Japan. This is why central banks seek 2 percent inflation rather than zero. They *hate* perfect price stability because it risks demand-side deflation and stagnation.

But, you ask—is there good deflation? There is indeed. It is supply-side deflation, driven by falling costs and rising productivity. When goods cost less to make, people buy more, output rises, and so do income and employment. This is the basis of a theory known as supply-side economics. Boost the supply curve, lower costs, boost productivity, and good things happen. The main problem is, we really do not know much about how to use policy tools to raise productivity. Productivity is mostly the terrain of businesses and depends on their decisions.

Let's now resume our round-the-world tour, making use of our new-found understanding of 'flation cholesterol—good and bad varieties.

Venezuela: Hyperinflation, the kind that sees prices rise by 65 percent, or 615 percent, is always a *demand-side phenomenon*. People know that things will be more expensive tomorrow than they are today, so they buy more today, and that expectation itself drives prices up, sometimes in an uncontrollable fashion. Usually, such rapid inflation occurs when governments expand the money supply, when they pay their bills by borrowing from the central bank rather than raising tax revenues. It is a case of severe mismanagement. Of course, supply plays a role. Businesses hold back goods, knowing that they will be able to sell them at higher prices tomorrow than today. This too is driven by price expectations.

Venezuela had elections in the fall of 2015. The unpopular government that has mismanaged the economy got a message from the people at the polls. It is now in the midst of a severe political crisis. The government is blaming "foreign interests" for the chaos—but when hyperinflation occurs, governments can blame only themselves.

By the way, Israel too had a mismanaged economy in 1985, with 1,000 percent inflation. It managed to stop inflation in its tracks, with a severe package of wage restraint, currency devaluation, and a big cut in government spending. Let's look back and see how you stop rampaging inflation. This is what Venezuela needs to do (see the box below).

Case Study: Israel—How to Stop 1,000 Percent Inflation in Its Tracks

Israel's own existential economic crisis unfolded precisely 30 years before that of Greece, on June 30, 1985. Previously top-secret minutes from a dramatic 24-hour cabinet meeting have just now been released.

The background to the meeting, chaired by then Prime Minister Shimon Peres, was a stock market crash at the end of 1983, leading to the government nationalizing the major banks, a huge currency devaluation in 1984 that generated 500 percent inflation, and flight of capital out of Israel. Massive government budget deficits were financed by printing money, á la Greece. As Israel's foreign exchange reserves fell, there was doubt that Israel could pay its external debt, at the time 70 percent of GDP. (Today the figure is half that.)

A cabinet meeting was convened at 9:30 AM on Sunday, June 30, 1985, and adjourned at 9 AM on Monday. Before it was a stabilization plan devised by Professor Michael Bruno together with Professor Stanley Fisher, at the time an economics professor at MIT, later the Bank of Israel governor, and today vice-chair of the US Federal Reserve.

The plan included a massive $750 million budget cut. According to the business daily *The Marker*, Housing Minister David Levy protested at the time, "[How can

> ministers explain and argue when half of them are asleep?" Peres responded, "This is the best time to make decisions...I've been waiting for this moment for a long time."
> A new currency was inaugurated, called the New Israeli Shekel (NIS), in use to this day, and its exchange rate was fixed at NIS 1.5 to the dollar. After the meeting, most of the ministers went home to sleep. Peres, energized, spent the day implementing the cabinet decisions. The plan halted inflation in its tracks and stopped the capital outflow. The budget deficit dropped from an alarming 12 percent of GDP in the first half of 1985 to only 2 percent in 1986. Growth in the money supply fell from 12 percent a month to less than two. The plan later served as a model for other countries that got into similar hot water.
> The lessons are clear. When you have a major economic crisis, act quickly to resolve it fully, impose substantial economic pain if necessary, administer it in one big dose, rather than in a series of small doses. While doing this, explain what you are doing to the public to gain understanding and support. In July 1985, as a result of slashed subsidies and the devalued currency, prices rose by 27.5 percent, causing a deep cut in the Israelis' standard of living. There were a few strikes. But, in general, the public supported the plan and preferred temporary pain to ongoing chronic inflation (or in Greece's case, ongoing unemployment and deflation).
>
> *Source:* Sharkansky (1987).[5]

India: I think there is a key fact here. Some 40 percent of food in India is wasted, between the time it is harvested and brought to market. This is through spoilage, rats, poor transportation, and other factors. Indeed, worldwide a large fraction of food grown by farmers never reaches consumers. If some way could be found to control this wastage, it would help control food inflation, and inflation in general, in India. This food inflation is largely supply-side.

The Nobel economist Amartya Sen has shown that famines in India were not caused by a shortage of food, but simply by rising prices, making food unaffordable for the poor.[6] This suggests that supply-side factors play a key role here. Why are thieves stealing onions? Well, when their price has doubled, why not? A contributing factor is price sensitivity. Onions are a key part of Indian food. At least in the short run, there are few substitutes. So insensitivity of demand to price, plus supply-side problems, combine to boost prices and make theft attractive.

Russia: When prices rise and output falls, we detect "stagflation." This must be a supply-side phenomenon, in part. Costs rise in Russia because when other countries refuse to sell to Russia (EU sanctions caused by Russia's adventures in Crimea and Ukraine), substitutes are expensive. This makes the value of the ruble fall, and this again makes imports (when you can get them) costly. Add to that some demand-side psychological inflation (people anticipate higher prices and so buy more than they need, which boosts prices) and you get a destructive inflationary spiral.

Japan: It all began here with a property bubble bursting. That left people with big debts (mortgages), but without big assets, because housing values plummeted. This curtailed demand. Japan's deflation has been the bad kind—demand-side deflation. And, ironically, the government and the central bank have done everything possible to battle it, increasing credit and lowering interest rates to zero. But it just doesn't help. People remain gloomy about the future and burdened with debt. Unlike in the US, where if mortgage payments are not paid, the bank forecloses on the property and the owners "walk away," in Japan, mortgage debt is like a diamond—it is "forever," unforgiven. Businesses too carry large debts and receive new loans from banks to pay off old loans; this funnels credit to failed companies when growing companies really could use it. So, today Japan finds itself with massive public debt, 230 percent of GDP, compared with only 50 percent in 1981. Japan has painted itself into a corner and is having major difficulty extricating itself. Its demand-side deflation has been an object lesson for many countries who battle to avoid it.

European Union: Blame both demand and supply. Productivity has been poor in Europe for some time. Costs have risen. Demand is weak, as Europeans see a weak job market and flagging economies. The European single market has not managed to sustain growing demand. Only Germany, Europe's largest economy, has benefited, as one of the world's major exporters, from the weak euro; and now even Germany's economy is slumping. The ECB wants to stimulate demand-side inflation, and is doing so by massive credit expansion, but so far it has not had much effect and inflation in Europe remains nearly zero. Europe clearly is suffering from demand-side deflation. With an atmosphere of chronic pessimism, it is very hard for governments and the central bank to restore growing demand.

Summing Up

So, let us summarize what we've learned so far from our Around the World tour.

What is good inflation, and why is it good? Good inflation is moderate price increase, say 2 percent yearly, driven by rising demand, reflecting a growing economy and underlying consumer optimism. Demand-driven inflation, when moderate, boosts output, employment, growth, and income. There is also a money-illusion effect—when people's wages rise by 2 percent, even though prices also rise by 2 percent, there is the illusion that we are better off, even though in real terms we can buy no more than before.

What is bad inflation? Why is it bad? Inflation caused by rising costs and falling productivity. This is known as "stagflation"—stagnation + inflation. It reflects lower output, lower incomes, and rising unemployment. Stagflation afflicted the world in the late 1970's, when oil prices rose, driving costs upward and leading to a global recession, in fact, two of them—1973–74 and 1977–79. This is supply-side inflation. The cure is easy to state but difficult to implement: Higher productivity. When workers are more productive, costs fall, prices fall, output increases, incomes rise, and the economy grows. Stimulating productivity is a powerful way to battle supply-driven inflation, but few countries are very good at boosting productivity through public policy.[7]

What is good deflation, and why is it good? Good deflation is falling prices driven by higher productivity and lower costs. It is good because when the costs of making goods fall, output rises, exports grow, people buy more, incomes increase, and, in general, the economy grows. In other words, good deflation is supply-side deflation. We have not seen much of this kind of deflation in recent years. Indeed we have seen the opposite, mainly in Japan, which is a poster boy for bad deflation.

What is bad deflation, and why is it bad? Bad deflation is falling prices driven by falling demand—people become pessimistic, uncertain, fearful, curtail their spending, buy less, and drive down output, production, employment and incomes. In Japan, a two-decade bout of such deflation began with a disastrous collapse of the Nikkei stock market in 1990, driven in turn by a property bubble that burst. (This happened 17 years later, in the US). As Japanese people struggled to pay heavy mortgages on properties worth half or less than before, they cut back on their spending. Strenuous efforts by the Bank of Japan, to cut interest rates and boost credit, were to no avail. Japan's economy has basically stagnated for two decades, owing to "bad deflation."

'Flation: It's Like Cholesterol (Good and Bad)

If our "cholesterol" approach to good and bad inflation and deflation is valid, and truly useful, it should help us understand some of the mysteries of history. And one of the biggest, the 800 pound gorilla, is the strange behavior of the US stock market, from 1950 to the present. We present it as a true Sherlock Holmes whodunit.

I guess it must have been the 'bad' inflation after all!

A Challenge for Sherlock:
The world's central bankers, meeting at 221B Baker Street, London, gathered in a small circle, sipping single-malt whiskey. One of them, a central banker from tiny Iceland, spoke up:

"Sherlock, this 'flation notion is all very enlightening, very basic. But it barely tests your powers of reasoning. We'd like to pose a real challenge, one worthy of your intellect. And it is a historical puzzle, one we have not solved."

"So, here it is. Suppose we look at a chart showing the US Dow Jones 30-stock industrial average, over a long period of time, about 80 years (see Box 3.2)."

Box 3.2: The Dow Jones Industrial Average (DJIA)

The Dow in Dow Jones comes from Charles Henry Dow, who founded the Dow Jones & Co. in 1882. Dow started calculating an average of prices of stocks to track movements in individual stocks. He first published his average on July 3, 1884. It included 11 stocks. The first average comparable to today's 30 industrial stocks appeared on October 1, 1928. *The Dow Jones industrial average is not really an average at all, but simply the sum of the prices of 30 stocks, continually adjusted for stock splits.* The 30 Dow industrials are chosen to be representative of their industry, and the market, and comprise around 20 percent of the market value of all stocks, and about a fourth of the value of all stocks listed on the New York Stock Exchange. Only three of the original 30 stocks from 1928 remain. They are Exxon-Mobil (once Standard Oil of NJ), General Electric, and General Motors. The list of 30 companies changes fairly frequently. In 2009 it was: 3M, Alcoa, American Express, AT&T, Bank of America, Boeing, Caterpillar, Chevron, Citigroup, Coca-Cola, DuPont, Exxon-Mobil, GE, GM, HP, IBM, Intel, Johnson & Johnson, JP Morgan Chase, Kraft, McDonald's, Merck, Microsoft, Pfizer, Procter & Gamble, Home Depot, United Technologies, Verizon, Walmart, and Walt Disney.

Source: https://en.wikipedia.org/wiki/Dow_Jones_Industrial_Average, accessed September 20, 2016.

Consider Figure 3.2, showing 80 years' history of the Dow Jones Index. An unsuspecting manager might inspect it, and reason as follows: "Stock prices have risen strongly in the US, until the year 2000. They declined from around 11,000 to about 8,000, then recovered again until 2008, when they fell again from 14,000 down to below 8,000."

"This of course would be highly incorrect," the central banker explained. "It would be comparing oranges and apples—1935 dollars (the sum of 30 Dow Jones stock prices in 1935) with 2010 dollars (the sum of 30 Dow Jones stock prices in 2010). Clearly, to compare 1935 with 2010, one would need to correct for inflation. Fortunately, this is easily done. Simply divide the annual DJIA number with the consumer price index.

"Now, when you do that," the central banker went on, gesturing toward Sherlock with his whiskey glass, "you get an entirely different picture—a puzzling one." (He points to a graph on a nearby flipchart; see Figure 3.3.)

"So Sherlock, here is the mystery. In the US, during the post-World War II economic recovery, common stocks rose (adjusted for inflation) from 1,000 to 3,000, or more than 200 percent, between 1950 and 1966. Then, stocks fell

Figure 3.2 Dow Jones 30-Industrial Stock Average, 1930–2010: Unadjusted for Inflation

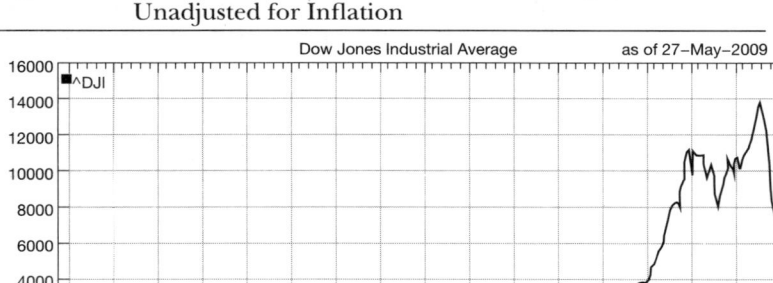

Source: Based on data from://schwert.ssb.rochester.edu/volatility.htm, accessed February 3, 2010.

Figure 3.3 Dow Jones Industrial Average, Divided by the CPI: 1950–2010

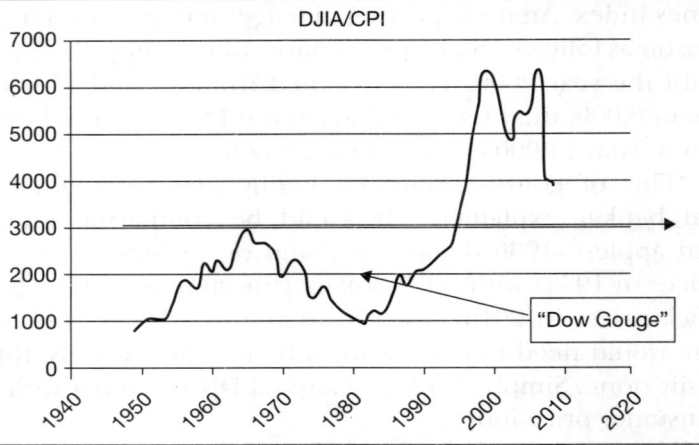

Source: Authors.

sharply, during 1966–81, from 3,000 back to 1,000, erasing all the gains! Then, stocks rose even more sharply, during 1981–2000—from 1,000 in 1981 to over 6,000 in 2000. Then they fell in the dot.com bubble, rose again, then fell during the global financial crisis during 2008–12."

"Sherlock, can you explain this? Does this have anything to do with your good-and-bad cholesterol 'flation theory?"

The central banker sat down, sinking into a leather easy chair and chuckling softly at the question he had posed for the renowned British sleuth.

Sherlock looked closely at the chart (Figure. 3.3), and gestured toward it with his pipe. He had a slight bemused smile on his face, as if he were enjoying every moment of this meeting.

Sherlock: "Hmmm, yes. Very strange. Bull market, 1950–66. Bear market, 1966–81. Bull market 1981–2000…. Yes, interesting. A superficial answer to the question is this: The unadjusted Dow Jones industrial average fluctuated in the range of 800–1,000 for 15 long years. Meanwhile, inflation, like the Colorado River chewing out the Grand Canyon, gradually eroded the real value of the 800–1,000 Dow. The consumer price index nearly tripled, from about 33 in 1966 to 97 in 1982."

"But," Sherlock asked, "what *caused* the inflation? And why was inflation at times good for stocks (1945–66, 1982–97), and at times disastrous (1966–82)? Why did equities not keep pace with inflation? How come equities were a great hedge for inflation in the 1950s and early 1960s—and stopped being so in 1965–66?"

"The key to solving the 'whodunit,' as the Americans like to call them, "of the mysterious bear market, 1966–81, lies in distinguishing between two types of inflation: Demand-pull inflation: Rising prices owing to excess demand for goods and services, originating with expansions of demand, as businesses, households, and consumers choose to spend more. As household's disposable incomes, and willingness to spend them grow, demand curves shift upward and outward. While prices rise, GDP increases. To produce more, more workers must be hired. Hence, in the case of demand-pull inflation, higher inflation is accompanied by lower unemployment. This inverse relation between inflation and unemployment is known as the Phillips curve relation, and it did prevail in the US during the 1950s and 1960s. Yes, it is clear. The Great Bull Market of 1950–66 was a demand-side phenomenon. Demand-side inflation is always good for stock prices. And it certainly was in 1950–66."

"On the other hand," continued Sherlock, "cost-push inflation is rising prices owing to rising costs of labor, capital, energy, and materials, originating with contraction in supply, higher unit costs, and the resulting increase in prices. Supply contracts when it costs producers more for each unit of output they make. This occurs when energy prices rise, wages increase, interest rates rise, taxes rise—in general, when the unit costs of factors of production and other business expenses increase. When unit costs rise, producers charge more for their products and raise prices. This shifts the aggregate supply curve inward, and to the left. The result is higher prices and, at the same time, a lower level of GDP. Here, unlike demand-pull, inflation is not at all a mixed evil; the level of economic activity contracts with inflation. As a result, output and profits also shrink. So, this kind of bad inflation, supply side, is very bad for stock prices. It shrinks profit margins, lowers revenues, and hurts company prospects. It causes stocks to fall. This is what happened during 1966–81. We had two oil shocks (1973, 1977) and we had food inflation before that; in short, we had massive troubles on the supply and cost side of the economy."

"Two very different forces are capable of pushing up prices and causing inflation. One operates on the demand side of the economy. The other finds expression on the supply side. Both are at work, in varying degrees, at any point in time. It is important to understand the nature of each, and to know which is dominant, in every country where global managers operate or plan to operate. I've prepared a simple Table to explain all this." Sherlock motions to a table he has pinned to the wall, near the walnut breakfront (see Table 3.2).

Table 3.2 Two Inflationary Forces

Demand-Pull	Cost-Push
* higher disposable income	* slower productivity growth
* lower personal taxes	* higher wages and interest rates
* higher budget deficits	* higher food and energy costs
* baby boom	* wage-price spiral
* investment boom	* falling dollar or currency

Source: Authors.

Sherlock continued with his explanation: "The periods 1945–66 and 1982–2000 were episodes of demand-pull inflation. Demand-pull inflation implies growth plus inflation—generally favorable for profits, and, hence, for stock prices. The period 1966–82 was one of cost-push inflation. Higher unit costs began with rising food prices in the early 1970s. Then came the two energy crises in 1973–74 and 1979–80, followed by higher wages and interest rates. Higher costs mean resources are less productive. GDP stagnates or declines as a result. Thus, cost push inflation implies GDP stagnation plus inflation. This is almost always unfavorable for profits and, hence, for stock prices."

"One of the main culprits was the collapse in productivity growth. Between 1948 and 1965, output per hour in the private business sector grew by more than 3 percent a year. From 1965 to 1973, it grew by only 2 percent a year, and from 1973–78, less than 1 percent a year. The recovery of productivity growth to 2 percent a year in the 1980s has contributed a lot to price stability, by matching wage increases, and offsetting their effect on costs and prices. Since 1982, the US economy has been undergoing very moderate demand-pull inflation, with little or no cost pressures."

"Demand-pull inflation is consistent with the behavior of the stock market in the 1950s and 1960s. Budget deficits were good for stocks because they were expansionary, raising GDP and economic activity, and with it profits. Inflation too was good for stock prices because it too signaled an increase in GDP and employment. But the 1970s and 1980s were quite different. While prices rose, GDP contracted. This is known as stagflation: stagnation + inflation. The cause was cost-push: Inflation caused by a contraction in supply rather than an expansion of demand."

"Cost-push inflation can indeed explain the causalities of the 1970s and 1980s. If inflation is contractionary in its impact on the economy, then higher inflation will hurt stock prices. Higher monetary growth will be seen as inflationary and will result in lower bond prices as investors demand higher interest rates. Lower bond prices will attract investors to shift their money from common stocks—another reason why inflation might hurt stocks. Cost-push inflation ended in 1982. In the 1980s and 1990s, US firms invested unprecedented sums in information technology and computers. Those investments generated remarkable gains in productivity in 1995–2000."

Global Managers: Know Your P's and Q's

If we agree that the *cause* of 'flation (both "de" and "in") is crucial to understanding the impact of 'flation, then how can managers tell whether it is cost-push inflation, demand-pull inflation, cost-push deflation, or demand-pull deflation that is dominant at any given moment, and in any given country? Here is Sherlock's "take" on this prickly question.

"One approach is to track the footprints of supply and demand—trace the price index against real GDP. By observing prices and GDP over time, we can grasp where the economy has been, and why, and, perhaps, where it and the stock market may be headed.

- When prices (P) rise and GDP (Q) falls—stagflation—it is cost-push.
- When prices rise and GDP rises, it is demand-pull (see Figure 7.5).

If the Q, P (Quantity, Price) point moves, for instance, northeast, from one year to the next, that suggests that the primary driver was an outward shift in demand, through higher spending by consumers, businesses, and governments. This is a demand-driven change, leading to demand-pull inflation and growth. The diagram shows the strong expansion in demand that occurred in the US from 1982 through 1990, propelled through tax cuts and higher consumer spending. If the Q, P point moves, for instance, in a northwest direction, that suggests that on a stable demand curve, the supply curve contracted, moving leftward and upward (recall that supply curves are really cost curves—so rising wages without comparable increases in productivity could cause supply curves to shift inward, leading to higher unit costs at each level of GDP). This occurred in 1981 and 1990—a phenomenon known as stagflation."

"Note that this good-bad inflation analysis applies to deflation as well. There is good deflation, driven by productivity gains that lowers costs and, hence, prices, while expanding GDP. There is bad deflation, driven by contractions in demand, leading to lower prices, but also to lower GDP and unemployment. In the global crisis of 2007–09, there has been widespread deflation driven by demand pull. It has been an unmitigated evil: declining GDP along with rising unemployment. Many companies have responded to resulting falling profit margins by aggressively seeking to lower costs by raising productivity. If sufficiently widespread, this could lead to good cost-push deflation: declining prices, but accompanied by rising GDP, and rising employment."

SUMMARY AND CONCLUSION

All over the world, countries are struggling with price stability. In some, like Venezuela, prices are rising far too quickly. In others, such as Japan, and perhaps Europe, prices are not rising quickly enough. At the center of the stage lie the central banks, whose job it is to maintain the stability of the currency and its purchasing power, using the three bears principle: the "porridge" must not be too hot (inflation) nor too cold (deflation). This has proved to be far more difficult than the French tight-rope walker who delights in walking a thin rope high in the air, often stretched between tall buildings.

Global managers must work hard to make sense of the inflation numbers. As with all economic data, they need to dive deep below the press releases, usually stating the monthly change in the CPI, and discover the underlying causes. They need to ask themselves whether the drivers of rising prices, or falling prices, lie on the side of demand (what businesses and people want to spend, based in part on what they expect will happen to future prices) or on the side of supply and costs (the cost of producing goods and services, driven by wages, materials, taxes, interest rates, energy prices, and so on, in turn driven strongly by productivity or output per hour of labor). A press release announcing 1.5 percent inflation for August 2015, for example, will have utterly different implications if the causes are growing demand or rising costs; indeed, the implications will be quite opposite, diametrically opposite, in each case.

For those with high levels of "bad" cholesterol, there are drugs available to treat the condition, known as statins. But for bad inflation and bad deflation, there is no such simple medicine. The best medicine, for global managers, is a perceptive, insightful diagnosis, understanding the underlying causes. And as with illness, a wrong diagnosis can lead to destructive, wrong decisions.

In the background of this discussion is the crucial issue of money, credit, and interest rates—a topic we have skirted, purposely, in this chapter. This is the subject of Chapter 4. It will explain how central banks control the money supply, expand or contract credit, and raise or lower interest rates, all of which is relevant for inflation and economic growth.

NOTES

1. Sherlock Holmes was a fictional London-based private detective, good at using logic to solve puzzling mysteries, invented by author Arthur Conan Doyle. Holmes wore a now-iconic double-peaker cap. Tiring of his protagonist, Conan Doyle once killed him off in a story—and fierce protests by his readers forced him to resurrect Holmes.
2. The trading economics website is free and is a fast and easy source for global economic data. Available at http://www.tradingeconomics.com/country-list/inflation-rate, accessed September 20, 2016.
3. http://www.breitbart.com/national-security/2015/07/11/venezuela-faces-hyperinflation-death-spiral-as-inflation-hits-615/, accessed September 22, 2016.
4. K. Nishizaki, T. Sekine, Y. Ueno, and Y. Kawai, "Chronic Deflation in Japan," Bank of International Settlements, paper no. 70, 2012.
5. Ira Sharkansky, *The Political Economy of Israel*, (Piscataway, New Jersey: Transaction Publishers, 1987), 125–26.
6. See the book by the Nobel laureate Amartya Sen, *Poverty and Famines: An Essay on Entitlement and Deprivation* (Oxford, UK: Oxford University Press, 1981).
7. See B. Cahill and S. Maital, *Britain's Productivity Challenge: Toward an Operations Innovation Revolution* (London: Trinity Horne, 2012).

Money: What It Is, What It Does

 **Tool 4: Economic Momentum**

Learning Objectives

- *What is money? How has the nature of money changed in the US (and elsewhere in the world) and why?*
- *How does money affect output, income, growth, and employment?*
- *What is economic momentum, and why is the velocity of money a crucial—and often overlooked—variable?*
- *How do central banks control the supply of money and the rate of interest?*
- *How are money, interest, and inflation related? Why are interest rates today the most important single macro variable in the US, Europe, and many other countries?*
- *How can managers track interest rates globally? Why should they?*

Money: What It Is, What It Does

- *How do interest rates affect the economy?*
- *How do central banks influence interest rates? Which rates can they determine?*
- *What is the fatal flaw in the current "dollar standard" global financial system?*

For all their miscalculations and the distrust that now surrounds their profession, economists will continue to exert a powerful influence over how we live.

—Alfred Malabre Jr.[1]

INTRODUCTION

The words that begin this chapter were written over two decades ago. They remain truer than ever. Economists' ideas have led to policies that have done the world harm. Unbridled free competition in financial markets has not proved utopian. Despite this, they remain influential. A key way economists influence how we live is through their control of the money supply, credit, and interest rates. This chapter focuses on how this is done.

A good approach to getting to the bottom of any hard question, is the method of seven "why's"—used universally by seven-year-olds. For them, a "why?" question, even if answered carefully, often leads to a second "why?" and a third, fourth, and so on, until the parent's patience wears thin.

This is a superb method for learning about matters in depth. By the time you have answered the seventh why, you generally have a fairly good understanding of the subject.

So, let us apply this method to understanding money and interest.

1. What is money? Why is money so important for the economy? What is economic momentum?
2. Why do some experts think that money and economic momentum are closely linked?

3. What are interest rates? Why do they get so much close attention from everyone?
   4. Who controls the supply of money? How do they do it? Why do they sometimes create vast amounts of money? How do they do this?
   5. Why is the world so keenly interested in the question of when will America's federal reserve begin to raise interest rates? Why were interest rates kept so low for so long anyway?
   6. Why has the mountain of money created by central banks in America and Europe not generated inflation, as it has done in the past? When will this "mountain" indeed begin to cause prices to rise—if at all?
   7. Why is the global economic and financial system so fragile, even after temporary repairs were made following the 2008 global financial crisis?

We will do our best to supply some clear answers to these questions in this chapter. Our data and examples will focus mainly on the US, not the least because the US dollar remains the world's dominant currency (a fact that reveals both the strength and the weakness of the global trading system).

WHAT IS MONEY?

For many, "money" is coins and paper notes. This is the concrete representation of purchasing power. But, in fact, for many years money has been mostly an accounting convention—a digital entry stating ownership of an amount of purchasing power in a financial account.

Figure 4.1 shows the various components of the US money supply, at the end of 2015.

Coins and notes amount to about $1.4 trillion. Demand, or checking, deposits add another $1.6 trillion. Savings and time deposits add another $9.3 trillion. Together, these three

Figure 4.1 Snapshot Data for Each of the Three Definitions of "Money" for the US, as of December 31, 2015

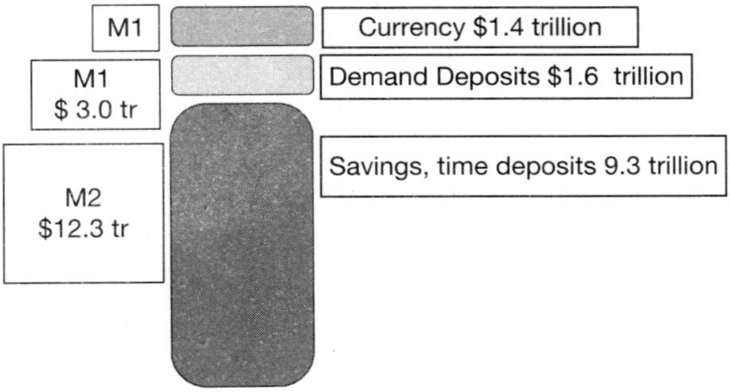

M1		Currency $1.4 trillion
M1 $ 3.0 tr		Demand Deposits $1.6 trillion
M2 $12.3 tr		Savings, time deposits 9.3 trillion

Source: Economic Report of the President. 2016 (US Government Printing Office, Washington D.C., January 2016).

components comprise what is known as M2 (the second tier of liquid assets), or a total of $12.3 trillion, at the end of 2015.

More than half of the over 40 billion paper notes in circulation, worth about $1.4 billion, are comprised of $50 and $100 notes. The US Bureau of Engraving and Printing prints about 6 to 8 billion new notes every year, to replace worn ones. The worn notes are shredded and discarded. Sometimes, visitors to a federal reserve bank receive a small package with shredded money. A large number of US dollar notes circulate abroad, in foreign countries, where the local currency does not enjoy stability or trust.

THE OTHER SHOE

Before we begin to explain the mechanics of money and interest, we want to set the stage, to show the vital importance of a deep understanding of monetary macroeconomics.

Those living in crowded tenement housing in New York City, for example, had several stories of apartments, with one bedroom atop another. It was common to hear a neighbor above removing their shoes and to hear them hit the floor. As one shoe dropped, with a "thud," there was an expectation of the second to follow. This expression, waiting for the "other shoe," has come to mean awaiting a widely expected event that may be delayed.

Just such a "second shoe" is the decision of the Federal Reserve Open Market Committee (FOMC), and its chair, Janet Yellen, to begin raising interest rates.

As we write this chapter, the world—financial markets, investment advisors, bankers, companies, governments, ordinary people—is literally holding its breath, waiting for the long-delayed decision of the US FOMC to "bite the bullet" and begin the long-awaited process of raising interest rates from their near-zero level. That decision will signal similar interest rate rises, probably, abroad, though possibly not in Europe, where the ECB struggles to fight European deflation and stagnating economies.

Reuters news agency reports:

> Federal Reserve Chair Janet Yellen on Wednesday (Nov[ember] 4, 2015) pointed to a possible December interest rate "liftoff" but said rates would rise only slowly from then on to nurture the U.S. economic recovery. In her first public comments since the Fed's meeting last week Yellen laid out what now appears the base case at the U.S. central bank—that low unemployment, continued growth and faith in a coming return of inflation means the country is ready for higher interest rates.

Faith in a coming return of inflation? Why? How? When?

Her remarks pushed bond yields higher and stocks lower. They also caused investors to reset their expectations of a December rate hike above 60 percent, a sign that markets are finally taking the Fed's language seriously after a period in which US central bankers were frustrated by the gap between their own outlook and market bets about their likely course of action.

Why did her remarks make interest rates on bonds (yields) rise? Why did "markets" not take the Fed's language seriously until recently?

"What the [Open Market] committee has been expecting is that the economy will continue to grow at a pace that is sufficient to generate further improvements in the labor market and to return inflation to our 2 percent target over the medium term," Yellen said at a House Financial Services Committee hearing. If the incoming information supports that expectation then our statement indicates that December would be a live possibility [for raising interest rates].[2]

> **Box 4.1: FOMC**
>
> The Federal Reserve Open Market Committee is a 12-person committee headed by the Fed Chair, Dr Janet Yellen. Seven members of the committee are Presidential appointees, for a seven-year term. Five members are presidents of the 12 Federal Reserve banks, scattered through America's leading cities, for example Dallas, Boston, New York, Chicago, Cleveland, St. Louis, San Francisco, and so on. The committee meets every six weeks, examines masses of data provided by Federal Reserve economists, and assesses the state of the economy, then votes on interest-rate policy. In the vote held in Oct. 2015, one member dissented against the decision not to raise interest rates. Decisions are usually unanimous, but there is dissent at times.
>
> *Source:* http://www.federalreserve.gov/aboutthefed/structure-federal-reserve-system.htm, accessed September 20, 2016.

Let us assume that Fed Chair Janet Yellen indeed acts to raise interest rates on December 16, 2015, with the approval of the FOMC. This indeed is what happened, as the Fed tentatively, gingerly, and rather fearfully, began raising interest rates to signal the end of the global crisis—and then quickly stopped doing so, as the economy proved softer than anticipated.

How does this actually happen? What is the mechanism that leads from a decision of a 12-person committee to the price of borrowing in the credit market?

HOW CENTRAL BANKS CREATE MONEY AND CHANGE INTEREST RATES

How, in fact, will the Fed raise interest rates? How does the Fed expand the money supply and lower interest rates? It is very important for Smartonomics global managers to understand the mechanics of this process.

Let us begin by analyzing "quantitative easing"—the process through which central banks in the US and Europe have greatly expanded the money supply in response to the global economic and financial crisis that began in 2008.

> On Jan. 25 2008, the Federal Reserve announced that it would purchase up to $600 billion in agency mortgage-backed securities (MBS) and agency debt. On December 1, Chairman Bernanke provided further details in a speech. On December 16, the program was formally launched by the FOMC. On March 18, 2009, the FOMC announced that the program would be expanded by an additional $750 billion in purchases of agency MBS and agency debt and $300 billion in purchases of Treasury securities.

This announcement was highly dramatic. It indicated an aggressive monetary policy to battle the negative impact of the global financial collapse—far more aggressive than the policy adopted, for instance, by the ECB.

What precisely happened, that brought interest rates down and increased the supply of money and credit in the wake of that dramatic Fed decision on November 25, 2008?

Here is the explanation, blow by blow:

Money: What It Is, What It Does   93

1. The secretary of the FOMC calls the New York Fed, at 33 Liberty Street in Manhattan, close to Wall Street in lower Manhattan. The New York Fed is the operational arm of the Fed, and runs a very large bond trading room. The secretary informs the head trader of the FOMC's decision.
2. The New York Fed buys $100 billion bonds from commercial banks in the open market. Banks deposit the New York Fed check in their Fed reserve accounts.

Here is how the two balance sheets look immediately after this transaction, on, say, January 23, 2016.
IMMEDIATELY AFTER (JANUARY 23):
(USD billion)

Commercial Banks		Federal Reserve	
Assets	Liabilities	Assets	Liabilities
Reserves $1,100	Deposits $10,000	Bonds $2,100	Currency $1,000
Loans 7,000			Reserves 1,100
Bonds 900			
S. Equity 1,000			

Note that the commercial Banks have "excess reserves"—reserves are $1,100 billion, while they are required to hold only $1,000 billion, or 10 percent of deposits.

Bank managers, thus, call their clients, saying: "Sir, or madam, you recall calling me last month and asking for a loan?" And the client replies, "Sorry, I cannot, we are loaned up to our reserve limit at present." "Well, today, I'm happy to say, I can make that loan. Please drop in to my office at your earliest convenience." These new loans simply create money, when bank managers give borrowers passbooks with the amount of the loan written in them as the new bank balance—the borrower's asset and the bank's liability, offset by the value of the loan, on the asset side. This credit creation is limited by the constraints of available reserves. The key to understanding the events of January 22, and, in general, to hearing what money is saying, lies in understanding how to read the balance sheets of both commercial banks and the federal reserve. Stylized highly-simplified versions are shown.

The initial balance sheets, on January 21, 2008, could be: (USD billion)

Commercial Banks		Federal Reserve	
Assets	Liabilities	Assets	Liabilities
Reserves $1,000	Deposits $10,000	Bonds $2,000	Currency $1,000
Loans 7,000			Reserves 1,000
Bonds 1,000			
S. Equity 1,000			

There are two key facts embodied in these balance sheets.

1. Banks make money by lending money. Loans are their principal assets. Deposits are their principal liabilities. Loans are made when bank managers lend money to clients, in the course of which deposit accounts are created. In this sense, money is not printed (except for a relatively small amount of paper currency), but created, when banks make loans.
2. Banks, however, cannot lend money without limit. They are limited by reserve requirements—the need to hold money to back the loans they make. These reserves are held as deposits in the central bank (Fed). Reserve requirements are always a fraction of deposit liabilities. In the previous example, reserves are 10 percent of deposits. The commercial banks whose balance sheet is shown cannot increase lending, because to do so would expand deposits beyond what their $1,000 in reserves permit.

Central banks lower interest rates and expand credit and loans by influencing the so-called monetary base, which is the amount of reserves held by commercial banks. They do this by what is known as open market operations—buying and selling bonds in bond markets.

Let us now track the events of January 22, 2008, blow-by-blow, to fully understand the financial engineering of credit expansion and interest-rate reduction. This credit expansion, when it is fully played out, will boost deposits by $1,000 billion (10 times $100 billion) and will boost loans by the same amount, $1,000 billion. The new balance sheets will become (by, say, January 30).

ONE WEEK LATER (JANUARY 30):
(USD billion)

Commercial Banks		Federal Reserve	
Assets	Liabilities	Assets	Liabilities
Reserves $1,100			
Loans 8,000			
Bonds 900			
S. Equity 1,000	Deposits $11,000	Bonds $2,100	Currency $1,000
			Reserves 1,100

The money supply has risen by $1,000 billion as a result of the FOMC's decision and the operations of its operational arm, the New York Fed. Money has not been "printed"—it has been created by bank managers, but only to the extent permitted by law, in accordance with the available bank reserves.

As a result of money being more plentiful, and more credit being supplied to markets, by the law of supply and demand the price of money (interest rates) will decline. This is known as the credit multiplier: A dollar of reserves can support, say, ten dollars of new deposits and loans. The New York Fed will continue its open market operations until interest rates decline to the target rate. The New York Fed may also lend money in the federal funds market to directly lower interest rates by boosting the supply of offered credit.

Box 4.2: The Crucial Role of Velocity and Momentum

"Pull over!" the traffic cop said to the 10-dollar banknote.

"But officer," said the note. "I was not speeding. I was barely doing 10 km per hour (6 mph)."

"Sure," said the officer. He was tough and grizzled and had heard it all. "That's exactly the problem, buddy. You were going too slow!"

"Too slow?!" said the note.

The stunned note fell silent, then recovered.

"Officer, believe me. I want to be a Ferrari. But these bankers, these people. They turn me into a turtle. They hang on to me. They used to spend and lend me like there was no tomorrow. Now? I can sit in a pocket or a vault for days! Weeks! I can't get no…momentum!"

Source: The fevered twisted mind of the authors.

In physics, high school students learn that the momentum of a moving body is the product of its mass (M) times its velocity (V).

Momentum equals Mass times Velocity, or M × V

High momentum can result either from having a heavy body move slowly or a light body move rapidly. According to Einstein's special theory of relativity, a tiny elementary particle like an electron gets heavier and heavier (higher and higher mass), theoretically, as it speeds up and approaches the speed of light. By the same token, in cricket, the ball can vary in weight, legally, from 5.5 to 5.75 ounces. So a 5.5 ounce ball bowled by a pace bowler at 100 mph (the fastest ever recorded) has the same momentum as a 5.75 ounce ball thrown by a spin bowler at only 95.7 mph.

The same relationship holds true in economics. This theory is one of the oldest in the history of economics, dating back to David Hume's famous 1748 Essay 12, and before that, even to Nicholas Copernicus. This theory states that the economic momentum of a nation, measured by its GDP, is the product of its money (M) times the velocity of money (V), or the number of times a unit of money changes hands during a year. This is definitional, or tautological, because velocity is identically equal to (defined as) GDP divided by money. But it is also a behavioral theory, because perceptions, psychology, and minds determine how fast money turns over.

This simple yet powerful economic relationship is shown in Figure 4.2.

This tool explains why central banks everywhere are struggling to combat the ongoing economic downturn. If they could, they would legislate a minimum speed limit for money. But they cannot. M is rising. But V is often falling even faster than the rate at which M is rising. So the product of M times V is falling. This is why we see, in several major countries, seemingly inflationary growth in money but falling prices.

Figure 4.2 Economic Momentum: Money Times Velocity

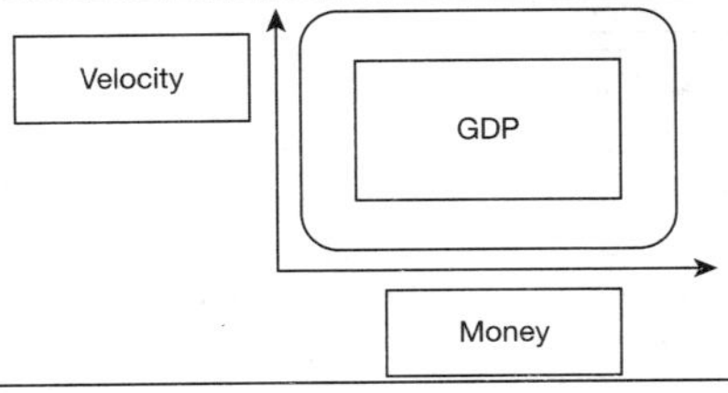

Source: Authors.

In his book on the Great Depression, *The Great Contraction, 1929–1933*, University of Chicago Professor Milton Friedman noted that between 1929 and 1933, the stock of money in America fell by a third as many banks closed their doors. But, he notes, the velocity of money also fell by almost a third. As a result, America's GDP declined by more than half. Apparently, history does repeat itself. This has occurred again, at the end of 2008. Central banks have learned from the 1930s how to prevent bank failures and the collapse of the money supply. But they have not yet found the secret for overcoming the slowing of money velocity, which greatly blunts the positive impact of more money.

Figure 4.3 shows graphically that despite the large expansion in "M", the money supply in the 4th quarter of 2008, in response to the financial collapse, economic momentum declined, because the velocity of money fell sharply, as panicky people and businesses held on to their cash and liquid assets, not knowing what the future would hold.

Mark Blyth and Eric Lonergan write that, in the 1930s, Keynes proposed burying bottles of bank notes in old coal mines; Once unearthed (like gold), the cash would create

Figure 4.3 The Impact of the Decline in Velocity: 4th Quarter 2008

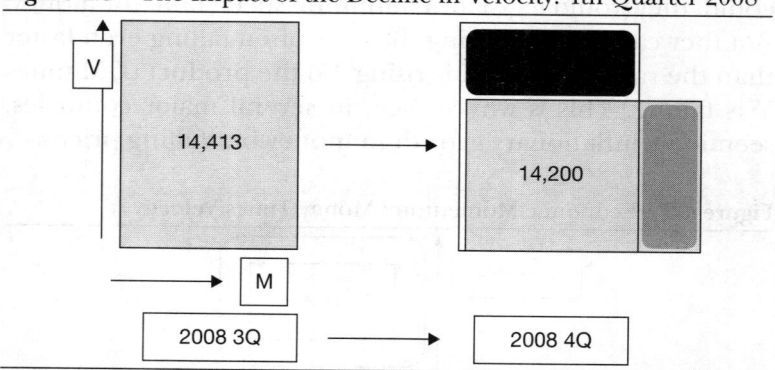

Source: Authors, based on data from The Economic Report of the President, U.S. Council of Economic Advisors, (Washington D.C., February, 2016).

new wealth and spur spending. The conservative economist Milton Friedman also saw the appeal of direct money transfers, which he likened to dropping cash out of a helicopter. Dylan Mattews writes that the idea is most closely associated with former Fed Chair Ben Bernanke, who first raised the proposal in the context of Japan's economic malaise in 1999 and repeated it in 2002 at a Federal Reserve board meeting.

THE MOUNTAIN OF MONEY: WHEN WILL IT BEGIN TO MOVE

A folk saying speaks about "the mountain coming to Mohammed." That saying is highly relevant today. There is a mountain of money. The key question is: when will it begin to move? When will the mountain come to the economy? When it does, to paraphrase what Napoleon said of an awakening China—the world will quake.

Why?

There are far too many dollars sloshing around in world markets.

The US money supply today totals more than $12 trillion, up from $8.5 trillion five years ago. That is a 7.3 percent annual growth rate, more than three times the rate of growth of the GDP. Under Federal Reserve Chairman Ben Bernanke, and now under his successor Janet Yellen, the US engaged in "quantitative easing" (massive credit creation) to spur its sluggish economy.

The resulting mountain of dollars has spread throughout the world and helped fuel property bubbles abroad, in China, Singapore, and perhaps indirectly in Israel, and ultimately will shake confidence in the dollar. We are unlikely to see an end to this policy soon; US economic growth slowed to 1.5 percent in the third quarter, down from 3.9 percent in the previous quarter.

"The dollar is our money—and your problem," US Treasury Secretary John Connolly said to foreign reporters in 1971, when the US stopped backing the buck with gold. That is America's policy to this day. Other nations' well-being demands a stable dollar and moderate credit expansion because world trade and finance requires a secure, solid currency. America perceives its interest lies in credit expansion. The world be damned.

America has for decades been under-saving, under-investing, and over-borrowing. The piper will eventually have to be paid.

Of 60 globally competitive nations, the US ranks 46th in capital formation as a percentage of GDP and 55th in domestic saving. Mainland China ranks first in both. As a result, America's infrastructure is worn and frayed. The US ranks 29th (out of 60 nations) in road infrastructure, 27th in bandwidth speed and 31st in railroads. The US continues to borrow heavily abroad, mainly from Asia, not to invest in the future but to consume in the present, further undermining the credibility of the dollar.

Again, the US Congress staged an 11th-hour showdown, on October 30, 2015, before raising the legal debt ceiling, barely avoiding another government shutdown like that of 2013. US government debt is today equal to the GDP; in 1974, the ratio was only 31 percent. The same ratio in Israel is 67 percent—an all-time low. In contrast, Spain, regarded as a country in fiscal trouble, has a lower debt-to-GDP ratio than the US.

There is a strong disconnect between America's dominance in financial markets, which has actually grown, and its ever-weakening economy. No country's money has remained a key world currency without a strong underlying economy.

US stock markets trade shares with a market value of $24 trillion, six times larger than that of China. US financial markets powerfully impact on markets in Europe and Asia. American fund managers run well over half the world's total assets under management, up from 44 percent a decade ago, according to the UK magazine *The Economist*. Some 60 percent of world output is produced in a dollar zone, in countries whose currencies are tied to the dollar.

Meanwhile, the US imports nearly $800 billion more than it exports annually, and has been doing so for decades. Only a country that can freely print (and borrow) the world's currency could do this.

In history, no nation's currency has remained dominant when that nation's economy was weak. Britain's pound sterling ruled the world for more than a century, until 1920, as Britain led the Industrial Revolution. But between 1920 and 1945, Britain lost its empire and the pound gracefully gave way to the dollar. This transition was smooth, partly because Britain and the US were strong allies, and partly because Britain facilitated it. But today, the US, the EU, and China act more like rivals than allies as each pursues its own self-interest. Thus, the transition to a new world currency is likely to be rocky.

There is a quiet but fierce currency war underway as major countries (Japan, Europe, and China) try to solve their economic maladies by devaluing their currencies. While this has temporarily strengthened the dollar, it is very bad in the long-run for the world economy.

We can hear critics saying, if the dollar is so weak, how come it is so strong? Since mid-2011 the trade-weighted dollar index (the value of the dollar measured against six other key currencies) has risen nearly 40 percent. Once, the euro was worth $1.45 (in mid-2011); today it is worth only $1.09. (The shekel–dollar rate has been on a roller coaster ride; the dollar strengthened from 3.40 shekels per dollar in mid-2011 to nearly 4.0 in 2012, fell to 3.40 shekels in mid-2014, rose back to 4.0, and is now around 3.86.)

Why is the dollar so strong? Largely because the other major moneys are weak.

Japanese Prime Minister Shinzo Abe launched an economic blitz to devalue the yen and spur Japan's economy in 2012; the yen did fall by a third, relative to the dollar, but the so-called "Abenomics" has not worked so far.

In August 2015, China made its renminbi depreciate by about 3 percent and in Europe, ECB Head Mario Draghi has promised to do "whatever it takes" to spur Europe's economy, including massive credit creation, zero interest rates, and a falling euro. Europe and the US seem to be in a losing competition to see who can print money fastest.

Despite a World Bank study showing that devaluing a country's currency does little for its economy, nations continue to attempt it. Some countries, such as Greece, locked into the euro, wish they could. One reason currency devaluation fails is that, today, trade is one big global value chain. If your currency falls, your exports are cheaper but your imports are more costly, and if you import components, that soon makes your exports more costly, as well.

THE FATAL FLAW IN THE WORLD'S MONETARY ARCHITECTURE

There is a fatal flaw in the architecture of the Bretton Woods agreements, signed in 1944—the dollar cannot be simultaneously America's money and the world's money.

The world has not yet addressed a crucial design flaw originating in 1944. At the 1944 Bretton Woods conference, held at a lovely New Hampshire resort, Hotel Mt. Washington, British economist J.M. Keynes proposed creating a world central bank and a world currency. That made sense. A lot of mischief would have been prevented had he been heeded.

But the chief US representative, Harry Dexter White, insisted that the dollar would be the world's currency. At the time, much of the world's economy had been destroyed by World War II while the US economy had doubled twice during the war. In 1945, the US produced fully 75 percent of the total world GDP. Hence, America called the shots.

Today, US monetary interests diverge from the rest of the world. A weak US economy seems to need piles of money and near-zero interest rates. So, this is what the US Federal Reserve does. And it has been for seven years. Financial markets nervously await the first hint that Yellen will begin raising interest rates—a bullet she has repeatedly refused to bite.

CRUNCHING THE NUMBERS: WHY THE MOUNTAIN DID NOT MOVE

Here is yet another mystery for Sherlock Holmes, whom we called upon in a previous chapter. This one will barely challenge his powers of deduction.

Between 2008 and 2014, in the United States, the money supply (M2) rose by 42.2 percent (see Table 4.1) This was a result of the quantitative easing described previously—the federal reserve's massive purchases of bonds (later imitated by the ECB, under head Mario Draghi), injecting huge amounts of liquidity and credit into the monetary system. Normally a 42 percent rise in money would generate considerable inflation.

Yet the GDP Price Index (P) rose by only 9 percent during the whole six-year period. In the US, the price index rose by far more in a single year during the double-digit inflation of 1978–80.

Why?

Sherlock has the answer. Velocity. The mountain of money not only did not move, but it slowed down. It stopped moving as fast as it did before. Velocity declined by 16.7 percent.

We can use the following equation to understand history—and to help predict and understand the future:

$$m + v + m*v = p + q + p*q$$

Table 4.1 Money Supply, Velocity, Price Index and Real GDP: Economic Momentum, 2008–14

Year	M2	Velocity (V)	Price Index (P)	Real GDP (Q)	Momentum MV
			1.000		
2008	8177	1.80	1.020	14430	14719
2009	8482	1.70	1.028	14024	14419
2010	8783	1.70	1.040	14382	14964
2011	9636	1.61	1.062	14607	15518
2012	10424	1.55	1.081	14945	16163
2013	10985	1.53	1.098	15276	16768
2014	11626	1.50	1.113	15651	17421

Source: Authors' calculations, based on data in Economic Report of the President 2016.

That is, the percent change in M plus the percent change in V, plus the cross product, is identically equal to the percent change in P, plus the percent change in Q, plus the cross-product. (Normally when m and v, or p and q, are small, the cross-product can be ignored; but in our case, both are quite large, as we are looking at a six-year period, rather than a single year).

Tables 4.1 and 4.2 show that economic momentum, measured by both MV and PQ, rose by 18.5 percent between 2008 and 2014. Half of that, approximately, was the rise in real GDP, 8.5 percent—a very small rise for a six-year period. (China's GDP growth in some years equaled that in a single year, during 1995–2005). Half was the rise in prices, 9.1 percent.

On the money side: Money supply rose by a startling 42.2 percent. This reflects the desperation of the Fed to counteract the 2008 global crisis and stimulate the economy with easy money.

Why then did this huge expansion in credit not stimulate the economy more?

Because of fear. As President Franklin Roosevelt said, during the Great Depression, "[T]he only thing we have to fear is fear itself." In fact, there are far more things to fear than just fear—but fear itself can create the damage it is fearful of. Through a slowdown in the rate at which money changes hands. When people are risk-averse, fearful of the future, they would rather hang on to their money than spend, borrow, and invest. So the change in momentum was the product of a rise in money, 42.2 percent, a fall in velocity, minus 16.7 percent, and the cross product, m*v, minus 7 percent, or 18.5 percent.

Table 4.2 Percent Change in M, V, P, and Q, 2008–14

% Change in: (2008 to 2014)					
M	V	Cross-product	P	Q	Cross-product
42.2%	–16.7%	–7.0	9.1%	8.5%	0.9%

Source: Authors' calculations, based on Table 4.1.

What we learn from this number-crunching, counsels Sherlock Holmes, is that a very old theory, mocked by some economists (an early version of this book was rejected by a leading economist, as reviewer, on the grounds the "velocity is merely technical"), very long in tooth and well over two centuries old, is highly relevant to understanding today's quandaries. And moreover, most important of all, counsels Sherlock, velocity of money is vital, not just useful, in determining and predicting the future.

When will economic momentum increase in the West?

When the mountain of money comes to Mohammed, and begins to move faster, that is, when velocity speeds up. When will that happen? When people overcome their fear, reduce their risk-aversion, and begin to spend and invest. That increase in velocity will, in turn, spur real economic activity, that is, Q, but also will generate some inflation, which is not a bad thing—central banks in America and Europe both have inflation targets and the actual inflation rates today are well below those targets, while the central banks seem unable to reach the desired level of inflation, needed to stimulate the economy and create jobs.

What this tells practitioners of Smartonomics is this: Do not wait for official figures to tell you what has happened to velocity. That will take far too long.

Instead, track velocity on your money. One trick: Simply look at the paper money. Crisp new bills indicate low velocity. In countries with high inflation, the money is tired, dog-eared, worn, torn, and scuffed. Just looking at the money tells a story.

Walk through markets and shopping centers. Observe people. Are they just strolling or sightseeing (as is the habit among young people, for whom shopping malls are a form of social entertainment)? Or are they buying? Are they carrying armfuls of packages?

When velocity begins to rise, when you sense it is rising, it may be a time to shift from deflationary survival policies (hang on to money, get out of debt, reduce borrowing, or stop borrowing totally), and begin inflationary thrive policies (borrow, because inflation will reduce the real inflation-adjusted interest rate).

Figure 4.3 shows vividly how the velocity of money fell sharply from the onset of the global financial crisis in 2008 through 2014, thus, largely offsetting the impact of the massive expansion in money and credit (M) during this period.

A Picture: A Thousand Words

Figures 4.4 and 4.5 tell an important story, based on our "velocity" and "momentum" tools. A rather complete economic history can be written, for the US, using these two diagrams.

Money velocity rose steeply from around 1984 through 1996. These were high-growth high-spending years, with the exception of the 1990–91 recession, stimulated mainly by the Reagan-era income tax cuts, which generated Keynesian consumption spending (not the supply-side higher saving that Reagan and advisors anticipated). Velocity then dropped steeply, during the 2000–01 dot.com crisis, rose again as the economy recovered, then in 2008, at the onset of the global financial crisis, velocity

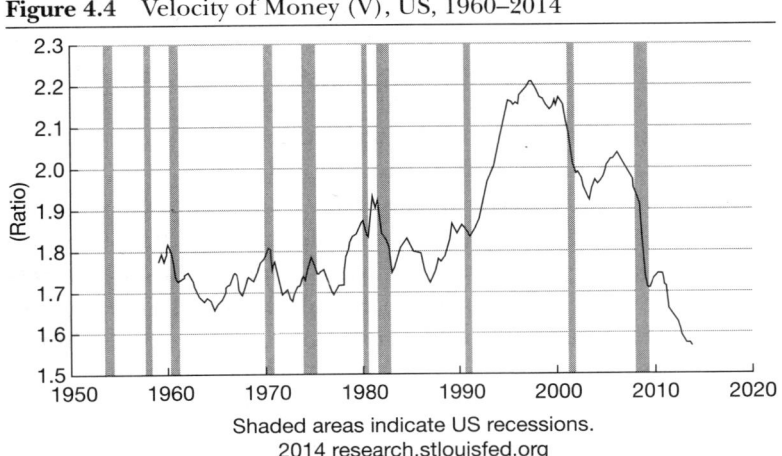

Figure 4.4 Velocity of Money (V), US, 1960–2014

Source: Federal Reserve Bank of St. Louis. Available at https://fred.stlouisfed.org/series/M1V, accessed September 22, 2016.

Figure 4.5 Federal Reserve Short-term Interest Rates, United States, 1953–2009

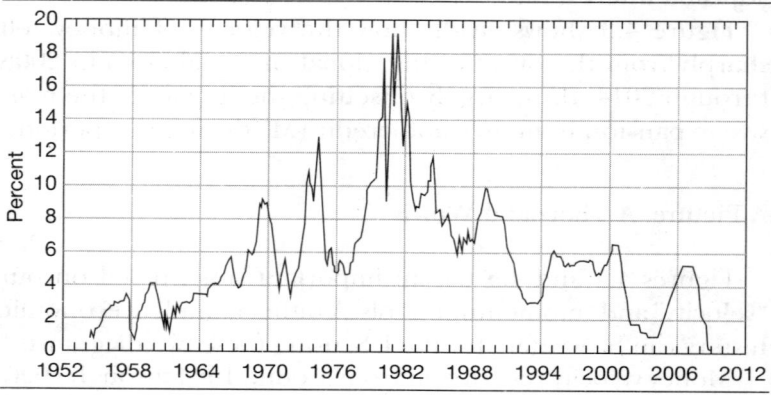

Source: Federal Reserve Bank of St. Louis. Available at https://fred.stlouisfed.org/series/INTGSTUSM193N, accessed September 22, 2016.

again plummeted, as fear replaced greed. Velocity continued to decline to historically unprecedented low rates in 2014 (as did interest rates). This fall in velocity explains why economic momentum has been very weak.

Figure 4.5 shows the federal reserve short-term interest rates for the period 1953–2009. What we see is a long-term trend toward higher interest rates, peaking in 1982, as the federal reserve used unprecedented 21 percent interest rates to fight double-digit inflation in 1978–80. This brought a US recession in 1980–81, and the federal reserve as a result lowered interest rates drastically and rapidly.

Later, in 2004 Federal Reserve Chair Alan Greenspan, fearing "irrational exuberance," in his words, that is, excessive speculation in financial markets, sharply raised interest rates, after having even more drastically lowered them during 2001–04. This massive credit expansion may have contributed to the eventual global financial crisis, which the interest-rate cut did not forestall or even mitigate. Later, the drop in world interest rates to near zero (indeed, to negative levels in Europe), and ensuing credit expansion, has done little to spur economic momentum, owing to the slowdown in velocity noted previously.

One conclusion that leaps out immediately from Figure 4.5 is that while US interest rates should be treated like an enormous cargo ship that shifts and turns very slowly and gradually, in fact, they were treated by the federal reserve chairs, especially Alan Greenspan, as if they were a Formula 1 race car, turning on a dime. It is paradoxical that even while the US economy has gradually weakened, shifting from providing fully 75 percent of world GDP in 1946 to just over 22 percent in 2015, US capital markets and financial services providers continue to dominate the world. US hedge fund managers still manage a very large proportion of global assets. This means that with the dollar as the world's key currency, US interest rates also to a large degree are world interest rates.

But, failing to recognize this, the US has managed its rates almost entirely focused on the US economy and its needs. The rapid fall in interest rates, for instance, after the 2000–01 dot.com bubble burst, created the disastrous housing bubble, and indeed was designed to do almost that—to boost demand for housing in order to stimulate the economy. The result was a global financial collapse that began in 2008. The resulting collateral damage to the rest of the world, and to the US itself, was massive.

CONCLUSION

We conclude this chapter with a case study.

In conversations with foreign exchange traders, we learned about the importance of having an "idea." That is, having a sense of a shift in the market in asset prices, a shift which others do not see or do not believe will happen. This is done by understanding underlying forces, the "plate tectonics" underlying global money and financial markets.

John Arnold had just such an idea. In fact, he had two of them. And they made him a billionaire. According to *Bloomberg Business*,[3] "Arnold wanted the truth, the cold, hard truth, and embraced the power of an idea no one else was seeing. Then he bet nearly everything he had on it."

In 2006, Arnold's hedge fund, Centaurus Advisors, bet that the price of natural gas would fall drastically. It did. The fund, and Arnold, made billions in profit. Hedge funds are investment funds that invest in virtually anything, globally; they can profit, for instance, by selling short natural gas contracts (selling gas they do not yet own, then buying it at lower prices to fulfill the contract and pocketing the profit).

In 2008, Arnold's hedge fund anticipated that the price of commodities, which had risen steadily, and some sharply, for many years, would collapse. They did. The fund profited immensely. In hindsight, perhaps this was quite obvious. A global financial crisis is always followed by an economic slowdown, which slashes demand for commodities, using in economic production. But it was not that obvious to most of us, except for a handful of those who sought "the cold truth," like John Arnold, who made courageous bets.

These bets made Arnold very unpopular as an investor. No one likes seeing other people being smarter than oneself, and making profits as a result.

Arnold was able to identify crucial turning points, known as "strategic inflection points." And it may well be that the world today, as we write this late in mid-2016, is at just such a crucial turning point.

Strategic Inflection Points

John Arnold spotted a strategic inflection point (SIP). Long-time Intel CEO Andy Grove developed this concept, to describe situations in which a major shift occurs in markets. Using the language of mathematics, when you look at a curve, an SIP is a point at which the curve shifts from rising more and more steeply to one in which it rises but less and less steeply, eventually flattening out completely. In other words, the first derivative of the curve with respect to time is positive, and so is the second derivative; but at an SIP, the second derivate shifts from positive to negative.

Spotting a strategic inflection point, when others do not, is something Smartonomics practitioners try to do regularly. It is difficult, but it gets easier with practice. To do it, you need tools and courage.

Smartonomics practitioners have great ideas. They analyze the situation, through number-crunching and Smartonomics tools, and keep sharp observational skills, cross-checking what the numbers say with what the "field" (the marketplace, the consumers, the psychology, and the mood) says. They develop ideas, based on teleology—cause and effect, using basic economic reasoning—using the method of consecutive "why's," only focused on the future, rather than on understanding the past.

And then, Smartonomics practitioners implement their ideas with courage, strength, and independent thinking to protect their investments and those of the organizations that employ them.

This combination of "think for yourself" and Smartonomics tools that assist in this process is, we believe, a winning one.

On October 11, 2015, *Wall Street Journal* reported on a meeting of central bankers, held in Lima, Peru, with the headline, "Central Bankers Urge Fed to Get On With Interest-Rate Increase." For months, or years, the US Fed had held interest rates at near-zero levels, and Europe followed suit. Capital markets had long expected that policy to end, with interest rates rising in order to offset expected rising inflation generated by the massive expansion of money and credit. Smartonomics readers now understand why that inflation has not occurred, but if velocity begins to rise, even slightly, it will occur and, in fact, that result is inevitable in the future. But when?

 **Action Learning: Read—and Have Ideas!**

On December 16, 2015, the US Fed began to raise interest rates. Here is the press account of that momentous event:

> Bloomberg Business News: Dec. 16, 2015: Fed Ends Zero-Rate Era; Signals 4th Quarter-Point 2016 Hikes. "For the first time in almost a decade, the Federal Reserve has increased interest rates while signaling the pace of subsequent increases will be 'gradual.' One percent increase in rates is intended for 2017. The publication of the full year's rate increase program is unusual, and is intended to allay capital market fears of the rate hikes, as it weans itself from addiction to zero-interest money."

Every Smartonomics practitioner should have immediately, on reading that news, begun having "ideas"—cause-and-effect reasoning, using the basic Smartonomics tools.

(a) What will be the impact on bond prices? Equity prices? (b) How will Europe react? Asia? (c) Will there be a "relief rally" (capital markets, long fearing higher interest rates, may actually applaud once they have started to rise)? Or will there be a "dread" "doom" decline, as the long addiction to near-free money begins to end? (d) Will the velocity of money rise or fall, or remain stable?

How do you believe global capital markets will see future events? Do you, Smartonomics practitioner, agree with the market consensus? Do you have a "contrarian" (opposite) idea, as John Arnold did? Do you see a SIP differently from most others? And do you have the courage to act on your beliefs?

For students of economics, macroeconomics can at times seem like a variation of theoretical physics. For Smartonomics practitioners, it is reality itself, and a great deal hinges on using it cleverly to understand what is going on. Much is at stake. In this chapter, we have analyzed the macroeconomics of money and interest rates in the context of the 2008 global financial crisis and the efforts of central banks in the US and elsewhere to respond to it. As with many macroeconomic topics, this chapter raises new questions. Why are there periods of boom and bust? Are they permanent aspects of economic behavior? Can they be predicted? What causes them? Are there similarities (and differences) in historical sequences of growth and decline? This is our next subject.

NOTES

1 Alfred Malabre Jr, *Lost Prophets: An Insider's History of Modern Economists* Boston, MA: Harvard Business School Press, 1994) 224.
2 www.reuters.com/article/2015/11/05/us-usa-fed-yellen-idUSKCN0ST-22V20151105#3rAqDRZZRLIodAdb.99, accessed September 20, 2016.
3 *Bloomberg Business*, "Giving Back Has Made This 41-Year-Old Retired Billionaire Less Popular," *Bloomberg Business*, November 19, 2015.

Booms and Busts: What Comes Next?

Tool 5: Four Key Questions

Learning Objectives

- *Understand why booms and busts recur, always have and always will*
- *Know the main economic theories that explain business cycles. Which one or ones do you personally favor?*
- *Understand in what ways are business cycles similar, and in what ways is each unique*
- *Know how trade deficits and budget deficits impact the real economy, and how are these two deficits interrelated*
- *Know what "animal spirits" are and how they drive the global economy*

A global recession is on the way. This truism of economics holds at any point in which the world is not in the grips of a contraction. The real question is always, when and how deep the next downturn will be.

—Mehreen Khan, *The Telegraph*[1]

INTRODUCTION

For global managers, there is bad news and good news. And it is far from being a joke.

First, the good.

In human history, "booms" (periods of economic growth, rising asset prices, optimism, rising profits, and, in general, prosperity) inevitably follow "busts" (downturns, recessions, and depressions, characterized by unemployment, falling incomes, falling asset prices, pessimism, and deficits). Admittedly, the "boom" that followed the Great Recession, 2008–12, has been very weak—but nonetheless, some markets have recovered strongly and some managers have profited from them.

Now the bad.

In human history, "busts" follow "booms." It is baked into the cake. There have been times when global managers, especially young ones, have been tempted to believe that the boom–bust cycle has ended forever, reinforced by statements by eminent economics. They inevitably are subject to a rude, painful, and memorable awakening.

All Smartonomics practitioners would do well to remember, and perhaps even post on their wall: *The next bust is on the way* (except when it has already just begun). But when? How? How deep? How long?

In this chapter, we explore the Smartonomics of the boom–bust cycle—causes, effects, and, especially, issues of timing and insight—how to answer the pervasive, imminent question, what next?

As we write these words, in March 2016, a thick fog has settled over the global economy. The weak global recovery from the Great Recession of 2008–12 seems to have stalled. In December 2015, the US Federal Reserve, led by Chair Janet Yellen, began tentatively and hesitatingly to raise interest rates—a signal of global recovery—only to suspend any further increases as the US and global economies sputtered. The price of oil has reached a 12-year low; this is normally positive, as it leaves more spending power in consumers' pockets but, instead, lower crude oil prices have dampened global optimism and driven asset prices down. China's stock market has plunged, followed by equity markets worldwide, and China's economy has slowed. A horrible pathetic flood of human beings from Iraq, Syria, Libya, and Afghanistan moves daily toward Europe, through Greece and Turkey, testing the EU and fracturing the member states' common borders. Britain moves toward a vote on whether or not to remain in the European Union.

Is another recession on the way? When? Why? How deep? For global managers these questions are mission-critical. Like sailors on a yacht in the North Atlantic, global managers scan the horizon, looking for storm clouds. Should they continue to enjoy the sailing? Or quickly head for port in advance of a looming storm? Take on additional debt, enjoying historically low (even negative) interest rates? Or, as rapidly as possible, get out of debt, pay off obligations, strengthen the balance sheet, and prepare to wait out the coming storm?

Bailing out of debt prematurely can truncate major global opportunities if the recession simply fails to happen, because most investment projects require borrowed money and credit. Failing to bail out of debt can lead to bankruptcy, if it does happen, when revenues decline and finding the cash to pay the banks and the bondholders becomes difficult or impossible.

In this chapter, and indeed in this whole book, global managers are urged to practice the fundamental tenet of Smartonomics—think for yourself. We will show how, repeatedly, highly esteemed economists and Nobel laureates have offered disastrous advice and utterly misread the business cycle (see Box 5.1).

Box 5.1: "We Won't Do It Again"

On November 8, 2002, the University of Chicago hosted a conference to honor Nobel laureate in economics, Professor Milton Friedman, on the occasion of his 90th birthday. Among the luminaries to address Milton Friedman was Professor Ben S. Bernanke (then a governor of the US Federal Reserve, and later to become Fed Chair). In his remarks Bernanke referred to the book by Friedman and Anna Schwartz, *A Monetary History of the United States*, which declared and proved that the Great Depression of the 1920s and 1930s was manmade. Bank failures led to a drastic fall in the money supply, which the federal reserve (founded in 1913) was unable (and, at the time, unwilling) to prevent or even address. Bernanke, then Professor of economics and Department Chair at Princeton University, said: "I would like to say to Milton and Anna: Regarding the Great Depression. You're right. We did it. We're very sorry. But thanks to you, we won't do it again."

In 2008, we "did it again," with the sub-prime mortgage crisis causing collapse in global markets and the Great Recession; the stock market decline was initially sharper and deeper than the crash of 1929. The proximate cause of the Great Recession was the failure of financial regulators, including the Fed, to restrain uncontrolled, often hysterical, speculation in financial markets.

And ironically, the person on whose shoulders it mainly fell to tackle the pain and risks of the Great Recession was Bernanke himself, as head of the Fed, for two four-year terms, from 2006 through 2014. Bernanke perhaps found new meaning in the old adage "never say never."

> Fortunately for the world, Bernanke was perhaps the ranking world expert on the Great Depression, having written his doctoral dissertation on the subject at MIT. He was aware of economists' past mistakes, and tried desperately to avoid them.
> *Source:* http://www.federalreserve.gov/boarddocs/Speeches/2002/20021108/default.htm, accessed September 25, 2016.

Our message to global managers is: Master the basic concepts of macroeconomics, Smartonomics, so that you can think critically about events and develop your own view.

It is far less painful, we believe, to be wrong about an independently constructed worldview than to be wrong after being misled by advice of "experts" whom we blindly trusted.

DEFINITIONS

We begin with some basic definitions related to the boom–bust cycle.

- Business cycles are short-term fluctuations in GDP and unemployment—cycles of recession, recovery, growth, and recession again, around a long-term growth trend, over periods of about four to eight years. They involve shifts between periods of relatively rapid growth (expansion, or boom) and periods of relative stagnation or decline (contraction, recession, or bust).
- Recession: Once defined as "two consecutive quarters of decline in real GDP," the most recent authoritative definition is: "a significant decline in economic activity spread across the economy, lasting more than a few months, normally visible in real GDP, real income, employment, industrial production, and wholesale–retail sales."[2]
- Downturn: Loosely used phrase referring to the contraction phase of the boom–bust cycle. A downturn can mean either an actual decline in real GDP (as occurred in the US, Europe, and Japan in 2009) or a significant slowdown in the rate of growth of GDP (as occurred in China in 2009).
- Depression: A prolonged severe economic contraction that lasts longer than a typical recession and afflicts economies in many parts of the world; a global economic contraction.
- Trends are long-term movements in GDP, prices, income, and employment, with consistent direction and nature, over the course of a decade or more.

There has been considerable controversy over what to call the 2008–12 downturn. Was it a recession? A depression? The consensus view now is that it was a serious prolonged recession—the Great Recession. But for ordinary people, as Shakespeare's Juliet observed, a rose is a rose by any other name, and so is a depression. What matters much more than what we call it, is, first, why did economists not foresee it? (Why did Queen Elizabeth, a paragon of protocol and polite discretion, bluntly ask the world-famous economics of London School of Economics in November 2008: "[W]hy did no-one see it [the downturn] coming?") And second, why did economists not know how to respond to it, when it occurred?

WHAT WENT WRONG WITH ECONOMICS?

In the BBC World Service's excellent program, global business, journalist Peter Day chatted with UK economist Paul Ormerod, something of a maverick within the economics profession, who professes to know what is wrong with economics and why it has failed. Here is a short summary of their conversation.

In 2003, Nobel laureate (in 1995) Robert Lucas said this: "Macroeconomics...has succeeded. *Its central problem of depression prevention has been solved, for all practical purposes,* and has, in fact, been solved for many decades."

The global Great Recession that began with the Lehman Bros. bankruptcy in September 2008 contradicts Lucas. If the boom–bust problem is solved, for many decades, why did former European central bank governor Jean Claude Trichet say, "[A]t the time of [the global crisis] policy-makers felt abandoned by economic theory, which was of no use whatever."

Why did former federal reserve Chair Ben Bernanke recently say that economic theory is wonderfully good only at explaining why we made mistakes in the past?

Why would an intelligent human being ever say that any complex social problem was solved forever?

So what is wrong with economics?

Ormerod in his new book *Positive Linking: How Networks and Incentives can Revolutionize the World*,[3] explains it simply.

Economics ignores other people. Decisions are made by one highly rational person. In reality, we copy others. We do what they do. That means that there are persistent bubbles, because people do what other people do, as all of us belong to networks, groups of persons who influence one another. That's why so many people destroyed themselves and their companies by investing in credit default swaps and mortgage-backed securities. Everybody else was doing it. So the lesson here is, while you are copying others, THINK INDEPENDENTLY. And if you want to remain creative, reserve part of your brain for creating NEW CHOICES, rather than just blindly going with existing ones everyone favors.

A part of the conversation between Peter Day and Paul Ormerod:

"Network," in Ormerod's book, refers not just to the Internet, but to all forms of social communities—any grouping of humans who influence each other's behavior. Ormerod says:

> There are serious limitations in the way conventional economics is taught and written about. Most serious: It treats people as if they were operating *in complete isolation from each other*. You make choices solely based on your own views, as if you were Robinson Crusoe. With the development of the Internet, it is a poor description of the world.
>
> Macroeconomics models weren't just academic, they had traction among Central Bankers, based on the idea of a single individual. When the financial crisis came, it was a *network* problem; the financial viability of one bank impacted on others, we worried about the cascade effect. *Economists' models omitted from the models this network effect.* Big companies have rebuilt their balance sheets. They're sitting on cash. Nobody wants to be the first one to move. As soon as one starts spending, others will follow—we'll get an investment boom. But when???
>
> When we think of any market where there is popularity, for example fashion, books there are crowd effects. We are like sheep. Investment markets behave like this. The book The Madness of Crowds was written 172 years ago, by Charles Mackay, 1841. Keynes called it "animal spirits." This governs

how the economy performs. It is the job of policymakers to intervene, to counteract animal spirits when they go bad. How do you make people more optimistic? The analysis here is psychological.

Herbert Simon, Nobel Laureate in Economics, was at his peak in the 1950's. The essence: He observed how firms really took decisions. He developed an alternative theory—he is the founder of the behavioral economics school. In 1955 his article built the foundation for it. In general, firms do not behave as economists say, rationality. The world is too complex. They use some reasonable rules and use them until they fail. They "satisfice"—chose a satisfactory alternative, rather than seek the absolutely optimal one.[4]

Ormerud continues:

The rational copying person should replace the rational economic agent. Copying is the way the network effect works. The number of choices available today are phenomenal. McKinsey, a consulting firm, says that on any single day, in New York City a consumer faces 10 billion potential choices! That cannot be done in an economically rational way. You cannot gather information on all these 10 b. choices. So you do what Herbert Simon said, you form short-cuts, heuristics, simple rules. If you choose a restaurant, you ask your friends. Copy what they do. It's a short-cut to deal with the world's complexity. Get a group of people whose opinion you trust, and you copy them. There is a lot of this on the internet. It is visible now: "those who like this, bought that…" This is left out of conventional macroeconomics. In the macro model, one person makes decisions, a representative agent. He/she represents the entire economy. They have to take rational decisions.

In the U.S. choice is regarded as a badge of freedom. A part of democracy. But this bewilders people. Choice has now exploded, grown exponentially. In the 1950s, Simon discussed this—there are so many alternatives, how can I decide? Even looking back, in most situations I can never know if I have made the best decision. All I can do is to hope to make a reasonable decision. The way to do that is to copy people's behaviors whom I respect.

Mid-price laptops in the German market: There are 3,500 possibilities. How can you possibly choose? How do you choose a smartphone? Ask a couple of young people, what's yours, and...I'll have that. More sensible than trying to evaluate 3,500 possibilities. *When people copy, when their behavior is driven by networks and social effects, we get cascades, bubbles...and sometimes collapse.*

One can surmise that in an increasingly connected world, we will no longer see recessions confined to one geography. Network effects, and the nature of human psychology, will spread them from where they began, to other parts of the world.

J.M. KEYNES AND "ANIMAL SPIRITS"

John Maynard Keynes was a British economist whose theories changed the world. Troubled by the Great Depression (1929–39), and the terrible suffering it brought, Keynes was aggrieved that conventional economics of the time could not supply an effective answer.

In a famous hearing in the House of Commons, a leading Cambridge economist was asked whether further wage declines would resolve the soaring unemployment rate, at a time when wages had collapsed disastrously. His answer: Yes. Today we know that falling wages destroys workers' purchasing power and weakens the economy, creating a "doom loop" leading to further wage falls. But, at the time, this was not understood. Conventional economics saw wages as the price of labor, and, like all prices, when the price of labor fell, it should raise demand. But, of course, it did not. Why employ a worker, at any price or wage, if there is no demand for what the worker can make?

Keynes wrote a landmark book,[5] in which he explained the underlying causes of booms and busts and the correct policy approach to deal with them. In it, he wrote:

> There is instability due to the characteristic of human nature that a large proportion of our positive activities depend on spontaneous optimism rather than mathematical expectations....Our decisions to do something positive...can only be taken as the result of *animal spirits*—a spontaneous urge to action rather than inaction.[6]

In other words, ultimately, every market is driven by psychology. Markets will continue to rise and fall with the animal spirits of human beings. Those spirits are the ultimate drivers of trends and cycles. And it is those spirits that explain why boom–bust cycles are a permanent part of the business landscape. Animal spirits also explain why predicting the onset and depth of recessions is so difficult—because basically animal spirits, the psychology of human moods and emotions, are volatile and hard to predict.

'NATIONAL MOOD IS A KEY DETERMINANT OF BOOM AND BUST'

For global managers, the key issue here is whether animal spirits—spontaneous urges to spend, buy or sell assets or houses, and engage in other economic activities—are rational and predictable, or whether they are essentially random. The title of a powerful bestselling book by Dan Ariely supplies the answer: *Predictably Irrational.*[7]

RATIONAL IRRATIONALITY

Many elements of consumer behavior are what economists regard as irrational. Yet they are not random—they are predictable. As Ariely observes:

> What we've learned is that relying on standard economic theory alone as a guiding principle for building markets and institutions might, in fact, be dangerous. It has become tragically clear that the mistakes we all make are not at all random, but part and parcel of the human condition. Worse, our mistakes of judgment can aggregate in the market, sparking a scenario in which, much like an earthquake, no one has any idea what is happening.[8]

In recent years, the concept of viral marketing (employing social networks to create rapid communication from one person to many others, about products, brands, and so on) has become widely used. There may also exist something called viral animal spirits. Ariely cites research by Nicholas Christakis, a physician and sociologist at Harvard University. Using data from a study that tracked about 5,000 people over 20 years, Christakis found that happiness, like the flu, can spread from person to person.

> When people who are close to us, both in terms of social ties (friends or relatives) and physical proximity, become happier, we do too. For example, when a person who lives within a mile of a good friend becomes happier, the probability that

this person's good friend will also become happier increases by 15%. More surprising is that the effect can transcend direct links and reach a third degree of separation: when a friend of a friend becomes happier, we become happier, even when we don't know that third person directly.[9]

We surmise that the animal spirits and optimism that fuels consumer spending, and rising asset prices, spread virally in the same way Christakis found that happiness spreads. The opposite, Christakis found, is less robust; sadness spreads more slowly than happiness—but nonetheless, it spreads. Political leaders sometimes try to manipulate this effect, by speaking optimistically when the economy is in a downturn. This rarely works, because instead of imbuing optimism it breeds skepticism, cynicism, and mistrust, which sometimes becomes pessimism.

Another key element of animal spirits is the effect of perceived uncertainty. When consumers and investors feel certain about the future, they are happier. When they are uncertain, they are unhappy. It turns out, according to research by Harvard psychologist Daniel Gilbert, that the unhappiness caused by the economic downturn in the US is not directly because people have less wealth and less income, but rather because they simply do not know what the future holds and are troubled by this uncertainty. He observes:

> Our (America's) national gloom is real enough, but it isn't a matter of insufficient funds. Americans have been perfectly happy with far less wealth than most of us have now, and we could quickly become those Americans again—if only we knew we had to.[10]

What does this brief discussion of animal spirits imply for global managers who practice Smartonomics? In a previous chapter, we discussed the rather vague notion of national energy as a key determinant of economic growth and dynamism. Here, we argue that *national mood* is a key determinant of booms and busts.

Booms are characterized by optimism, perhaps excessive, and busts are characterized by pessimism, also frequently excessive. Optimism and pessimism spread rapidly, like influenza epidemics. The bust ends and becomes a boom, when optimism returns, when uncertainty dissipates, and when consumers and investors feel sufficiently confident and secure about the future to engage in new spending and investment.

This animal spirits boom–bust theory is a cause for both optimism and pessimism among global managers—pessimism, because national mood is very hard to quantify and measure (see Box 5.2), and optimism, because managers who interact daily with workers and customers, who diligently cultivate listening skills, and who become skilled at hearing and empathetically feeling the national mood can gain insights and foresee developments even better than experts equipped with thousands of hard data sets. The soft stuff (national mood) is, indeed, the hard stuff—both in terms of the difficulty entailed in gathering information, and in terms of its strong, real impact on the prices of assets, including common shares.

Keynes' animal spirits theory of boom–bust can be summed up in a single paragraph.

Economic activity is driven by human emotion; normally greed prevails, as individuals try to gain income and wealth, and the resulting optimism overstretches the normal constraints of economic production and consumption. At certain points in time, when greed reaches excess and overextends the bounds of our understanding and abilities, the growth process stops and then declines. At this point, the dominant emotion in world markets shifts from greed (and optimism) to fear (and pessimism). This shift becomes a self-fulfilling prophecy, in that the behavior engendered by fear generates the result that is feared and expected. After a certain period, long or short, it is human nature that fear subsides and greed again prevails, as the unused capabilities of economic activity offer opportunities seized first by intrepid individuals, and later, by others who are influenced and energized by them.

And then, the entire process begins again. And on it goes, probably to the end of human history.

Box 5.2: Consumer Sentiment

One of the strongest attempts to assess animal spirits and link national mood with consumer spending is a measure known as the index of consumer sentiment. Such an index exists for the US and for major European countries. Two organizations in the US measure consumer sentiment: University of Michigan and the Conference Board, a nonprofit consulting organization. The methods are the same—a brief questionnaire asks a monthly random sample of people whether they are better off now than six months ago, whether they expect to be better off in six months than they are now, and whether they plan to make a major purchase (car, house, or appliance). This has proved to be a useful, though not infallible, indicator of the future direction of the economy.

Source: Authors.

Action Learning: Taking the Economy's Pulse

Global managers who practice Smartonomics constantly measure the pulse of business sentiment first-hand, by talking to clients, fellow workers and the man or woman in the street, as well as by tracking surveys of consumer sentiment and business sentiment.

- Do you regularly engage in such informal conversations?
- Do you cross-check by matching survey data with your own observations?
- Can you acquire a sense of animal spirits through these conversations?

Some excellent sources of such data are: taxi drivers (taxis are sensitive to the business cycle, because people walk or take public transportation when their incomes decline); restaurants (also sensitive to business conditions); and shopping malls (are they crowded, and are people carrying packages or simply window shopping?)

A SHORT HISTORY OF BUSINESS CYCLES

There is strong evidence that business cycles have been an integral part of economic activity for well over a century and a half. An economic research organization, the National Bureau of Economic Research, carefully tracks US business cycles and offers data on them dating back a century and a half to 1854. The data are shown in Table 5.1. They cover the period up to 2007, when the latest Great Recession began.

The boom cycle from March 2001 through December 2007 lasted 81 months, somewhat longer than the average cycle length in the post-World War II period. This may have deceived many global managers into thinking that the boom–bust cycle had been forever "ironed smooth." Those who thought and acted thus paid a heavy price.

One key reason that even brilliant Nobel Prize economists have prematurely eulogized the business cycle is that each business cycle has elements similar to the previous one, but, also, crucial elements that are uniquely different and new, never seen before. Like generals, economists battle the next "war" (downturn) using insights and tools used in the previous one—tools that may be inappropriate, obsolete and

Table 5.1 Number and Duration of Business Cycles, US, 1854–2007

Period	Number of Business Cycles	Average Duration (Months)*
1854–1919 (65 years)	16	49 months
1919–1945 (26 years)	6	53 months
1945–2001 (56 years)	10	67 months
Total:	32	55 months
March 2001–Dec 2007 (6 years)	1	81 months

Source: National Bureau of Economic Research, www.nber.org/cycles.html
Note: *Number of months, to peak of economic activity from the previous peak.

ineffective. The Great Recession, for instance, of 2008–12, was driven by financial innovations, collateralized debt obligations, and credit default swaps that were nonexistent, or at least far less important a decade ago. Human nature finds new and unique ways to exploit human greed and engage in excessive risk and, inevitably, the "bust" brings people down to reality.

THE COMPLEX MOSAIC OF BOOMS AND BUSTS

While the underlying cause of boom–bust cyclicality may be human emotion, nonetheless it is vital to track other key elements that can exacerbate or mitigate the boom–bust cycle.

- *Government policy:* It is sometimes argued that government policy itself exacerbates, or even causes, rather than mitigates, business cycles. In what has been called the stop-go cycle, promulgated especially by critics of Britain's economic policies in the 1950s and 1960s, it was argued that Britain's monetary and fiscal policy (known as "stop–go") braked, or stimulated, the economy very vigorously, but always too late. This made the business cycle worse than it would have been in the absence of any policy, braking the economy when it was already slowing or stimulating it when it had begun to grow.

Today there is controversy over what is known as "austerity": Efforts by governments in Europe to slash budget deficits and reduce debt, as a response to the Great Recession, even though demand remains weak and austerity further weakens it. It seems clear to many that austerity has prolonged the Great Recession rather than resolved it.

- *Politics*: Related to stop-go is the so-called political cycle. Democracies have elections every four years or so. In the two years prior to the election, governments stimulate the economy, creating a boom in order to be elected or re-elected. In the two years after it, they brake the economy, creating a bust, to resolve the problems created during the boom. This so-called political cycle has been documented in nearly every democracy. One researcher noted, "U.S. Presidential elections every four years have a profound impact on the economy and the stock market. Wars, recessions and bear markets tend to start or occur in the first half of the term and bull markets, in the latter half." Another study found that "[F]rom 1941 through 2000, (U.S.) stock market lows have occurred surprisingly close to mid-year congressional elections, or approximately two years before presidential elections."[11]
- *Cyclical responses to initial shocks*: This theory, due to J.M. Keynes and expanded by MIT Professor Paul Samuelson, shows how the complex interaction between consumers (personal consumption) and businesses (investment) can create cycles. Each added dollar of consumer spending multiplies into three or four dollars of added spending, as spending creates successive rounds of spending, output, added

employment, higher income, more spending, and so on. This is known as the multiplier (discussed later).
- For businesses, booming sales lead to higher investment, in turn creating higher output, income, and spending, leading to higher investment spending to expand productive capacity. This mechanism is known as the accelerator. The multiplier and accelerator interact to create boom–bust cycles. When both spending and investment become excessive, consumers and businesses brake their demands, leading to economic decline which is amplified by reverse multiplier and accelerator effects.
- For instance, in a downturn, businesses have excess productive capacity and so may cease buying new assets completely (rather than simply reduce investment spending by 5 or 10 percent). This implies that investment is a highly volatile component of GDP, more so than other components.
- *Real business cycles*: External innovation shocks occur as new technologies replace old ones and economies decline then boom, as investment pauses and then accelerates. In this theory, business cycles are not a sign of inefficiency or market failure, but rather a sign of rejuvenation, implying that governments should not try to intervene or smooth the cycle. If they do, they just make things worse. In the 2008–12 Great Recession it is evident that the world has not yet discovered the next huge consumer appliance—though the smartphone may be making a strong bid for that title.
- Radios, TVs, computers, and cell phones in turn drove waves of expansion, but their successor has, many believe, not yet made its appearance. However, it will. TV was invented in the 1930s. And personal computers were born during the 1977–79 and 1980–82 stagflation (falling GDP, or stagnation, accompanied by rising prices, or inflation), and recession periods.

- *Karl Marx:* He wrote that capital accumulation causes profit rates to fall, leading businesses to merge and create monopolies, to reduce wages, leading to economic crisis. While Marxist economics has been largely discredited, the growing global inequality of wealth and income distribution suggests that there are elements of Marx's boom–bust theory present and at work in today's global markets.
- *Credit cycles:* In boom times, banks overlend, businesses and people over-borrow, as interest rates fall and real (inflation-adjusted) rates may become negative. When borrowing halts, as a result of over-leverage, investment slows, asset prices decline, and the economy dives into recession.

In the face of so many different elements of boom–bust cycles, we clearly need an eclectic perspective that adapts and integrates the most valid parts of other theories. In addition, it is a key part of Smartonomics that global managers never ever become wedded to boom–bust theories that worked in the past but may be obsolete in the present and irrelevant in the future.

It has been said that nothing is more useful than a good theory, and nothing is more destructive than a bad theory. Good macroeconomic theory is a theory that helps us understand what is going on and what is next, and aids us in seeing through the thick fog that seems to perpetually cover global markets (and perhaps, growing ever thicker). Only if you have a theory can you constantly test, correct, and improve it. Having no theory places us at the mercy of the "experts" and their own theories, which often no longer work.

Four Questions

We conclude this chapter with Tool 5: Four Questions.

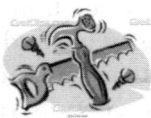 ## Tool 5: Four Key Questions

In thinking independently about boom–bust cycles and trying to track them, managers would do well to avoid the fierce theory wars of economists, and to simplify by focusing on four key practical market-based questions that drive boom–bust cycles and underlie all of the business-cycle theories listed previously:

- Do people have money and are they optimistic and keen to spend it? Or are they concerned about debt and pessimistic about losing their jobs?
- Are businesses making profits and are they keen to reinvest them in creating new assets (buildings, machineries, equipment, and software)?
- Do governments have money and are they keen to spend it, beyond what they absorb in tax revenues?
- Are businesses selling more abroad to other nations than is being bought from abroad, that is, do exports exceed (or fall short of) imports, and is the gap widening or shrinking?

The first two questions require managers to track the underlying sentiment that drives personal consumption and business investment. The latter two questions require that we track (and perhaps forecast) two key deficits: The budget deficit and the trade deficit. This, it emerges, generates a simple and powerful tool for tracking national economies.

For the country in which you live or work, answer the four boom–bust questions. How can you find data that generate accurate answers? How can you supplement such data with your own observations in stores, malls, and workplaces?

Do your answers lead you to conclusions that differ from those of the forecasting experts? Why?

Above all, can you anticipate major shifts in consumption, investment, public spending, and trade?

THE TWIN DEFICIT APPROACH

The basic logic of this tool brings us back to Chapter 1 and the definition of GDP. Readers will recall that GDP is defined as the sum of:

> *Personal consumption +*
> *Gross capital formation +*
> *Public consumption +*
> *Exports − imports*

Let us engage in a small algebraic manipulation. Subtract net personal taxes from both sides of this definition. Net personal taxes is the amount of taxes people pay, less the transfer payments they receive (negative taxes, such as social security, welfare and unemployment insurance). GDP, which is also gross domestic income, less personal taxes, is equal to disposable (i.e., spendable) income.

Disposable income equals:

> *Personal consumption* +
> *Gross capital formation* +
> *Public consumption* − *Net personal tax* +
> *Exports* − *imports*

In the four-question Tool 5, the first two questions relate to personal spending and business spending. The second two questions relate, respectively, to:

1. The government budget deficit, or public consumption minus net personal taxes.
2. The trade surplus, or exports minus imports.

A rising government budget deficit adds demand and spending to the economic system and tends to push the system toward "boom," or at least to emerge from "bust." So part of the four-question tool requires Smartonomics practitioners to track carefully the government budget deficit or surplus. Fortunately, most governments publicize their budgets well in advance so that the trend can be identified (though the planned budget is not always the one that actually occurs). If the budget deficit is likely to grow, the trend will push toward "boom." If it is to decline, that the trend will push toward "bust."

With regard to the trade surplus, a surplus of exports over imports adds spending and demand to the economy and, hence, is pro-boom. A large and growing trade deficit (imports exceed exports) is pro-bust, because it increases the "leakage" of spending and demand from the economic system in favor of other countries.

So, in essence, Smartonomics asks global managers to track these two key numbers: the budget deficit and the trade deficit, and the expected changes. If, for instance, the budget deficit grows faster than the trade deficit, the net effect will be "boom." If the opposite, then "bust."

Published data always appear with a time lag, often a considerable one. So Smartonomics requires us to be vigilant and to spot changes in these twin deficits in advance, if possible, of publication of official data.

We can, therefore, add, perhaps, a fifth question to Tool 5:

In summary, is the budget deficit growing faster than the trade deficit, or vice versa? What is the net impact?

Figure 5.1 shows the path of the "twin deficits" (budget deficit and trade deficit) for the US, 1980 to 2006, just before the onset of the global crisis. We see a 30-year pattern of growing dissaving among government (budget deficit), with the very short and temporary exception of the dot.com crisis of 2000, parallel to the growing proportion of net imports (which in turn is the mirror image of foreign borrowing).

Figure 5.1 US Trade Deficit and Budget Deficit, 1980–2006

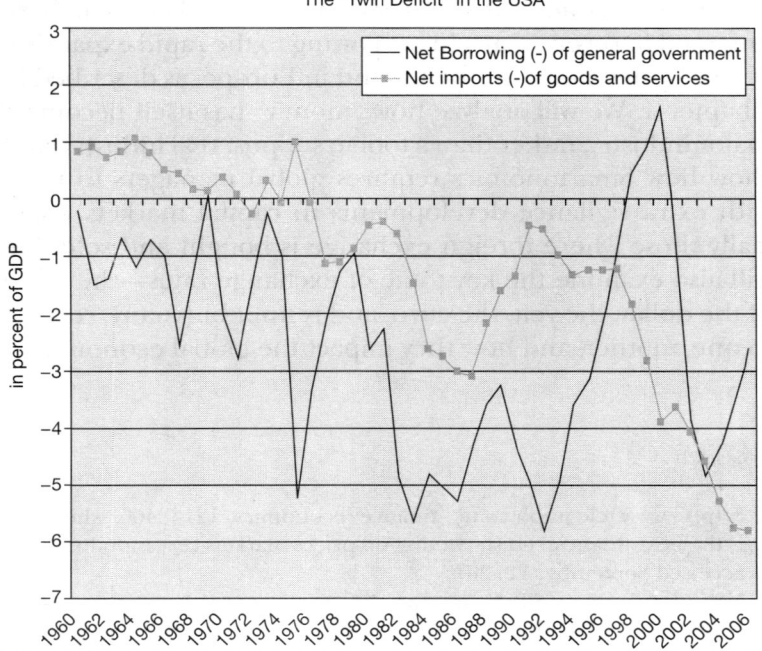

Source: Authors.

Note the upturn (decline) in 2006 in the government budget deficit, along with the continued rise in the trade deficit. This might have been a signal for a worsening economy—and perhaps, impending recession?

For example: China's economic growth has slowed in 2016 to below 7 percent, lowest in perhaps two decades. The Chinese government is planning a strong pro-active policy to stimulate growth. China's export surplus has declined in recent years, as the world economy has failed to recover. This decline has slowed China's economy. The government intends to offset it with some deficit spending. A Smartonomics prognosis for China's economy, which in the most recent period has been the world's main growth driver, can be built simply on an assessment of whether China's deficit spending will offset its declining export surplus.

In the next chapter, Chapter 6, we will focus on the immense and growing flows of capital between countries and the huge volatile and often speculative markets that have emerged in recent years, in part owing to the rapid expansion of the money supply in the US and in Europe, as described in Chapter 4. We will analyze how "money" has itself become a major industry, rather than a tool to support real industry, and show how Smartonomics requires global managers to track with extra vigilance developments in capital markets, especially those where foreign exchange is bought and sold. We will also examine the key topic of exchange rates—the value of the dollar, the yen, the euro, and renminbi (yuan), relative to one another, and how they impact the global economy.

NOTES

1 http://www.telegraph.co.uk/finance/economics/12138466/when-is-the-next-financial-crash-coming-oil-prices-markets-recession.html, accessed September 22, 2016.
2 National Bureau of Economic Research, www.nber.org, accessed September 22, 2016.

3 Paul Ormerpd, *Positive Linking: How Networks can Revolutionize the World* (London: Faber and Faber, 2012).
4 Herbert A. Simon, "Theories of Bounded Rationality". Chapter 8, in C.B. McGuire and R. Radner, Decisions and Organizations (Amsterdam: North Holland Publishing Company, 1972).
5 J.M. Keynes, *The General Theory of Employment, Interest and Money* (Palgrave Macmillan, London, 1936).
6 Keynes, *The General Theory of Employment, Interest and Money*, 161–62.
7 Dan Ariely, *Predictably Irrational: The Hidden Forces That Shape Our Decisions* (New York:, Harper Collins, 2008).
8 Dan Ariely, Blog: "2008 was a Good Year for Behavioral Economics", predictablyirrational.com, May 20, 2009; http://www.predictablyirrational.com/?page_, accessed September 22, 2016.
9 James H. Fowler and Nicholas A. Christakis, "Dynamic Spread of Happiness in a Large Social Network: Longitudinal Analysis Over 20 Years in the Framingham Heart Study", *British Medical Journal*, December 4, 2008, http://www.bmj.com/content/337/bmj.a2338, accessed September 22, 2016.
10 Daniel Gilbert, "What You Don't Know Makes You Nervous", *New York Times*, May 20.
11 Marshall D. Nickles, "Presidential Elections and Stock Market Cycles: Can you Profit from the Relationship?" (working paper, *Graziadio Business Report*, 7, no. 3 (2004), Pepperdine University), http://gbr.pepperdine.edu/043/stocks.html, accessed January 18, 2010.

6

Torrents of Capital

Tool 6: The Buck and the Big Mac

Learning Objectives

- *Know how vast amounts of money created by the US, EU and Chinese central banks are being transformed into capital, and how this is impacting global markets*
- *Learn why the world has become virtually addicted to zero interest rates*
- *Understand why falling crude oil prices have depressed global markets and economies, rather than revived and energized them*
- *Know why the US, EU and China cannot control exchange rates, even when they collaborate and work together*
- *Learn how to calculate whether a nation's foreign exchange rate (the rate at which its currency exchanges for other currencies) is too expensive, too cheap or just right*
- *Learn why the dominance of the dollar may be ending*
- *Understand the basic flaw in today's global markets—the chronic problem created in July 1944 and never truly resolved, now haunting the world*

Torrents of Capital 141

Even after 40 years of activity in the capital markets, I believe we are in a time we've never experienced before, characterized by extreme volatility. We are in uncharted territory!

—Zvi Stepak[1]

INTRODUCTION

The opening quote by a seasoned investment fund manager is true today—we *are* indeed in uncharted territory, as the global marketplace evolves, changes, and generates booms and busts, as Chapter 5 explained.

But it is important to understand that the above quote is *always* true—Smartonomics practitioners know they are *permanently* in uncharted territory, because in global markets history often repeats itself, but never repeats itself precisely in the same manner. So while it is important to understand the teleology (causality) of past crises, booms, busts, and uncertainty, it is equally crucial to know that the present and future will be different, probably very different, than the past.

This chapter focuses on global capital markets, their crucial role, why they have become exceedingly volatile, and, specifically, on the nature and impact of the torrents of capital now flooding the world, as central banks create money in unprecedented amounts to battle the Great Recession. We focus on the US dollar and its exchange rates vis-à-vis other currencies, because the dollar remains the world's currency, and the primary means of exchange in global capital markets. The US dollar embodies a deep-seated paradox, one that has existed since July 1944, that is endangering the global system of trade and investment, and is far from being resolved; the dollar has been doomed to chronic schizophrenia, serving both as the American national currency and the world's currency, with considerable conflict between those two roles. Smartonomics practitioners will always keep a close eye on this paradox, described in detail further.

We intend to answer these fundamental questions that Smartonomics practitioners ask, or should be asking themselves:

Why is the world flooded with money and how much of it has been created? Why has "austerity" been a flop? Why has zero-interest-rate money been a catalyst for often-reckless speculation? Why have plunging oil prices not been a boon to global markets, and instead of creating a bull market, as in the past, have been a "bear"? Why did global stock markets fall sharply in 2015–16, and then recover? Why has global trade stagnated? Why is the US dollar so strong when the US economy is so weak? How does the price of a hamburger provide Smartonomics managers with a powerful tool for assessing exchange-rate risk? What are the Black Swan scenarios? Why have the torrents of capital been a major cause of the enormous gap between rich and poor?

We begin with the torrents of capital themselves and their underlying causes.

- *Why is the world flooded with money and how much of it has been created?*

The world's primary currency, used in trade and investment, is the dollar. Dollars are created by the US Federal Reserve, as explained in Chapter 4. And they are flooding into world markets in unprecedented quantities—a virtual torrent. Figure 6.1 shows that the US money supply doubled, from the outbreak of the global financial crisis in 2008, to 2016. This is approximately a 10 percent annual rate of growth (using the "rule of 72," dividing 72 by the number of years, about seven, to find the constant annual growth rate), and is much higher than the slow growth of the economy. There is some evidence that this torrent has had influence far beyond America's borders, for instance in driving Singapore's housing bubble and perhaps even China's. The euro money supply (M1) grew from about 4 trillion euros in 2008 to 6.6 trillion euros in early 2016, a rise of 66 percent, not quite as

Figure 6.1 US Money Supply, 2006–16

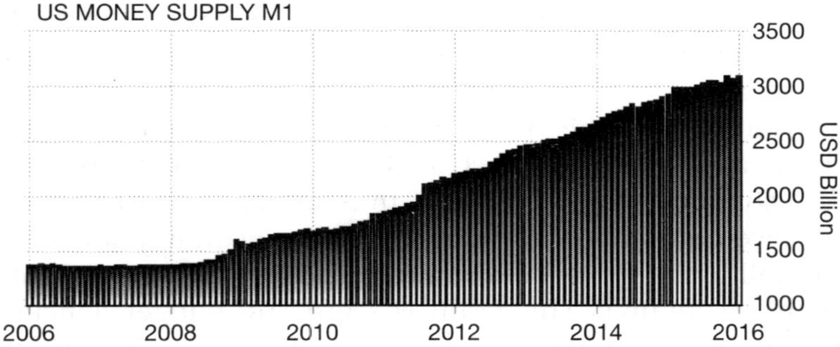

[Chart: US MONEY SUPPLY M1, values in USD Billion, rising from approximately 1200 in 2006 to over 3000 by 2016]

Source: Trading Economics, http://www.tradingeconomics.com/united-states/money-supply-m2, accessed September 22, 2016.

dramatic as the expansion of the US money supply, but still substantial. And according to the *Financial Times*:

> China's broad money supply growth between 2007 and 2013 was greater than that of the rest of the world combined, spurring the country's rapid economic expansion but creating the risk of asset price bubbles and widespread loan defaults. Analysis by Ousmène Jacques Mandeng, a former deputy division chief at the International Monetary Fund, suggests *China's broad money rose by $12.9 tn in the seven years to 2013*, outstripping the $11tn rise of the rest of the world.[2]

The policy that generate this torrent has been dubbed "quantitative easing (QE)" by economists because it involves purchase of bonds by central banks, which injects liquid reserves into the banking system and enables rapid expansion of credit and, hence, money. It is practiced by the US central bank, though it appears it might now be slowly coming to an end, and is still being practiced and even expanded by the ECB.

It is significant that the two main world currencies, the dollar and the euro, are somewhat out of sync. While the US Federal Reserve has begun to raise interest rates, the ECB continues to lower them and even move toward "negative interest rates" (i.e., as a borrower you pay less money back at the end of the year than what you borrowed at the start of the year).

What drove the US and ECBs to implement QE? Desperation. The global crisis that began in 2008 brought the economy to a grinding halt, thus, impacting government tax revenues (which are sensitive to the economy, and rise and fall much more than in proportion to the rise and fall of the economy). The result was growing budget deficits, which further rattled capital markets. Thus, at a time when economies were stagnating due to deficient demand and spending, governments were contracting their expenditures to slash budget deficits, a policy known as "austerity," thus, worsening the demand deficiency. The only tool available was expansion of credit. And because this basically was the only impactful policy left in the government's armory, it was used aggressively and perhaps even excessively.

Action Learning

Smartonomics adherents think and act like a world-class football midfielder. They position their thinking not where the world is today but where it will be tomorrow and next year, just as a top midfielder passes not to the striker but to where he will be in two seconds.

1. How well did you anticipate the "flood of money" (credit creation) which began shortly after the global financial crash in 2007–08?
2. How well have you used this torrent of money in your future narratives, or scenarios, for the coming three to five years?

- *Why has "austerity" been a flop?*

Austerity flopped, because you cannot battle a drought by turning off all the taps. Figure 6.2 shows the sharp decline in world GDP growth from 2010 through 2012. The world lost two percentage points of GDP growth annually. This may not seem huge, but global growth has fallen by half. Looking closely at the causes, revealed in Figure 6.2, it is clear that while China and the US have continued to drive growth as before, the "rest of the world" has not, and "rest of the world" is mainly Europe. Europe's austerity program, slashing government spending to cut deficits, has brought even greater deficiency of demand and slowed rather than expanded European economies. It is unclear why anyone would expect a different result. And it is even more unclear why top mainstream economists supported Europe's austerity programs, long after it was clear they were a failure.

Nobel Laureate Paul Krugman, a severe critic of pro-austerity macroeconomics, offers the following remedy:

Figure 6.2 World GDP Growth, 2010–15, and Sources of Growth

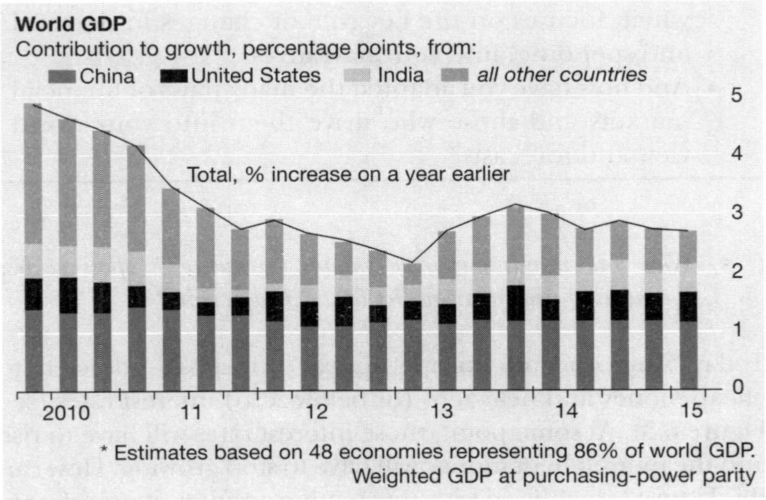

Source: The Economist.

Here's what economists have to do. First...face up to the inconvenient reality that financial markets are subject to extraordinary delusions and the madness of crowds. Second...admit that Keynesian economics ([s]ee Chapter Four) remains the best framework we have for making sense of recessions and depressions. Third...incorporate the realities of finance into macroeconomics.[3]

Action Learning

Krugman offers economists three pieces of advice. It is applicable in particular for Smartonomics practitioners

- How have you integrated the "delusions and madness of crowds" in your understanding of financial markets?
- How have you integrated Keynesian economics, which focuses on the key role of changes in demand and spending, into your narratives?
- And how have you adapted the many flaws of financial markets and those who drive them into your world view and forecasts?

- *Why has zero-interest-rate money encouraged often-reckless speculation and near-addiction to cheap credit?*

Today, America and Europe appear hopelessly addicted to cheap money and near-zero (or below-zero) interest rates (see Figure 6.3). At some point, those interest rates will have to rise and the mountain of money will have to stop growing. How can this U-turn be achieved without creating another massive financial crisis and, in Israel, without bursting the housing bubble?

Figure 6.3 Short-term Interest Rates in the US, UK, Eurozone, and Japan, 1990–2015

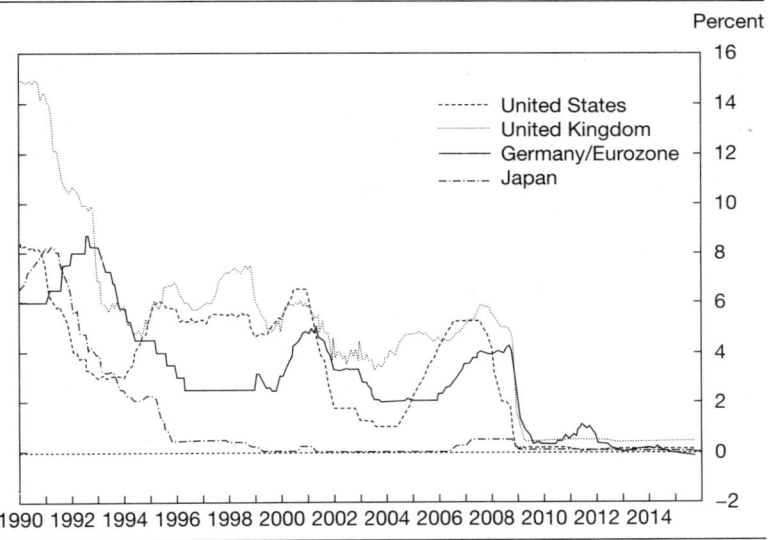

Source: Gourinchas and Rey (2016).[4]

America and Europe have both run out of ammunition to fight sluggish economies. In its February Monetary Report, the Bank of Israel says, "[T]he interest rate tool is nearly fully exploited." In Switzerland, the central bank has imposed negative interest rates to keep its Swiss franc from getting too expensive relative to dollars and euros. And now the ECB is about to follow suit.

It is interesting that Japan provides an object lesson for the world that has largely been ignored. Japan's property bubble burst disastrously in 1990, with the Nikkei Stock Index falling by three quarters as a result. Japan responded by drastically lowering interest rates, and expanding the money supply and credit. Short-term interest rates in Japan have been close to zero for two decades. Yet, it has not significantly spurred economic growth in Japan, which remains in stagnation.

Sometimes, tragically, ill persons treated with painkillers become addicted to them. This is what has happened to the US and Europe.

In Europe, the ECB has announced that it too has implemented a program known misleadingly as "QE" (quantitative easing, or buying bonds to inject liquidity and expand credit). We suggest a different term than QE: money bonanza (MB). It is a bonanza for the financial services industry.

Banks and businesses have become addicted to near-zero interest rates. It has enabled many of them to make profits through financial speculation; it is hard to lose when you borrow money almost for nothing. But low interest rates have done little for the real economy, to spur real investment, infrastructure, and capital formation. They simply benefit what the world's smartest investor, Warren Buffett, calls the "money shufflers."

The main idea of cheap money was to spur investment. But why would businesses build more factories when the current ones can make more output than they can sell?

Even companies that make real products, instead of shuffling money, benefit. For instance, Teva, Israel's largest global company, recently bought back some of its high-interest dollar bonds (issued years ago when interest rates were high) and instead will sell bonds in Europe, where interest rates are much lower. In doing so, Teva will make some $170 million in lower interest costs. This is, of course, smart finance; but it is worth noting that small investors and households do not have the same opportunities. According to Mike Dolan, writing in the *New York Times*, "[C]ompanies have made a killing by borrowing for next to nothing just to buy back their own shares, boosting the equity prices further in the process." This was not the intended goal of low interest rates.

Households too have become addicted to cheap money.

At some point, central banks in the US and Europe will have to start raising interest rates, when the huge bulge of money they created begins to generate inflation. Banks, businesses, and households will have to break their cheap-money addiction. It will not be easy.

Once, the global bond market was sleepy and small. Today, after governments and companies flooded the market with bonds, it is enormous, larger than the capitalization of global stocks and equally or more volatile, amounting to over $80 trillion, about the size of annual world GDP. When interest rates rise, as they must, bond prices will fall, simply because the relation between bond yields and bond prices is inverse. This effect alone will cause huge paper losses to bond holders, especially pension funds and other funds belong to pensioners.

Addiction to cheap money is crashing headlong into a long-run global trend: Aging populations and falling saving. According to studies by three investment banks, Barclays, Goldman Sachs, and Morgan Stanley, there has been a global glut of savings owing to a 30-year expansion of workers in peak saving years (the "baby boomers"). This glut helped lower bond yields and interest rates. But this global savings boom is ending, as the baby-boomers grow older and retire, and shift from saving to spending. In the next few years, predict the banks, that end to the savings glut will bring "a potentially seismic reversal of financial markets," with falling bond and stock prices.

There are two ways to cure a money addiction. One is "cold turkey"—a well-coordinated carefully-staged global increase in interest rates, by central banks in the West, so that money cannot ruinously flee from one country to another. This is highly unlikely.

Another approach is that "each country tackles its own addiction in its own way and in its own time." This is more likely and more dangerous. Cheap money has already flowed from the West to Asia, helping to infect China and Singapore with the same housing bubbles that America suffered.

Smartonomics practitioners are watching carefully the risky and difficult transition, that has only just begun, from low or zero (or negative) interest rates to higher rates. This transition is occurring as another "Black Swan" (unexpected event) is roiling global markets: The sharp fall in crude oil prices.

- *Why have plunging oil prices not been a boon to global markets, and instead of creating a bull (rising) market, as in the past, have been a "bear" (falling market)?*

We must first understand why oil prices crashed, between 2014 and late 2015, from over $100 a barrel to under $30 (see Figure 6.4). Only then can we examine why this fall in the price of oil has not stimulated the world economy.

The proximate cause, of course, is simply supply and demand. Supply of oil outpaced demand for it. But why? [5]

The key to crude oil prices has been held by one country for over 50 years: Saudi Arabia. The reason? Saudi Arabia has vast oil reserves under its desert sand and pumping that oil is very inexpensive, perhaps less than $10 a barrel—compared with, for instance, the enormously high cost of "fracking" ("fracturing" shale oil deposits deep underground with steam and hot water, to enable the crude oil to flow) or the

Figure 6.4 Crude Oil Prices, 2006–15

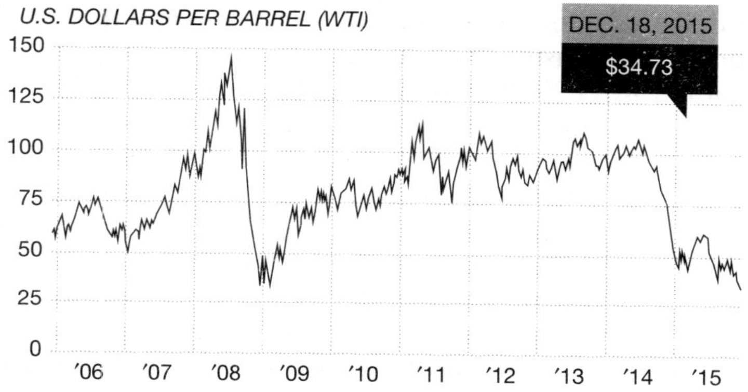

U.S. DOLLARS PER BARREL (WTI)

DEC. 18, 2015
$34.73

Source: http://thechronicleherald.ca/business/1307188-big-price-change-at-nova-scotia-gas-pumps-coming-tonight, accessed September 22, 2016.

high cost of pumping oil from beneath the seas and oceans using drilling platforms.

Oil is for Saudi Arabia a geopolitical weapon. Its leaders have stated repeatedly that they regard the oil market as their key weapon in the battle of Sunni Islam, led by the Saudis, against Shia Islam, led by Iran. By flooding world oil markets, Saudi Arabia can lower the price of crude oil and deeply wound its enemies who rely crucially on oil revenues. Of course, so does Saudi Arabia, and therein lies the dilemma.

In 2014, Saudi Arabia again engaged in its favored policy, flooding an already glutted oil market with crude oil. The goal was to hurt Iran, and to some extent Russia, Iran's ally, and to cripple America's fracking industry, which produced high-cost oil. It worked in part. Russia's economy has been deeply hurt. So has Iran's economy. But, indeed, so has Saudi Arabia's economy.

Ali al-Naimi, Saudi Arabia's fabled oil minister for 21 years, perhaps one of the longest reigns of a government minister anywhere, is out of a job, fired on May 7, 2016. As the main architect of the oil price war against Iran, al-Naimi did not succeed in crippling American oil production; producers there have fought to lower costs and remain in the business, contrary to expectations.[6] Saudi Arabia had a record budget deficit in 2015 and its currency, pegged to the US dollar, is under great pressure. The IF warns that unless Saudi Arabia slashes government spending, it will run out of money by 2020. But if Saudi Arabia's ruler, King Salman, does cut spending, he runs the risk of creating instability in a kingdom already threatened by unrest.

Normally, when oil prices fall, gasoline prices fall too. Gasoline prices in the US were a dollar a liter in early 2014 and fell to less than half that in early 2016. That should comprise "good deflation" (see Chapter 4), by leaving purchasing power in the pockets of consumers, money that is then spent elsewhere instead of being funneled to Mideast oil producers. It used to be a "rule of thumb" that a 10 percent fall in oil prices boosts global growth by 0.1 to 0.5 percent.[7] Between mid-2014 and January 2016, crude oil fell by 75 percent, from $110 a barrel to around $27. But, global capital markets fell and global GDP growth stagnated (see Box 6.1).

Box 6.1: How Economists Got It Wrong—Again!

"As oil prices have fallen to levels not seen since 2003, sagging below $27 a barrel on Wed., Jan 20, 2016… many…experts now say they do not expect lower prices to bolster the U.S. economy significantly in 2016. 'We got this wrong,' John C. Williams, president of the Federal Reserve Bank of San Francisco, [said]…. Economists at J.P. Morgan Chase, who predicted last January (2015) that lower oil prices would add about 0.7 percentage points to the U.S. economic growth rate, [now estimate that lower prices might have shaved 0.3 percentage points off the growth rate."[8]

Source: Appelbaum (2016).

Why did economists "get it wrong"—again? Here are a few reasons.

- Falling oil prices cause immense geopolitical instability in sensitive parts of the world, damaging economies in South America, in Russia, the Mideast, and elsewhere.
- In the past, when oil prices fell, money was transferred from low-spending producers to high-spending consumers. But after the global 2008 crisis, that may no longer be true. Consumers are saving more of their windfall, or borrowing less, and producers too are tightening their belts, causing some demand-deficiency stagnation.
- Low crude oil prices have hurt investment spending in oil exploration in the Arctic, off Brazil, and off West Africa.
- Global banks are sitting on loans for oil exploration that could well become non-performing, that is, default on payment.

"The oil shock comes as the world economy is still coping with the aftermath of the [2008] financial crash," notes *The Economist*. "[T]he world could yet be laid low by an oil monster on the prowl."[9]

- *Why has global trade stagnated?*

In the remarkable period of rapid global economic growth in the two decades up to 2008, the engine of growth was world trade, which grew twice as fast as global GDP. Today, experts note that global trade is having perhaps its worst period since the Great Depression, when world trade virtually disappeared in the wake of repeated retaliatory currency devaluations and tariffs.[10] Exports from China were 11 percent lower in January 2016 than a year earlier. Imports fell even more, by 18.8 percent, the 15th straight monthly drop. India's exports were 13.6 percent lower in January 2016 than a year earlier, and in 2015, South Korea's exports were 8 percent lower than the year before, the worst decline since 2008.

According to James Saft, "[B]etween 1950 and 2008, global trade grew at three times the rate of the global economy, reflecting the postwar expansion and eventual integration of China and the Soviet bloc. That all stopped with the global financial crisis." World trade is now forecast by the World Trade Organization to grow by a weak 3.3 percent in 2016, roughly the growth rate of global GDP. This "mid-life crisis" of globalization raises crucial questions.

- Will slow economic growth and rising unemployment lead countries to follow Great Depression strategies, devaluing their currencies and imposing tariffs (even though the latter are banned by the World Trade Organization)?
- One expert notes that "investment in China was yesterday's demand but is now today's supply." Has China's prodigious production capacity outpaced global demand?

Tool 6: The Buck and the Big Mac

- How does the price of a hamburger provide Smartonomics managers with a powerful tool for assessing exchange-rate risk?

Suppose we want to compare data, any data, between two countries. The data for each country are measured in local currency units—for instance, bolivars (Venezuela) and pesos (Mexico). How do we compare "oranges and apples"?

One way, of course, is to convert bolivars and pesos into dollars. But at which exchange rate? Often official rates do not truly reflect the underlying accurate "true" value of the local currency. That "true" value is measured by the purchasing power of the money—what a unit of currency can buy.

So, now, the question moves one level higher: How would we know what the purchasing power parity (PPP) value of the bolivar, peso, or renminbi, or yuan, is? How can we show, for instance, that the PPP rate of the Chinese RMB (yuan) is 3.53 per dollar in 2009, making the yuan far more valuable than the official exchange rate of 6.86? The answer is supplied by the PPP exchange rate.

PPP Exchange Rate: Definition: The basic idea behind the method for judging the true value, or PPP, of a currency, relative to that of the American dollar, is appealingly simple. Create a shopping list of things people ordinarily buy (food, clothing, etc.). Take the list to New York and other US cities and buy everything on it. Make a note of what the products on the list cost—say, a total of $1,000. Now take the same list to Shanghai, Beijing, Nanjang and Guangzhou. Buy everything on it. Say the same shopping list costs 3,530 yuan (RMB) to buy.

If $1,000 buys what 3,530 yuan buys—then $1 is equivalent in purchasing power to 3,530 yuan:

USD 1,000 = 3,530 Yuan

Therefore: USD 1 = 3.53 Yuan

If your shopping list was a basket of items that enter into US–China trade, then your shopping expedition offers a clue about "underlying" or "true value" exchange rates between dollars and yen. This simple idea is known as purchasing power parity and it says that exchange rates should reflect underlying prices and costs in each country, and each unit of currency should buy roughly equal amounts of goods and services in the two countries. (Parity means equality).

If the shopping basket wasn't too big and bulky, one could arbitrage it. Arbitrage is the operation of buying low and selling high, to make a profit. If, say, the actual dollar–yuan exchange rate were 8 yuan per dollar (a level it maintained for over a decade, until 2007) one could invest 3,530/8=$441, buy the basket of goods in China for 3,530 yuan, take it to America, sell the goods for $1,000, and pocket the sizeable profit of $1,000−$441=$559. A 56 percent profit—not bad for one trip.

And, of course, this is precisely what occurs, though it is not called arbitrage and largely it happens when, for instance, the US retail chain Walmart buys goods from its over 6,000 suppliers in Shanghai alone, then ships them to the US, and sells them in its huge stores.

Burgernomics

How can the PPP notion be implemented in practice? No one is going to travel the world weekly with shopping lists. In 1986, *The Economist* found an amusing and original way to compute true rates, known as burgernomics or the Big Mac exchange rate. Their idea was to use Big Macs, consistent in quality and weight in place of the cumbersome shopping list. "It is not a precise predictor of currencies," *The Economist* puns, "simply a tool to make exchange-rate theory a bit more digestible." The Big Mac Index was invented by *The Economist* 30 years ago in 1986, as a "lighthearted guide to whether currencies are at their 'correct' level." But it turned out to be a fairly serious tool for macroeconomists and for Smartonomics practitioners.

Big Macs, the large-selling hamburger of the McDonald's hamburger chain, are sold in 80 countries around the world. (It is not sold in India due to the widespread taboo on eating beef, stemming from the Hindu religious belief. However, the Maharaja Burger in India is equivalent, and can be used for the same purpose). In each country, the Big Mac has a price in local currency. For instance, in China a Big Mac cost 12.50 yuan in January, 2009. At the same time the average price of a Big Mac in New York, Chicago, San Francisco, and Atlanta was $3.54. Hence, what 12.50 yuan buys in Beijing, $3.54 buys in the US.

The Big Mac PPP exchange rate is simply the ratio of those two numbers: the ratio of the dollar price of a Big Mac, and the yuan price:

$$USD\ 3.54 = 12.50\ yuan = ONE\ BIG\ MAC$$
$$Therefore: USD\ 1.00 = 12.50\ yuan/USD\ 3.54 = 3.53\ yuan$$

The Big Mac exchange rate of the yuan, when compared with the official exchange rate (6.84 yuan per dollar on January 30, 2009) shows the purchasing power rate (3.53 yuan per dollar) is only 52 percent of the official rate (6.84 yuan). In other words, the yuan is undervalued by about half. If Chinese goods were priced locally at the Big Mac exchange rate, rather than the official rate, they would cost twice as much in US dollars.

The Big Mac exchange rates are calculated at regular intervals, and published in *The Economist* (see Figure 6.5). They reveal an interesting pattern. Like China, many countries purposely undervalue their currencies, that is, foster exchange rates relative to the dollar, so that dollars are very expensive in terms of local currency. Far more currencies in the world are undervalued (that is, the price of local currency in terms of US dollars is very cheap) than are overvalued. This is simply another way of saying that the American dollar is still overvalued (too expensive), despite its sharp decline. The message of the Big Mac tool is not solely that many world currencies exchange for dollars at prices that make dollars too expensive (overvaluation), but that dollars are exchanged for nearly every foreign currency at rates that greatly overstate the true underlying value of the dollar.

Figure 6.5 Big Mac Index: Percent Currencies are Overvalued (+) or Undervalued (−) Relative to the US Dollar, January 2016

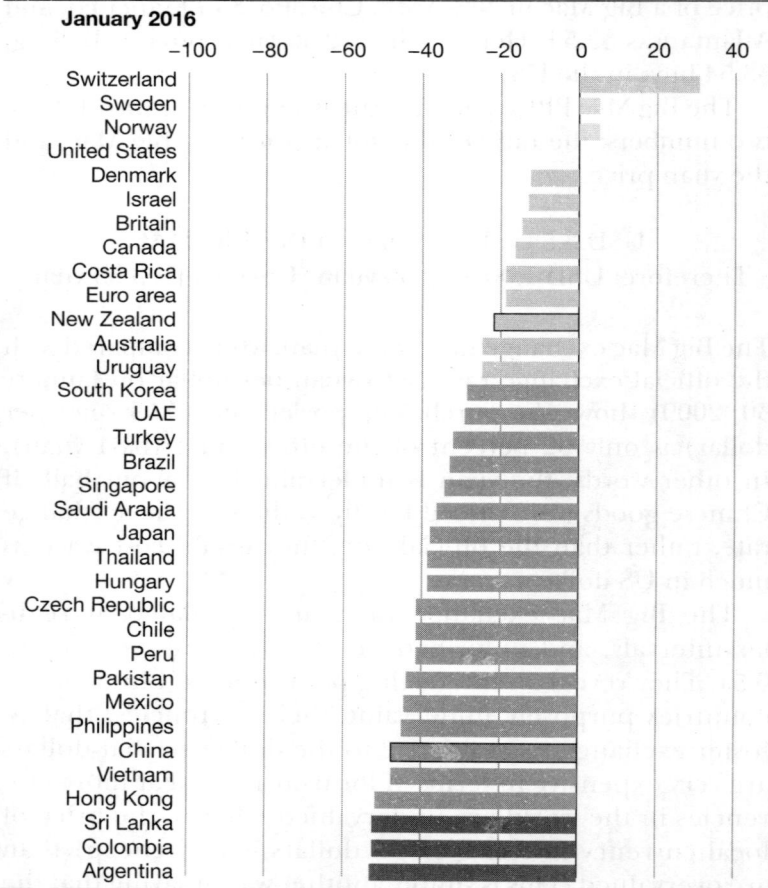

Source: The Economist, http://www.economist.com/content/big-mac-index, accessed September 22, 2016.

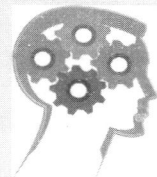 **Action Learning**

When will the buck "pass"? When will its exchange rate reflect the true underlying strength and buying power of the dollar? When will the dollar fall? What is your view? Why? For some assistance see the section: Is the Buck Passing?

- *Why is the US dollar so strong when the US economy is so weak, relatively?*

There is a very short answer. The more unstable the world becomes, geopolitically, the more US capital markets appear as islands of stability and "safe havens" for money, despite the destabilizing speculative actions common on Wall Street. "Safe haven" investment in the US implies exchanging foreign currencies for dollars; this creates demand for dollars and raised the exchange-rate value of the dollar. Once upon a time, a currency's strength or weakness depended on the demand for the currency in order to buy this country's goods (trade). Today, a currency's external value in foreign exchange markets is driven far more by largely speculative flows of capital, part of the torrents of capital, and not by trade. Capital flows between countries (money transferred for investment and speculative purposes) exceed trade flows by a huge margin. This was once not the case. And it does seem like an instance of the tail wagging the dog.

IS THE BUCK PASSING?

This passage from a report by an American economist reflects widespread concern and even anxiety:

> The U.S. dollar has dominated the international monetary system since the end of World War II. While the U.S. economy has generated weak growth since 2009, and accumulated a large sovereign debt, the dollar's status as an international medium of exchange and reserve currency has not diminished. The Chinese renminbi (RMB, or yuan), however, barely visible in international trade or financial flows just three years ago, appears to be blossoming. China is now the world's largest trading nation, and more corporations, particularly in Asia, are beginning to invoice their business in RMB. The Chinese regime is calling for a reform of the international monetary system to expand the internationalization of the RMB. Speculation has begun about whether the U.S. dollar could be supplanted by the RMB. Such a development would jeopardize the enormous economic advantages that the U.S. has enjoyed by possessing the world's dominant currency.[11]

It is possible, even likely, that after 72 years, the reign of the US dollar in world markets, since the Bretton Woods conference in July 1944, is ending. Today some 87 percent of all global foreign exchange transactions involve the US dollar. But that may be about to change. And if it does, Smartonomics practitioners must be ready for it.

There are far too many dollars sloshing around in world markets. The torrents of capital flooding world markets are in large part (though not solely) dollars.

The US money supply today totals over 12 trillion dollars, up from 8.5 trillion five years ago. That is a 7.3 percent annual growth rate, more than three times the rate of growth of the GDP. Under Federal Reserve Chair Ben Bernanke, and now under his successor Janet Yellen, the US engaged in "quantitative easing" (massive credit creation) to spur its sluggish economy.

The resulting mountain of dollars has spread throughout the world and helped fuel property bubbles abroad, in China, in Singapore, perhaps indirectly in Israel, and ultimately will shake confidence in the dollar. We are unlikely to see an end to this policy soon; US economic growth has slowed to 1.5–2 percent.

"The dollar is our money—and your problem," US Treasury Secretary John Connolly said to foreign reporters in 1971, when the US stopped backing the buck with gold. That is America's policy to this day. Other nations' wellbeing demands a stable dollar and moderate credit expansion, because world trade and finance requires a secure solid currency. America perceives its interest lies in credit expansion. The world be damned.

America has for decades been under-saving, under-investing and over-borrowing. The piper will eventually have to be paid.

Out of 60 globally competitive nations, the US ranks 46th in capital formation as a percentage of GDP and 55th in domestic saving. Mainland China ranks first in both. As a result, America's infrastructure is worn and frayed. The US ranks 29th (out of 60 nations) in road infrastructure, 27th in bandwidth speed, and 31st in railroads. The US continues to borrow heavily abroad, mainly from Asia, not to invest in the future but to consume in the present, further undermining the credibility of the dollar.

Again, the US is bumping against its legal debt ceiling; when Congress is slow to raise it, the US government shuts down for lack of cash—which is what happened on October 1–16, 2013.

US government debt is today equal to its GDP; in 1974, the ratio was only 31 percent. In contrast, Spain, regarded as a country in fiscal trouble, has a lower debt-to-GDP ratio than the US.

There is a strong disconnect between America's dominance in financial markets, which has actually grown, and its ever-weakening economy. No country's money has remained a key world currency without a strong underlying economy.

US stock markets trade shares with a market value of 24 trillion dollars, six times larger than that of China. US financial markets powerfully impact markets in Europe and Asia.

American fund managers run well over half the world's total assets under management, up from 44 percent a decade ago, according to *The Economist*. Some 60 percent of world output is produced in a dollar zone, in countries whose currencies are tied to the dollar. Meanwhile, the US imports nearly 800 billion dollars more than it exports annually, and has been doing so for decades. Only a country that can freely print (and borrow) the world's currency could do this.

In history, no nation's currency has remained dominant when that nation's economy was weak. Britain's pound sterling ruled the world for over a century, until 1920, as Britain led the Industrial Revolution. But between 1920 and 1945, Britain lost its empire and the pound gracefully gave way to the dollar. This transition was smooth, partly because Britain and the US were strong allies, and because Britain facilitated it. But today, the US, EU, and China act more like rivals than allies as each pursues its own self-interest. Thus, the transition to a new world currency is likely to be rocky.

There is a quiet but fierce currency war underway, as major countries (Japan, Europe, and China) try to solve their economic maladies by devaluing their currency. While this has temporarily strengthened the dollar, it is very bad in the long-run for the world economy.

Critics say, if the dollar is so weak, how come it is so strong? Since mid-2011 the trade-weighted dollar index (the value of the dollar measured against six other key currencies) has risen by nearly 40 percent. Once the euro was worth $1.45 (in mid-2011); today it is worth only $1.09. (The shekel–dollar rate has been on a roller coaster ride; the dollar strengthened from 3.40 shekels per dollar in mid-2011 to nearly 4.0 in 2012, fell to 3.40 shekels in mid-2014, rose back to 4.0, and is now around 3.86.)

Why is the dollar so strong? Largely because the other major moneys are weak.

Japanese Prime Minister Shinzo Abe launched an economic blitz to devalue the yen and spur Japan's economy in

2012; the yen did fall by a third, relative to the dollar, but so-called "Abenomics" has not worked so far.

In August 2015, China made its renminbi depreciate by about 3 percent. And in Europe, ECB head, Mario Draghi, has promised to do "whatever it takes" to spur Europe's economy, including massive credit creation, zero interest rates, and a falling euro. Europe and the US seem to be in a losing competition to see who can print money fastest.

Despite a World Bank study showing that devaluing a country's currency does little for its economy, nations continue to attempt it. Some countries, like Greece, locked in to the euro, wish they could. One reason why currency devaluation fails is that today trade is one big global value chain. If your currency falls, your exports are cheaper but your imports are more costly, and if you import components, that soon makes your exports more costly as well.

THE FATAL INTERNAL FLAW

There is a fatal flaw in the architecture of the Bretton Woods agreements signed in 1944—the dollar cannot be simultaneously America's money and the world's money.

The world has not yet addressed a crucial design flaw originating in 1944. At the 1944 Bretton Woods conference, held at a lovely New Hampshire resort, Hotel Mt. Washington, British economist J.M. Keynes proposed creating a world central bank and a world currency. The world currency would be created and managed by a world central bank in the same manner that national central banks control national currencies. It would create international liquidity (for trade purposes, not for individuals) in a Goldilocks fashion—not too much, not too little—to maintain stability. That made sense. A lot of mischief would have been prevented had he been heeded. If central banks are a good idea for a country, why not for the world and the global economy?

But the chief US representative, Harry Dexter White, insisted that the dollar would be the world's currency. At the time, much of the world's economy had been destroyed by World War II while the US economy had doubled twice during the war. In 1945, the US produced 75 percent of total world GDP. Hence, America called the shots.

Today, US monetary interests diverge from the rest of the world. A weak US economy seems to need piles of money and near-zero interest rates. So, this is what the US Federal Reserve does. And it has been for seven years. Financial markets nervously await the first hint that the Fed, under Chair Janet Yellen, will begin raising interest rates—a bullet she has repeatedly refused to bite.

If the resulting money mountain shakes world confidence in the dollar, well, as Connolly said, "that's your problem." And indeed it is the world's problem. If the buck is indeed passing, the whole world has a problem. The machinery of global markets depends on having a stable acceptable world currency. As the dollar "passes," and the renminbi undergoes a difficult adolescence, world markets may be left without a stable viable currency.

For 72 years, since 1944, the US has enjoyed many advantages accruing to its "key currency" status of the dollar. According to William T. Wilson, it costs 12.5 cents to print a $100 bill. That bill, widely accepted because the dollar is the world's currency, can buy real goods and services or assets worth $100. This is known as "seigniorage"—the profit made by a government by issuing currency, especially the difference between the face value of money and its production costs. There are very few businesses that enjoy the net margin enjoyed by the US Federal Reserve and US government accruing to printing dollars: in the case of the $100 bill, which ironically has the image of the extremely frugal Benjamin Franklin on it, the profit margin is $99.875/$100 or 99.8 percent! Not many businesses have such a margin. A country like Venezuela, when it prints bolivars, its currency does not gain "seigniorage" but simply causes raging inflation (180.9 percent in 2015, in a world largely struggling with deflation, not inflation) and economic chaos.

TORRENTS OF SPECULATION

One of the main impacts of the torrents of capital flooding global markets has been the increase in financial speculation and asset-price volatility. With interest rates at record lows, the only way investment fund managers can generate adequate rates of return for their investors is by taking higher risk. The positive, near-linear correlation between risk and return is an inexorable fact of life in global markets, almost like Planck's constant or the speed of light.

Take, for instance, financial contracts that are based on "ICE Libor" (it stands for the tongue-twisting Intercontinental Exchange London Interbank Offered Rate, a benchmark interest rate). By one estimate, more than $350 trillion of contracts (three or more times annual world GDP) are based on Libor.[12] A major scandal broke out when in 2012, a number of banks' financial traders lied about the interest rates emerging from their transactions (and forming the basis of the Libor calculation) to help their own trading profits or to help their banks' financial positions. As a result, the British Bankers' Association gave up administering Libor, and the ICE Benchmark Administration took over.

Libor may indeed be "honest" today. But the assets based on Libor (many of them speculative in nature, such as interest rate options, swaps, and futures) total over three times annual world GDP. So for an untold number of years, this massive market was manipulated, by those who manipulated the underlying Libor rate that drove many financial contracts. And today, even if Libor is honestly determined and provides a "true" benchmark, the value of contracts based on it is truly enormous.

In short, the torrents of money have generated torrents of highly speculative capital, creating high and growing volatility (fluctuations) in global capital markets.

A kind of feedback loop has resulted—higher volatility (which implies potentially higher speculative profits, albeit with higher risk) attracts more and more capital, and such capital flows themselves increase the volatility. Such feedback loops often do not end well (see Box 6.2).

Box 6.2: $9 Billion Loss

A financial trader named Howie Hubler has become notorious for being responsible for perhaps the largest financial loss in history attributable to one person. As a senior manager for the investment bank Morgan Stanley, Hubler earned $25 million in pay in 2006. Hubler told his traders to sell "credit default swaps" (i.e., insurance against default) on $16 billion worth of what he thought were safe debt obligations—which turned out to be "opaque," hiding risky subprime mortgages.

> As the subprime mortgages collapsed in 2008–09, Hubler refused to "bail out" (swallow the losses), hoping the market would recover. But it didn't. In the end, the overall losses for Hubler's group totaled $9 billion, as Morgan Stanley was liable for the "insurance" against the bad debts. Morgan Stanley lost $58 billion in the financial crisis overall. And Hubler? He resigned, rather than be fired. He was paid $10 million in back pay when he left.
>
> Very little of what caused this massive trading loss has been changed or repaired in global financial markets. While the nature of such losses will involve different assets in future, other than credit default "swaps," the speculative nature of global capital markets makes huge trading losses still highly possible, and even likely.
>
> *Source:* http://blog.trejdify.com/2012/02/how-to-lose-9-billion-and-walk-away.html, accessed September 22, 2016.

Global managers who practice Smartonomics are, of course, aware that at times "contrarian thinking" (thinking diametrically opposite from the herd, or the market itself) is sometimes called for. When it becomes the basis for an investment strategy, it can be immensely profitable. (See the following box on The Big Short).

> **How A Handful Made Billions from the 2008 Crisis**
>
> A handful of people saw the 2008 financial crisis, driven by sub-prime mortgage collapse, coming.
> Dr Michael Burry, a medical doctor with Asperger's disease (and one blind eye, from a bout with cancer)

saw it. This is ironic—someone with one eye saw things those with two good eyes, and advanced degrees in economics, failed to see! [13]

He started a hedge fund in Cupertino, CA, and in 2005 foresaw the 2007–08 crisis in sub-prime mortgages. He invested in credit default swaps (CDSs) which are insurance contracts against bond default, betting on default—and made $720 million! How?

He took the trouble to read the sub-prime mortgage documents, while others did not. He saw through the scam in which Goldman Sachs investment bank persuaded the global insurance company AIG to issue CDS's in the amount of $20 billion and, later, another $30 billion, without highly paid AIG senior managers understanding at all what they were insuring (not a 1 in 1,000 event, but a 100% certainty of collapse, owing to the nature of the subprime mortgages).Why didn't others on Wall Street see it? "Wall St. is paid to delude itself," author Michael Lewis says. Berry explains why the bonuses paid to Wall Street investment managers are so huge.

"The top people there want to be paid huge sums, so they have to pay people below them very large sums," he explains. Berry thought, when he bought up CDS's, that others would copy him, eliminating the profit. But they did not. Perhaps 10 or 20 people acted like him, seeing the looming crisis coming.

Michael Lewis notes: "Wall St., in its present form, cannot be sustained. It is getting subsidized credit from the Fed, paying zero interest, then lending and investing at higher interest, and making billions. This cannot be sustained." "The (Wall St.) leaders have lost their sense of responsibility to society," he observes. "Wall St. has become disconnected from reality, from real productivity." It was an elegant form of theft, he believes. Wall Street bankers paid themselves $20 billion in bonuses in 2009—after the crisis! In 2007, they paid even more: $33 billion in bonuses!

The worst part of the global capital market is this: Nothing has been fixed. The bond rating agencies that rated sub-prime mortgage securities as AAA (Moody's, S&P) are still paid by the companies who issue and sell the bonds—the investment banks.

And credit default swaps? They still are unregulated, and no-one knows to this day for certain how much they total or what they are worth? And the icing on the cake? The same "experts" who caused the crisis are now cashing in, with huge consulting contracts for the government, because they are the only ones who really understand the flawed system they inflicted on society. "A neat trick Wall St. does often," Lewis notes, "charging fortunes for cleaning up the messes it created in the first place."

- *Why have the torrents of capital created an enormous gap between rich and poor?*

One of the consequences of "torrents of capital"—global efforts to battle economic stagnation in the wake of the 2008 crisis, by massive credit creation and zero (and now, negative) interest rates—has been to accelerate the trend toward growing inequality in the distribution of wealth. A tiny fraction of the world's population has access to the torrents of capital, the so-called "one percent," using it to make large speculative profits; and a very large fraction, the 99 percent, do not. This is the subject of Chapter 7.

NOTES

1. Zvi Stepak, investment fund founder and head, quoted by *The Marker*, Israel.
2. http://www.ft.com/intl/cms/s/3/c85cb7b0-62a1-11e5-9846-de406c-cb37f2.html#axzz43F0b6Zj2, accessed September 22, 2016.
3. Paul Krugman, "How Did Economists Get It So Wrong?" *New York Times*, September 6, 2009.
4. Pierre-Olivier Gourinchas, and Helene Rey, "Real Interest Rates, Imbalances and the Curse of Regional Safe Asset Providers At the Zero Lower Found." Working Paper 22618, NBER, Cambridge MA. http://www.nber.org/papers/w22618.pdf, accessed September 22, 2016.
5. This section is based in part on Andrew Scott Cooper, "How Saudi Arabia Turned Its Greatest Weapon on Itself", *New York Times* Sunday Review, March 13, 2016, http://nyti.ms/1LYTEMt, accessed September 22, 2016.
6. See Clifford Krauss, "Falling Prices for Cutbacks at the Smallest Oil Companies; Tiny Operators Reduce Expenses to Hold Down Debt in Troubled Times," *Global New York Times*, February 26, 2016, 19.
7. *Economist*, "Who's Afraid of Cheap Oil?", *The Economist*, January 23, 2016.
8. Binyamin Appelbaum, "Cheap Crude Is No Longer an Engine for U.S. Growth", *International New York Times,* January 22, 2016, 16.
9. *Economist*, "Who's Afraid of Cheap Oil?".
10. James Saft, "Tough Year Ahead for Global Trade", *International New York Times*, February 17, 2016, 16.
11. William T. Wilson, "Washington, China, and the Rise of the Renminbi: Are the Dollar's Days as the Global Reserve Currency Numbered?" http://www.heritage.org/research/reports/2015/08/washington-china-and-the-rise-of-the-renminbi-are-the-dollars-days-as-the-global-reserve-currency-numbered, accessed September 22, 2016.
12. *Daily Telegraph*, "These Banks Will Stop Banks' Libor Lies For Good", March 17, 2016.
13. Michael Lewis, *The Big Short: Inside the Doomsday Machine* (New York: W.W. Norton, 2010). A Hollywood movie has been made based on this book. Also: Michael Burry was interviewed on the American TV Network CBS's program *Sixty Minutes*, by Steve Croft. Available at http://www.cbsnews.com/news/author-michael-lewis-on-wall-sts-delusion/

7

The Gap

Tool 7: 1%/99%

Learning Objectives

- *Understand why wealth has become increasingly concentrated in fewer and fewer hands, both between nations and within nations*
- *Grasp the geopolitical impact of the growing rich-poor gap*
- *Know what solutions and palliatives have been proposed, and distinguish between those that are viable and those that are not*
- *Learn how the BOP (bottom of the pyramid, the poorest and least asset-rich people, income groups and nations) offers great potential for Smartonomics practitioners*
- *Learn how the top of the pyramid, the 1%, offers major opportunities, as does the bottom 99%*

> *Do the dynamics of private capital accumulation inevitably lead to the concentration of wealth in ever fewer hands, as Karl Marx believes in the 19th [century].? Or do the balancing forces of growth, competition and technological progress lead in later stages of development to reduced inequality and greater harmony among the classes, as Simon Kuznets thought in the 20th C.? What do we really know about how wealth and income have evolved since the 18th [century]., and what lessons can we derive...for the century now under way?*
>
> —Thomas Piketty[1]

INTRODUCTION

This chapter is titled simply "the gap." There are many gaps in this world—gaps between theory and practice, between formulated strategy and its implementation, and between what leaders say and what they do. But, to most people, it is obvious what we mean when we say "the gap"—it is clearly the large and growing gap between rich and poor, between wealthy and penurious, both within nations and among nations.

Understanding "the gap," its causes, nature, effects, and likely future course is a crucial part of Smartonomics. The gap will impact geopolitics, economics, financial markets, indeed every aspect of our lives, worldwide, for years to come. The gap is both a source of global risk and a potential source of immense global opportunities. This chapter will address both. The key tool is simply the deep understanding of the forces that are driving the one percent (wealthy) and the 99 percent (middle income and poor) farther and farther apart, especially in the distribution of wealth.

The direct ancestor of this book is our text, *Global Risk/ Global Opportunity* (SAGE, 2010). Chapter 9 of the book addressed "noneconomic risks," including political risk and terrorism. We have come to realize that one of the underlying sources of these noneconomic risks is "the gap"—and the growing desperation it arouses between the have and have-not nations. For example, the First Gulf War in 1991 is now regarded by many as a Malthusian war in which Iraq's dictator, Sadam Hussein, sought to grab the oil wealth of his small neighbor, Kuwait, through military invasion as a kind of quick short-cut to prosperity. The results were disastrous, for the Mideast and the world, and the "collateral damage" from this war is still ongoing.

Consider this single telling statistic:

> A new Oxfam report [shows that] the 62 richest billionaires own as much wealth [in aggregate] as the poorer half of the world's population…1% of people own more wealth than the other 99% combined.[2] The wealth of the poorest 50 per cent dropped by 41 per cent between 2010 and 2015, despite an increase in the global population of 400 million. In the

same period, the wealth of the richest 62 people increased by $500 b. to $1.76 trillion. Mark Goldring, the Oxfam Great Britain chief executive, said: "It is simply unacceptable that the poorest half of the world population owns no more than a small group of the global super-rich—*so few you could fit them all on a single coach*. In a world where one in nine people go to bed hungry every night, we cannot afford to carry on giving the richest an ever bigger slice of the cake."

One busload of people owns more assets than 3.6 billion people! If those people got off the bus and gave all their assets to the bottom 50 percent, the latter would no longer be poor. But instead, the one percent bus is getting less and less crowded.

The Oxfam report was timed to be released during the annual World Economic Forum in Davos, Switzerland, where the super-rich gather annually to pontificate about the state of the world.

Almost as we write these words, a crucial inflection point is taking place. The share of wealth held by the world's richest one percent is now greater than the total share of wealth held by the poorest 99 percent (see Figure 7.1). The two lines crossed in 2015. At current rates, in just a single decade, 2010–20, the share of world wealth held by the richest one percent will have risen by ten percentage points, from 45 percent to 55 percent.

Two important questions arise. Why is this growing inequality occurring? And what does it imply for global managers who practice Smartonomics?

The best answer so far has come from a somewhat surprising source: A French economist named Thomas Piketty, whose rather pedantic 700-page tome, packed with dense figures and limpid prose, has become a best-seller, albeit one I think that is more widely bought than is widely read to the bitter end.

But to truly understand "the gap," we need first to draw on two other path-breaking books: Hernando de Soto's book,

Figure 7.1 Share of Global Wealth: Top 1 Percent and Bottom 99 Percent

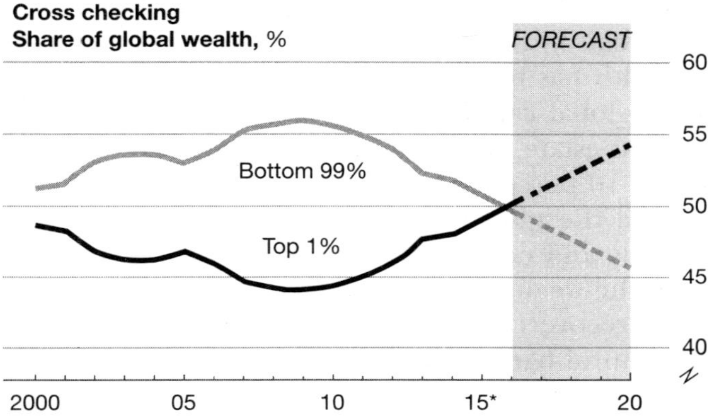

Cross checking
Share of global wealth, %   FORECAST

Bottom 99%

Top 1%

2000   05   10   15*   20

Source: *The Economist,* citing Oxfam.

The Mysteries of Capital: Why Capitalism Triumphs in the West & Fails Everywhere Else, and the late C.K. Prahalad's wonderful book, *The Fortune at the Bottom of the Pyramid: Eradicating Poverty Through Profits.*[3]

Together, these three books provide a clear "teleology" (cause-and-effect analysis). We begin with *The Mysteries of Capital* and de Soto's key argument.

> Poor countries are capital poor. But they are asset rich. They have valuable resources and valuable land. But in order for assets to become capital, there has to be a marketplace, in which forces of supply and demand determine value and pricing through purchase and sale. Unless ownership of an asset is clearly established and its title is legally established, it cannot be bought or sold in open markets. Poor countries lack such markets, because, for example, they lack an orderly corruption-free system of registering title to land. De Soto claims that giving the poor title to the land they farm would at one stroke strike a massive blow to poverty. But land reform has been slow and painful.

Figure 7.2 shows the other side of the de Soto story. We have come across this figure earlier, in Chapter 2 (Figure 2.3). In the West, mainly, and partly in Asia's emerging markets, enormous wealth has been created as physical assets were monetized in global capital markets and rose in value—stocks, bonds, real estate, mortgages, and so on. This wealth grew from only 10 percent of global GDP to nearly half in 2006, just before the global financial crisis derailed the process temporarily and destroyed some of the wealth—but far, far less than the wealth that was created since 1980. And as the world has recovered from the Great Recession, 2008–12, the world's central banks have created massive amounts of new money. This in turn has driven a steep rise in equity prices. According to a study by Deutsche Bank, "Global stock market capitalization has more than doubled since the Federal Reserve started its quantitative easing program in 2008."

Consider the global market for "derivatives," financial assets that are "contingent," derived from other assets, such as options—the option to buy or less 100 shares of IBM at a given strike price. This market virtually did not exist four decades ago. Then, a pair of brilliant economics, Myron

Figure 7.2 Global Wealth, 1980–2006

$ trillion'	1980	1990	1995	2000	2001	2002	2003	2004	2005	2006	CAGR, 1996–2006, %
Total	12	43	66	94	92	96	117	134	142	167	9.1
Equity securities	3	9	18	32	28	24	32	38	44	54	10.4
Private-dept securities	2	10	15	22	23	26	30	34	36	43	10.7
Government debt securities	2	8	13	14	17	17	20	24	24	26	6.8
Bank deposits	5	16	21	26	26	30	34	38	39	45	7.8
Nominal GDP, $ trillion	10.1	21.5	29.4	31.7	31.6	36.8	36.9	41.6	44.8	48.3	5.7
Financial depth, % of GDP	201	201	223	294	290	292	315	318	317	346	

17.4% increase

Source: McKinsey Global Institute. In: Seshadri and Maital, Global Risk/Global Opportunity, 2012, 127.

Scholes and Fisher Black, published a paper in 1973 in the *Journal of Political Economy* in which they showed that the fair price of an options contract depended of five easily-measurable parameters.[4] The result: A booming market in derivates, that today is estimated by some experts to be 10 times bigger than world GDP![5] Including everything, the derivatives market could be worth a staggering $1.5 quadrillion ($1,600 trillion).

So the first piece of the 1%/99% puzzle is this: Western economies, with some help from Asian emerging markets, have become an enormous machine for creating new capital by monetizing assets, a process driven by money creation (see Chapter 4). Poor countries have, in large part, not been a part of this process as they lack the infrastructure and underlying conditions to make it possible, claims de Soto.

This capital-creating machine created massive risky assets, known as credit default swaps, that nearly destroyed the global economy in 2008. To battle the Great Recession that ensued, world central banks used "QE" (massive money creation) that has restarted the capital-creating machine with a vengeance. In the great global soccer game, huge sums of money created by US, European, and Asian central banks sit on the sidelines, eager to enter the game. They eventually do, as enterprising bankers and financial services experts find ways to use low-interest money to earn high returns.

A revealing graph supplied by Bloomberg Business Week (see Figure 7.3) shows that the ratio of national capital (total public and private capital) to national income (i.e. GDP) in Europe, from 1870 through 2010, has followed a U-shaped pattern—initially falling, from 1870 to around 1950, and then, as the post-World War II recovery began, rising to close to 1870 levels. Karl Marx wrote his book *Capital* around the time Europe's capital-to-GDP ratio was about 600 percent. He predicted growing concentration of capital. He was wrong for about 80 years. Today, as capital grows faster than GDP, and is held in relatively few hands, Marx's 1867 prediction about the growing concentration of wealth is, after many decades, turning out to be accurate.

Figure 7.3 National Capital as a Percentage of National Income, Europe, 1870–2010

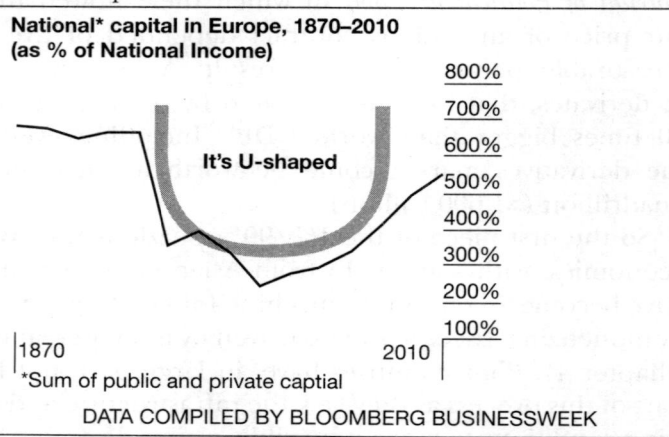

DATA COMPILED BY BLOOMBERG BUSINESSWEEK

Source: http://piketty.pse.ens.fr/files/capital21c/en/pdf/F4.5.pdf, accessed September 22, 2016.

The second piece of the puzzle is in the book by Piketty. He raises the question: Who is holding the vast majority of this new capital, the new riches created by the capitalist money machines? The answer, of course, is: The rich and the very rich.

As the share of capital held by the rich grows, so does the share of the *income* from capital. This is almost obvious. Figure 7.4 shows the cumulative distribution of global income from capital. In 1979, 80 percent of the total income from capital accrued to the *wealthiest 40 percent* of the population; in 2007, just before the global financial crisis, 80 percent of capital income accrued to *only 15 percent* of the population.

Based on income tax returns, Piketty shows that the wealthy earn, on average, real returns of about 8 percent on their capital investments. This is much higher than the rate of growth of world GDP, and far higher than the rate of return that the non-wealthy can earn, if they had significant savings to invest. The result:

The consequences for long-term dynamics of the wealth distribution *are potentially terrifying,* especially when one adds that the return on capital varies directly with the size of the initial stake and that the divergence in the wealth distribution is occurring on a global scale.[6]

Figure 7.4 Cumulative Distribution of Income from Capital (Lorentz Curve), 1979 and 2007

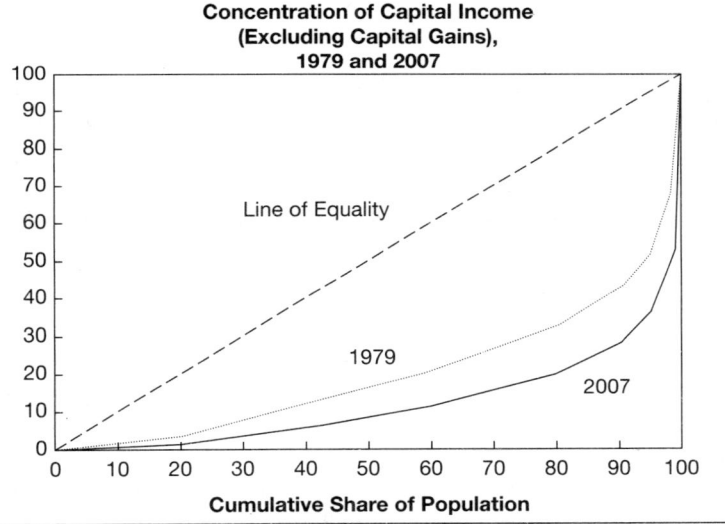

Source: Thomas Piketty (2014), *Capital in the 21st Century,* p. 571.

Wealth that earns 8 percent compound interest, and where the interest is reinvested, doubles every nine years. (This is the "rule of 72"—divide 72 by the real rate of return gives the number of years for wealth to double). So the wealth of the wealthy is doubling in less than a decade. The nonexistent wealth of the poor is not doubling because it is nonexistent, and the wealth of the middle class, earning one or two percent, is growing very slowly.

Let us carry out a simple hypothetical calculation. Suppose there are only two people in the world. They have equal wealth, equal to 100. The first, Alpha, and Alpha's descendants, earn one percent real return annually. The other, Beta, and Beta's descendants, earn eight percent real return annually. Here is their wealth and that of their descendants over a century:

Year	1	20	40	60	80	100
Alpha	100	122	149	182	222	270
Beta	100	466	2,172	10,125	47,195	21,998

After a century, Beta and descendants have wealth over 80 times greater than Alpha. Will Alpha and clan find violent, desperate ways to try to redress the imbalance long before the century is over?

So why does Piketty, a normally understated empirical macroeconomist, think that the dynamics of long-term wealth distribution are potentially terrifying?

Here is why. People with great wealth gain control of the democratic system, to perpetuate their wealth through tax breaks. The growing concentration of wealth in fewer and fewer hands cannot be corrected by the democratic system (the vast majority, who have no wealth) because the super-rich use their wealth to manipulate the democratic system. That statement does not come from Piketty. It comes from an article by a researcher, John Cassidy, "Is America an Oligarchy?"[7] He quotes two political scientists, Gilens and Page, who claim that: "Our analyses suggest that majorities of the American public actually have little influence over the policies our government adopts":

> Americans do enjoy many features central to democratic governance, such as regular elections, freedom of speech and association, and a widespread (if still contested) franchise. But...in the United States, our findings indicate, the majority does not rule—at least not in the causal sense of actually determining policy outcomes. When a majority of citizens disagrees with economic elites and/or with organized interests,

they generally lose. Moreover...even when fairly large majorities of Americans favor policy change, they generally do not get it.

On many issues, say the authors, the rich exercise an effective veto. If they are against something, it is unlikely to happen.

So here is where things stand. Wealth grows faster than income. Wealth concentrates in fewer and fewer hands. Wealth corrupts democracy.

Marx predicted that the concentration of wealth would grow so intolerable, that the proletariat would revolt. If the democratic system cannot repair itself, what other solution is there?

Piketty does propose a possible solution to growing wealth inequality and the resulting instability that emerges, after nearly 600 pages of analysis. The right solution is a progressive annual tax on capital—this will make it possible to avoid an endless inegalitarian spiral while preserving competition and incentives for new instances of primitive accumulation.... The difficulty is that this solution, the progressive tax on capital, requires a high level of international cooperation and regional political integration.[8]

We believe that Piketty himself does not believe that a global progressive tax on capital, with rising rates according to wealth, is feasible. If indeed the wealthy use their wealth to tilt the democratic process in their favor, what are the odds that legislatures will vote to impose a tax on those that fund their representatives' election? And if one country, say, Britain, does impose such a tax, which is highly unlikely, Britain's wealth will simply migrate instantly to low-tax countries so that, unless all nations impose a wealth tax, no nation truly can.

So far, this Smartonomics analysis has been deeply pessimistic, even alarmist. It is alarming not solely for the middle and lower class worldwide; it should be alarming for the rich and super-rich, because at some point, the evident extreme injustice will inevitably bring explosive change, hard to predict and harder to control once underway.

It is time to invoke the third piece of the puzzle, the book by C.K. Prahalad, *The Fortune at the Bottom of the Pyramid: Eradicating Poverty Through Profits*. Smartonomics sees opportunities where others see only risk. And Prahalad, who sadly passed away on April 16, 2010, definitely sees opportunities.

OPPORTUNITIES: THE BOTTOM OF THE PYRAMID

> *If we stop thinking of the poor as victims or as a burden and start recognizing them as resilient and creative entrepreneurs and value-conscious consumers, a whole new world of opportunity will open up.*
>
> —Thomas Piketty[9]

Smartonomics practitioners see opportunities where others see risk. "The gap" is a perfect example. C.K. Prahalad is a superb practitioner. He stresses that mindset—the way we perceive facts and contexts—plays a crucial role in our thinking and behavior. The prevailing mindset toward "the gap" has been to funnel aid, in a variety of ways, to poor countries. Instead, Prahalad suggests we rethink our basic assumptions:

> What is needed is a better approach to help the poor, an approach that involves partnering with them to innovate achieve sustainable win-win scenarios, where the poor are actively engaged and, at the same time, the companies providing products and services to them are profitable.

Prahalad points out that there are some four billion people at the bottom of the wealth-and-income pyramid, more than half the world's population, who live on less than $2 per day. One can see that fact as reflecting abysmal poverty. But turning the coin over, one can see it as a huge market of up to some $2 times 4 billion equals $8 billion daily, or 365 times $8 billion = almost $3 trillion annually.

In Box 7.1 are some examples of how global corporations are leveraging the bottom of the pyramid for win-win innovations, using "reverse innovation"—developing cost-efficient products in poor countries, then migrating them to wealthier countries, rather than the conventional reverse direction, from rich to poor:

Box 7.1: Reverse Innovations: From the Bottom to the Top

Professor Vijay Govindarajan's new book about "reverse innovation" has some valuable ideas for mining the "bottom of the pyramid" opportunities.[10] In his YouTube talk Professor Govindarajan provides some case study examples:

"Historically, MNC's design products in rich countries, and sell them in poor ones. Reverse innovation involves the opposite, innovating in poor countries and bringing the products to rich ones. Clearly poor people want what rich people have. But why would a rich man want a poor man's product? That is the essence of reverse innovation.

- Nestle: is remaking itself as a health and wellness company. The place they are looking to innovate is emerging markets, because of the size of the consumer base. They innovated under the brand name Maggi (noodles) in India, low fat healthy noodles. It created a huge market in India, but is now sold successfully in rich countries.
- Tata Nano: $2000 car. The cost of a DVD player in a BMW is much more! They target the two-wheeler population in India. Two-wheelers cost $1,500. A $2,000 car will win the two-wheeler population.

You are converting nonconsumers into consumers. This is fundamental innovation. Tata Motors plans to bring the Nano into Europe and the US. This will transform the global auto business. [Tata has since encountered serious difficulties in marketing the Nano, but its efforts have helped generate a whole new market in sub-mini inexpensive automobiles].
- GE: Five years ago GE pioneered an ultra-low-cost portable ultrasound machine in China. It costs $15,000. Contrast that with the premium ultrasound machines, sold for $350,000. Why do you need a portable machine in China? 90% of China is rural. You have no hospitals. The hospital has to come to the patient. So the machine must be portable. The low-cost portable machine, innovated for China, is now creating markets for GE all over the world, including the US. It is a $300 million global business for GE. In the US, you can put the portable ultrasound machine in an ambulance, when there is an accident. GE's premium electrocardiogram (ECG) machines were nonstarters in rural India, because patients didn't have the money to pay for the test, and small clinics and physicians couldn't afford the machine or the support costs. These constraints defined the sandbox for GE Healthcare to develop an $800 ECG machine for rural India that is portable, battery-operated, easy-to-use, and easy-to-repair. GE found many ways to cut costs. The high-end machine was custom-designed, so GE built a machine using commodity components, realizing huge cost advantages. For a cost-effective printer, GE used the kind of ticket printer found on public buses and in movie theaters. Since these printers are produced in the millions, GE could enjoy significantly lower costs due to economies of scale. The small printer reduced the weight of the

> machine—less than a can of Coke—and helped make it portable. By eliminating the monitor, GE reduced the need for huge power consumption. This, in turn, contributed to longer life for the rechargeable battery. [This low-cost ECG too can successfully migrate to wealthy countries, where health care costs are spiraling upward out of control]."
>
> Govindarajan goes on to observe:
>
> How come reverse innovation has become so important? It is because of the 2008–09 Great Recession. It has fundamentally reset the world. Growth has shifted from developed to developing countries, from rich to poor. 15 years ago, GE used to prepare its global strategy, so there was a strategy for the US, Europe, Japan and the rest of the world. Today GE has a BRIC strategy, for the Mid-East, and—the rest of the world. This is a fundamental change. MNE's have taken the 7 b. people on earth and divided them into 2 b. rich people, and 5 b. poor. The latter were left to government and charity. This is outmoded. We need to bring the 5 b. poor into the consumer base. *They cannot consume the same products consumed by the 2 b. rich base. There is no product created for middle America ($50,000 per capita income) that can be adapted to capture middle India ($800 per capita).*
>
> Source: YouTube video, Prof. Vijay Govindarajan, https://youtu.be/ztna1lt_LZE, accessed September 22, 2016.

OPPORTUNITIES: AT THE TOP OF THE PYRAMID

Each year, Boston Consulting Group, a leading global consultant, publishes a comprehensive survey of global private wealth (see Figure 7.5). This survey shows that private wealth, growing at about 8 percent annually, will continue to grow rapidly, far faster than global GDP, though the pace of growth will slow somewhat to 6 percent (which still doubles global wealth every 12 years) and by 2019 will total some $210 trillion.

Figure 7.5 reveals enormous opportunities for value creation at the top of the pyramid, where this private wealth is held.

Smartonomics practitioners can excel as managers of private wealth. To do so, they must ask:

- Can I see opportunities in global markets, that others cannot and do not?
- Can I communicate those opportunities to private wealth holders in ways that inspire confidence and understanding?
- Can I successfully implement my insights in bold long-run strategies that create value both for the holders of private wealth and those who benefit from it, in its investments?

Figure 7.5 Global Total Private Wealth, $ Trillion (2012–19) (Annual Growth Rates in Circles)

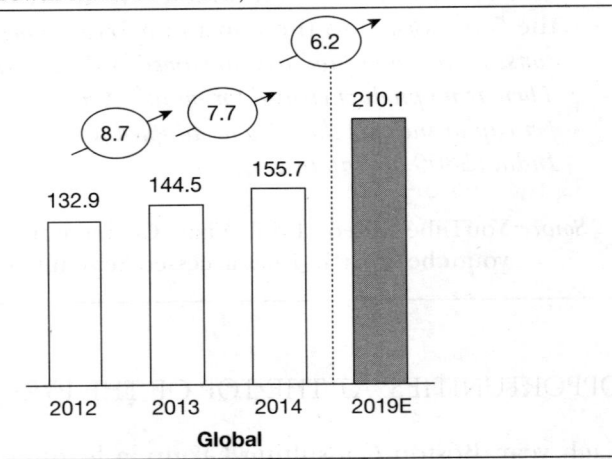

Source: Boston Consulting Group Global Wealth 2015.

The Gap 187

The opening sentence of the BCG Global Wealth Report 2015 is revealing:

> The wealth management industry has arrived at an inflection point. While one group of players seems to be guarding the status quo, another group is seizing the moment. These proactive institutions are doing more than their competitors to raise their game in ways that will ensure profitability and market-leading positions over the next five years and beyond.[11]

It is both obvious, yet not fully understood, that "the gap" has created an enormous industry built on managing wealth and that industry has two fundamentally different sets of players—those who are content with exploiting the low-risk advantages of vast wealth, earning high returns with relatively low risk, and those who are eager and able to leverage wealth to outperform the conservative play-it-safe wealth managers, to achieve above-average returns.

Private financial wealth is greatest in aggregate in North America, and will total $62.5 trillion by 2019, but it is growing very slowly, at 4 percent yearly, as is wealth in Western Europe, which will total just under $50 trillion by 2019. In contrast, Asia-Pacific private wealth (excluding Japan) will grow at 10.9 percent annually (2014–19) and will exceed that of Western Europe by 2019, at $55 trillion. Wealth is growing rapidly in Eastern Europe (8.7 percent annually), Latin America (11.3 percent), and the Mideast and Africa (8.4 percent).

What these figures imply is that the risk-return curve in private wealth is alive and well. Markets in which private wealth is growing the fastest are also the markets where risks of all sorts (political, financial, or economic) are also highest.

Smartonomics practitioners will do well to apply the tools of macroeconomics to conduct due diligence in the high-risk high-return parts of the world (Latin America, Eastern Europe, and Asia) and identify opportunities. The key, of course, is not to invest *along* the conventional risk-return curve but, to identify wealth management opportunities in which the return is at or above the trend line and the risk is significantly below the trend-line value corresponding to the relevant rate of return. This is what is implied by creating value for the holders of private wealth. To do so will require expertise in "country due diligence" (described in the next chapter), skill in communicating such insights (also described in the next chapter), and the courage to implement what may be a contrarian view of the world, that runs counter to the prevailing thinking. Investing money by following the crowd can be relatively risk-free (though not always, as for instance, during financial bubbles), but rarely offers well-above-market-average returns. Investing money by going against the prevailing wisdom can generate higher-than-average returns, but incurs risk that is very high if the market ends up going in the opposite direction. There is a clear choice here; Smartonomics favors the latter.

THE FOURTH INDUSTRIAL REVOLUTION

So far in this chapter, we have called upon the wisdom contained in four books—those by de Soto, Prahalad, Piketty and Govindarajan—to explore how "the gap" can lead Smartonomics practitioners to wise and profitable decisions that create value for themselves and their clients. We have tried to explain why "the gap" between rich and poor, especially in wealth holdings, will continue to grow.

But we have not yet explained the fundamental cause for this growing gap, other than the fact that great wealth earns on average 8 percent returns and doubles every 9 years, while those without such wealth fall behind or earn only 1 percent on their savings. What underlies this key differential? What is the basic "teleology" (causal mechanism)?

To understand it, we need to look back in history at the three past industrial revolutions, and the fourth one now underway.

- The First Industrial Revolution, in the late 18th and early 19th centuries, substituted electrical and water power for human and animal power. This directly benefited laborers by greatly enhancing their productivity.
- The Second Industrial Revolution, in the late 19th and early 20th centuries, used mass production and the assembly line to boost labor productivity. This too directly benefited laborers, raising their productivity and creating relatively high-paying jobs for growing middle class.
- The Third Industrial Revolution took place in the latter part of the 20th century and featured globalization, which drove costs down through global sourcing and trade. Major benefits accrued to workers in Asia, where much manufacturing migrated.
- The Fourth Industrial Revolution is unfolding now. Here, the focus is the digital revolution and the Internet of Everything, connecting all devices and all human beings through the Internet.

The Fourth Industrial Revolution is a major driving force underlying the growing global inequality of wealth and income, among nations and within nations. Those with the knowledge and skills required by the digital revolution grow wealthy. Those lacking them fall behind. Unlike the previous three industrial revolutions, this revolution is not a major creator of well-paying jobs, nor is it a trend that boosts labor productivity for large numbers of workers. Instead it is a labor-saving revolution that is replacing large numbers of jobs.

For example, the social network known as Facebook has a market capitalization of its shares equal to $310 billion, making it one of the most valuable companies in the world (as of March 13, 2016). In 2007, when Facebook was just getting rolling, it employed 450 workers. Today it employs 12,691 people. This is a miniscule number, relative to other leading global industrial companies with market capitalization similar to that of Facebook. Google has a market capitalization of $510 billion and employs 61,000 workers. Compare this with what was once one of the world's leading industrial companies, General Motors, a creature of the Second Industrial Revolution and mass production, which once employed 800,000 employees, mostly assembly line workers earning relatively high wages.

A key aspect of the Fourth Industrial Revolution is the so-called Internet of Things (IoT), or, as we prefer to call it, the Internet of Everything—the digital system that will connect everyone and everything, every person, family, and device, through the Internet (see Box 7.2). The Internet of Everything is at present a force that greatly increases inequality, because some four billion people in the world, the bottom of the pyramid, are not connected to the Internet at all. One of the biggest challenges now facing the world, and facing Smartonomics practitioners, is to find a practical scalable way to connect those four billion to the Internet.

Box 7.2: Internet of Everything

The global consulting firm McKinsey recently prepared an extensive report on IoT. According to the report,

> The Internet of Things has the potential to dramatically improve health outcomes, particularly in the treatment of chronic diseases such as diabetes that now take an enormous human and economic toll....Technology suppliers...are working to fill the gap between the ability to collect data from the physical world and the capacity to capture and analyze it in a timely way.

According to the study, IoT has a potential economic impact of $3.9 trillion to $11.1 trillion per year in 2025. And, at the extreme, the global IoT industry could be

> as large as 11 percent of the world economy by that year. A wide range of devices that talk to one another will exist, on our bodies, in our homes, shops, offices, factories, worksites, cars, cities, and outdoors. Some 26 billion objects (not including phones or PC's) will be Internet-connected in a decade. A whole new Internet protocol will be needed to provide sufficient Internet addresses for them all. And our cars? Road accidents and fatalities will decline by 80 percent. No IoT machine ever imbibed too much alcohol and ran off the road or into an oncoming vehicle.
>
> *Source:* Manyika et al., McKinsey Global Institute, June 2015.[12]

The 2016 World Economic Forum at Davos, Switzerland was devoted to the theme of "Mastering the Fourth Industrial Revolution". As part of this event, the WEF asked four Nobel Prize winning economists (Robert Shiller, Edmund Phelps, Michael Spence, and Alvin Roth), to define what they saw as the major challenges facing the world in the context of the 4th Industrial Revolution. Robert Shiller, 2013 laureate, noted: "We cannot wait until there are massive dislocations in our society to prepare for the Fourth Industrial Revolution". Yet, such dislocations have already occurred, massively, and will continue. And our society is far from prepared for them. Shiller urges a new tax and benefit plan "to deal with a possible huge increase in economic inequality." Such an increase is already upon us. And it will grow worse. Shiller recommends we view the issue as "developing a moral consensus now, from the original Rawlsian position." But what is the original Rawlsian position?

John Rawls was a moral philosopher who developed a simple, powerful notion of optimal inequality based on the "original position"—suppose each of us was born not knowing at all into which income and wealth bracket we would grow, a position behind "the veil of ignorance." What distribution of income and wealth would we choose from this "original position?" A study by Dan Ariely and colleague done on a group of Americans showed that, given the Rawlsian question, most would prefer an income distribution close to that of Sweden (relatively equal) rather than the income distribution prevailing at present in the United States.[13]

Interestingly, two of the Nobel laureates, Phelps and Spence, choose the slowdown in economic growth and productivity as the key world challenge. And Roth, in turn, the 2012 Laureate, focuses on the migration crisis, which in part is a reflection of global inequality and the desire of the poor to seek geographies where their lives will be better.[14]

Shiller has written a spirited defense of finance and the banking and financial services industries, badly maligned in the wake of the 2008 financial crisis brought on by (many perceive) commercial and investment banks who took on excessive risks.[15] His book concludes by affirming:

> [I]t is an illusion that it is personally advantageous to be aggressive and selfish in the financial dealings of one's life, or that one should expect such aggressiveness from others. The real interest that we all have is to see the varied activities of humankind amplified and enriched by the most effective financial arrangements we can devise, *improving our financial technology so that it helps create a powerful and generous financial society.* (213)

No better or clearer statement could be made of the fundamental credo of Smartonomics in the face of "the gap."

CONCLUSION

Chapter 6 recounted how a "torrent of capital" is flooding the world, with massive impact in the wake of the 2008–12

Great Recession and the desperate ongoing efforts of central banks, in the US, Europe, and China, to spur growth by massive credit creation. This chapter shows how the torrent of capital is in part related to, and a cause of, "the gap," the growing inequality of income and wealth distribution between rich and poor people, families, and nations.

In this chapter we have examined how "the gap" can create opportunities for Smartonomics practitioners, in two separate realms: the one percent (the wealthy and the super-rich) and the wealth management opportunities they offer and the 99 percent, the bottom of the pyramid, the poor, those largely without wealth. Creating value for those at the top of the pyramid, and those at the bottom of the pyramid, will require the clever use of macroeconomic tools, willingness to think independently, and high skill at translating insights into global trends and developments into plans of action that can be clearly communicated to others, whether clients or team members. It will require the ability to engage in "due diligence" of distant countries and markets, analyzing macroeconomic risks and opportunities.

This is the subject of the next chapter.

NOTES

1 Belknap Press, Harvard University, Boston, MA: 2014; published in 2013 as *Le Capital au XXI siècle, Editions du Seuil, Paris*.
2 Larry Elliott, Economics Editor, "Richest 62 People as Wealthy as Half of World's Population, Says Oxfam", *The Guardian*, January 18 2016.
3 Hernando de Soto, *The Mysteries of Capital: Why Capitalism Triumphs in the West & Fails Everywhere Else*. (repr., New York: Basic Books, 2000); C.K. Prahalad, *The Fortune at the Bottom of the Pyramid: Eradicating Poverty Through Profits* (New Delhi: Pearson Education India, 2006).
4 Black, Fischer and Scholes, Myron, "The Pricing of Options and Corporate Liabilities", *Journal of Political Economy*, 81 no. 3 (1973): 637–54.
5 "Along with credit default swaps and other exotic instruments, the total notional derivatives value is about $1.5 quadrillion—about 20% more than in 2008, beyond what anyone can conceive, let alone control if unexpected turmoil strikes". http://www.globalresearch.ca/global-derivatives-1-5-quadrillion-time-bomb/5464666, accessed September 22, 2016.

6. Thomas Piketty, *Capital in the 21st C.*, 571.
7. *The New Yorker*, April 18, 2014.
8. Thomas Piketty, *Capital in the 21st C*, 572–73.
9. Prahalad, *The Fortune at the Bottom of the Pyramid*, 1.
10. Vijay Govindarajan, *Reverse Innovation: Create Far From Home, Win Everywhere* (Boston, MA: Harvard Business School Press, 2010).
11. Boston Consulting Group, Global Wealth Report (Boston, MA: Boston Consulting Group, 2015), 3.
12. James Manyika, Michael Chui, Peter Bisson, Jonathan Woetzel, Richard Dobbs, Jacques Bughin, and Dan Aharon, "Unlocking the potential of the Internet of Things". McKinsey Global Institute, June 2015. http://www.mckinsey.com/business-functions/business-technology/our-insights/the-internet-of-things-the-value-of-digitizing-the-physical-world accessed September 22, 2016.
13. Norton, Michael I., and Dan Ariely, "Building a Better America—One Wealth Quintile at a Time," *Perspectives on Psychological Science*, 6 no. 1 (2011): 9–12.
14. https://www.weforum.org/agenda/2016/01/four-nobel-economists-on-biggest-challenges-2016/, accessed September 22, 2016.
15. Robert Shiller, *Finance and the Good Society* (Princeton, NJ: Princeton University Press, 2013).

8

Mining for Opportunities

 **Tool 8: Due Diligence Checklist**

Learning Objectives

- *Understand how to conduct "due diligence" for a country*
- *Learn how to combine macroeconomic analysis with microeconomic "opportunity mining"*
- *Become proficient in employing a checklist—a framework that integrates the previous seven essential tools and adds to them non-economic factors related to culture, politics, and ethics*
- *Know why major paradigm shifts occur in global markets and key industries and how and why such shifts can create exceptionally attractive new business opportunities*
- *Understand how to build a "global narrative"—a story that describes your view of how events will unfold in global markets in the coming 3–5 years and reveals the opportunities hidden in unfolding crises and uncertainty*
- *Learn where to find essential data and how to analyze it*

Ideas are the currency of the 21st [century]. Ideas, effectively packaged and delivered, can change the world.... Ideas are only as good as the actions that follow the communication of those ideas.

—Carmine Gallo[1]

Don't be trapped by dogma (living with the results of other people's thinking). Don't let the noise of other people's thinking drown out your inner voice. And most important, have the courage to follow your heart and your intuition. They somehow already know what you truly want to become.

—Steve Jobs, Commencement Address, Stanford University, 2005

INTRODUCTION

As we write these words, a quick scan of world economy and geopolitics reveals:

- An imminent threat to the EU as millions of refugees pour out of the Mideast and through Turkey and Greece, desperately trying to reach safe haven in Europe; European borders are no longer fully open to the "free flow of goods, services, money and people." Britain votes to leave the EU, partly as a result of the flow of migrants.
- A shaky Chinese economy, faced by state banks with massive nonperforming loans, a decline in manufacturing, slowing growth, an aging population, and severe environmental problems related to water, air, and land;
- Volatile global capital markets, as investment managers desperately accept high levels of risk to achieve minimal rates of return;
- The glut of oil, causing historically low oil prices and throwing whole countries into chaos, including Venezuela, Russia, and even Saudi Arabia; stagnating

world economy with growth rates unacceptably low, as world trade slumps;

...and the list could be much longer.

How can a Smartonomics practitioner, faced with so many global risks, manage money, people, and products in a responsible and smart manner, that sees opportunities in trends and crises that others see only as risk and uncertainty?

By the time this chapter reaches print, the list will have changed completely. An entirely new list of economic, financial and geopolitical "surprises" and uncertainties will have been born.

Faced with such rapid change and volatility, how can global managers use Smartonomics to navigate through the treacherous ups and downs? How can they use Smartonomics to endure, prevail, and survive? (See Box 8.1.)

> **Box 8.1: Survival**
>
> Today's managers focus on growth, profit, market share, and competitiveness. Survival is not in their lexicon. Yet, in today's volatile world, survival is not a certainty, for individuals, companies, or even small countries. Did anyone believe that a 165-year-old investment bank, Lehman Brothers, could disappear overnight? But it did, on September 15, 2008. Did anyone foresee the demise of the Soviet Union? Entire Sovietology departments at universities were dissolved in the wake of that debacle.
>
> The US can lose 50,000 soldiers in Vietnam, devastate Iraq, and bog down in Afghanistan, without endangering its survival in the least. But for individuals, and even large corporations, there is very little margin for error and no-one can ever take for granted their continued financial solvency.
>
> Survival has always been, still is, and will always be a primary concern. In an age where credit is cheap and plentiful, it is easy to pile up large amounts of debt, which in a sharp downturn become unmanageable. The response to such "paranoia" is not to "play safe," which itself is often the great risk of all, but to seek opportunities buried within risk, while maintaining constant vigilance (like meteorologists) for storm clouds—especially those not generally seen by "experts."[2]

In this chapter, we propose a systematic approach for Smartonomics managers, to use the preceding set of seven tools, and this chapter's eighth tool, as they explore risks and opportunities in global markets and sharpen their vigilance for risks and opportunities.

Definition:

Due Diligence:

An in-depth analysis of the economy, society, polity and financial markets of a new, and perhaps unfamiliar country, or even a highly familiar one, using a systematic checklist of questions that can help analyze that country's business prospects and "mine for opportunities."

Global managers may have experienced being part of an organization that acquires another company, or is acquired by one. The investigatory process that precedes a takeover is known as due diligence. It is exhaustive, and often exhausting. In part, it exists to avoid legal liability, lest the takeover fail and lead to shareholder litigation. But mostly, due diligence seeks to ensure that the management knows precisely what it is acquiring, and avoid unpleasant surprises.

Country due diligence is similar. Global managers who seek to do business in new geographies should follow a similar, thorough investigatory process. What follows is a kind of template, or framework, for analyzing the risks inherent in doing business in a new and perhaps unfamiliar market. When global managers do their homework well, they will be able to spot risks in markets where others see only opportunities, and in turn find opportunities where others see only risk.

China is a good example. One of the earliest American companies to invest in China was General Electric (GE). They found opportunities when others saw only risk. In global investment, as with management of technology, there is a classic dilemma of first-entrant advantage (the advantage of being first in a market, or in a new technology), and second-entrant advantage (the advantage of being second, or third, and, thus, learning from the mistakes of the pioneers). The resolution of this dilemma depends on solid fact-gathering and employment of the eight tools. Integrating the previous seven tools creates the eighth:

Tool 8: Due Diligence Checklist

Checklist for Country Due Diligence

When you next fly on an airliner, be assured that the pilot, co-pilot, and (if there is one) flight engineer have gone through a careful checklist, or protocol, before takeoff. The checklist ensures that every detail has been covered, for the safety of the passengers. Even if the pilot has flown hundreds of thousands of hours, the checklist is still mandatory.

Hospitals, too, are implementing "protocols." Fatigued doctors and nurses can easily slip up, and a structured list, or protocol, specifying what precisely is to be done for patients, can prevent errors that could be fatal.

We propose a similar checklist for conducting "due diligence" macroeconomic analysis on a business opportunity. The checklist corresponds, more or less, to the preceding seven chapters and the tools described therein. Before you launch your investment, or business idea, crunch the numbers thoroughly, methodically. It could be a matter of survival.

Macro Accounting—Chapter 1: A Country is a Business; Chapter 2: National Saving

- How large is the country's GDP and GDP per capita, measured in dollars, at prevailing exchange rates, and also using PPP exchange rates that reflect the real, underlying value of the currency?
- What does its GDP cash flow look like—the sources of GDP and its uses, the proportions of GDP bought by households, governments, businesses, and foreigners?

Mining for Opportunities 201

- Is the country's GDP growing? How fast? How is the annual increase in GDP—the growth dividend used: for consumption, for investment, or for exports?
- Is the country present- or future-oriented, as measured by how the GDP divides up between personal and government consumption, and investment and net exports?
- How large is the country's net addition to its stock of buildings, machines and equipment, and how does it pay for that investment—out of its own saving, or through borrowing the savings of foreigners?
- Overall, is the country investing abroad, or are foreigners investing in it? Where are its citizens and businesses investing abroad, how much, and in what way? Who, how much, and in what form are foreigners investing in the country? How have these patterns been changing?
- What key components of demand are driving the country's GDP growth, or slowing it?
- How fast is the country's capacity to produce goods and services (potential supply of GDP) growing, relative to demand growth? If demand is outpacing productive capacity, is there a threat of future inflation?
- How much of each additional GDP dollar is spent by households on personal consumption, and how much is saved? How have these important proportions been changing?
- How large is the budget deficit as a proportion of GDP? Are exports bigger or smaller than imports? How important is trade, and net exports expressed as a proportion of GDP?

Money, Interest, and Inflation—Chapter 3: 'Flation; Chapter 4: Money

- How does the country shape its monetary policy? Who is responsible? What are its key considerations?

- How fast is the money supply growing? How is the rate at which that money changes hands (velocity) changing?
- Is the central bank's monetary policy currently making it easier, or harder, to borrow money? Are real (inflation-adjusted) interest rates rising, or falling? How is this affecting GDP? Historically, are real interest rates relatively high or relatively low?
- Does the central bank have the freedom to lower interest rates, or is it seriously limited in this by the need to maintain a fixed exchange rate relative to another currency?
- In general, what degree of political pressure and influence is exerted on the central bank when it sets monetary policy and interest rates? How independent is it?

Cycles and Trends—Chapter 5: Booms and Busts

- What is the current direction and magnitude of the two key macroeconomic forces: prices and output? How have they been changing in recent years? How high is unemployment? How has it been changing?
- Is there inflation? How much? Is inflation driven mainly by demand-pull forces (rising spending)? Or by cost-push (rising wages, interest rates, energy prices, taxes and cost of materials) forces?
- How do long-term interest rates currently compare with short-term ones? Is the difference between short-term and long-term interest rates currently large, or small, and does this signal an impeding recession?
- What is the current level of inflation-adjusted common stock prices?
- How does this compare with historical levels? Are common-stock prices justified by underlying profitability, and future earnings prospects of the country's businesses?
- Is a recovery from the global recession likely soon? Are there any signs of this recovery now? How effective is the government's fiscal and monetary stimulus plan?

- How large and how efficient are the country's capital markets—specifically its equities (common stock) market?

Dollars and Deficits—Chapter 6: Torrents of Capital

- Is foreign trade important to the country's economy? Who are the country's main trading partners?
- Is the current account of the balance of payments in deficit, or in surplus? How has this deficit or surplus been changing in recent years? If in deficit—does this signal a future drop in the value of the country's currency, relative to the dollar?
- Is the country's official (legal) exchange rate bigger, or smaller, than the underlying (purchasing power) value of the country's currency relative to the dollar? Is there a black market in foreign exchange, and if so, how high are black-market rates relative to official ones?
- Are exchange rates fixed or floating? If they are floating, are they a cause of inflation? How sensitive is the country's exchange rate to speculative buying and selling? If they are fixed, is the current fixed exchange rate stable, or will there be devaluation (decline in the currency's value)?
- How are the twin deficits (budget, trade) changing, and how are these changes affecting the overall disposable income?

Integrating the Tools—Chapter 7: The Gap

- Are there enormous gaps between rich and poor? Is this a source of instability in the country?
- For this country, which variables serve as leading indicators, by signaling changes in business activity well in

advance of economic downturns? What are such indicators currently signaling?
- Do businesses and consumers have money, or can they borrow it easily? Are they optimistic and willing, and ready to spend? What is the country's overall mood?
- Is the country truly democratic? Is it politically stable, internally? Is it involved in potentially explosive disputes with neighboring countries? Is there a large, restive underclass?
- Does the country have national energy? Can individuals become wealthy through innovation and entrepreneurship? How well-educated are the people?
- Is your personal sense of the country's character and direction, based on your own observations and insights, consistent with the business profile provided by answers to the checklist questions? If intuition and analysis differ: Which is right?
- Demography: How rapidly is population growing? What is the age structure of the population? What fraction of the population is under the age of 15? What fraction is over the age of 65? What fraction lives in cities and urban areas? Is there emigration or immigration? One of the major future trends in the major industrial countries is the aging of the population. This will have important political and business implications. Japan, for example, has a rather old and aging, population. India's population is relatively young; so is Iran's.
- Health and Education: What is the average life expectancy of men and women? Child mortality rates? What fraction of youth complete primary and secondary school? University? What fraction of the population is literate?
- Energy and Resources: How high is energy consumption? Where are energy sources—especially oil and coal—obtained? Are there natural resources?
- Environment: Is the environment protected by strong policies? Is there ecological awareness?

- Political System: Is the country democratic? Is it politically stable? Are business and government allies or adversaries? Is political power concentrated or diffuse?
- Society and Culture: Is the country individualistic or collectivist? Egalitarian or hierarchical? Is there gender equality? Is there a strong work ethic?
- Religion: What are the major religions? Are there religious beliefs or taboos that could affect your products and marketing?
- Language: Do its people have a common language, or do they speak many dialects?
- Values and Attitude: How do its citizens view foreigners? How do they feel about globalization and competing in global markets?
- Competitiveness: How does the country rank in the tables of World competitiveness? How well does the country compete in global markets? How has this ranking changed? What are the country's competitive strengths and weaknesses?
- Corruption: How honest, or dishonest, is the business system and the political system.
- Freedom: How free are the country's markets? How well can individuals and companies pursue their business interests without the constraints of excessive regulation or bureaucracy?

From Macro to Micro: Zoom Out, then Zoom In

In the book *Cracking the Creativity Code,* Ruttenberg and Maital offer a structured approach for producing, and then implementing, creative ideas.[3] We call it: Zoom in/zoom out/zoom in. Zoom in begins with a close detailed analysis of the challenge, or problem, and our goals. Then zoom out—build the big picture, gather data, and explore the entire ecosystem in which your idea is embedded. Finally, after an intensive zoom-out analysis, return to "zoom in." Bring your insights back to the original problem, and apply them, recalling Carmine Gallo's observation that ideas are only as good as their implementation.

Let us apply this zoom-in/zoom-out approach, and the due-diligence checklist, to the case of India.

> **Case Study: Due Diligence for India**
>
> Forty years ago I worked on the Indian economy for the World Bank. Ever since, I have been fascinated by the place. The ability of this huge and poor nation to sustain a lively democracy has been among the world's political wonders. Yet its economic performance has fallen short of what it might have been. Despite improvements in policy and performance since the crisis of 1991, this remains the case. Nevertheless, India is now the world's fastest-growing large economy. What might it be in future?[4]

India had national elections in April–May 2014, won by the BJP Party led by Narendra Modi, with an absolute majority in Parliament. The government inherited high inflation and a large budget deficit; in 2013–14, the economy grew by only 5.3 percent. Growth in GDP in 2015–16 is forecasted at 7.5 percent (see Figure 8.1).[5] It is significant that India's economy is now growing faster than that of China. India, however, remains a very poor country, with GDP per capita at 11 percent of that in the US, compared with China's 25 percent of US levels.

India has a chronic trade deficit (imports exceed exports; see Figure 8.2), but this deficit has declined in absolutely value ($ million) by half since 2012–13 in early 2016, and this has contributed to rising growth (the trade deficit has reduced growth by much less than in the past).

India's budget deficit too has declined significantly, to 3.9 percent from a high 7.8 percent in the second half of 2008 (see Figure 8.3). The lower budget deficit implies less

Figure 8.1 India Annual GDP Growth Rate, 2012–16

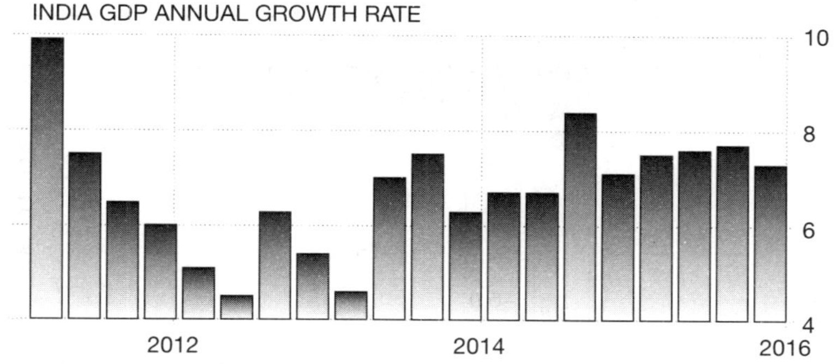

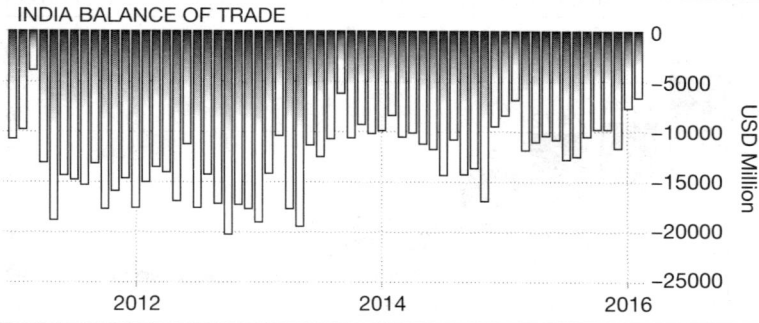

Source: Trading Economics, http://www.tradingeconomics.com/india/gdp-growth-annual, accessed September 22, 2016.

Figure 8.2 India: Balance of Trade (Exports Minus Imports), 2012–16

Source: Trading Economics, http://www.tradingeconomics.com/india/balance-of-trade, accessed September 22, 2016.

purchasing power injection, but has buoyed foreign investor confidence.

The shrinking government budget deficit has improved India's public debt position; government debt is now (2014) 66 percent of GDP, down from 78.5 percent in 2006, and lower than the comparable ratio in, for instance, the US or the EU (see Figure 8.4).

We now turn to money and interest. Table 8.1 shows that India's money supply (M1) doubled between 2006 and 2010, and grew by one-third between 2010 and 2014. Why then has

Figure 8.3 India: Government Budget Deficit as a Percentage of GDP 2006–16

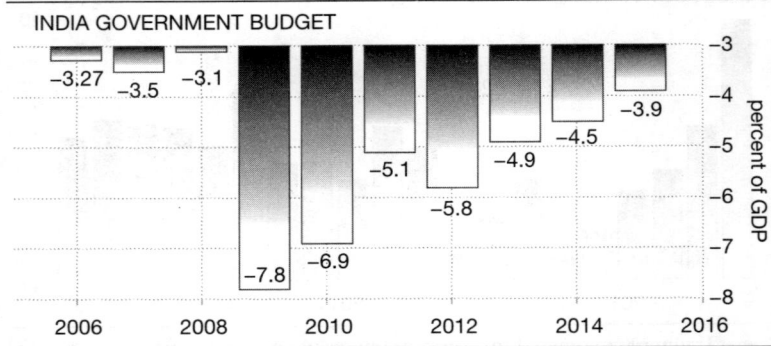

Source: Trading Economics, http://www.tradingeconomics.com/india/government-budget, accessed September 22, 2016.

Figure 8.4 India: Government Debt as a Percentage of GDP 2006–14

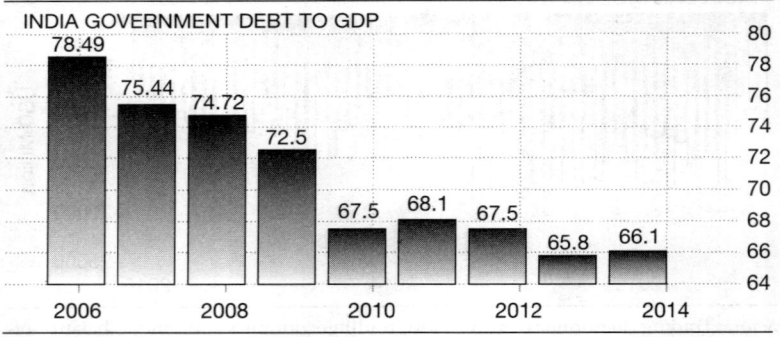

Source: Trading Economics, http://www.tradingeconomics.com/india/government-debt-to-gdp, accessed September 22, 2016.

inflation actually fallen, from 10 percent in 2013 to 5–6 percent today? The answer is revealed in Table 8.1: The velocity of money—the rate at which M1 changes hands in GDP transactions—declined sharply, from 12.65 in 2006 to 9.80 in 2013, a drop of 23 percent. There is clearly no sense of money losing its value rapidly among the Indian people. In addition, lower oil prices have also helped control inflation.

India's central bank has set its interest rate at 6.75 percent, down from 8 percent in 2014 (see Figure 8.5). It is likely that

Table 8.1 India: Velocity of Money (M1), 2006–14 (Billions of Rupees)

Year	Nom. GDP	M1	Velocity
2006	949	7500	12.65
2007	1239	10000	12.39
2008	1224	12000	10.20
2009	1365	12500	10.92
2010	1709	15000	11.39
2011	1836	16000	11.48
2012	1832	17500	10.47
2013	1862	19000	9.80
2014	2049	20000	10.25

Sources: Trading Economics Money: http://www.tradingeconomics.com/india/money-supply-m1, accessed September 22, 2016.
Nominal GDP: http://www.tradingeconomics.com/india/gdp, accessed September 22, 2016.

that interest rate will fall in the coming months, maintaining the downward trend and acting to encourage capital formation, which has fallen from 39 percent of GDP in 2011–12 (higher than in most countries) to 34 percent in 2014–15.

Doing business in India is not easy. The World Bank's Ease of Doing Business website, which measures 10 different business transactions (registering land, registering a business, obtaining credit, paying taxes, and so on), ranks India only 130th in the world (owing to a dense red-tape-tangled bureaucracy), somewhat improved from 139th in 2010 (see Figure 8.6).

How globally competitive is India's economy? After a steady decline, from 49th in the world to only 71st in the world (see Figure 8.7) in 2016, the ranking improved significantly to 55th in the world. This reflects the improvements in the Indian economy since 2014–15.

Corruption remains a problem. Figure 8.8 shows India's global ranking in the perception of corruption, down from 95th in 2011 but still at a relatively high 76th in the world in 2015.

Figure 8.5   India: Interest Rates 2012–16

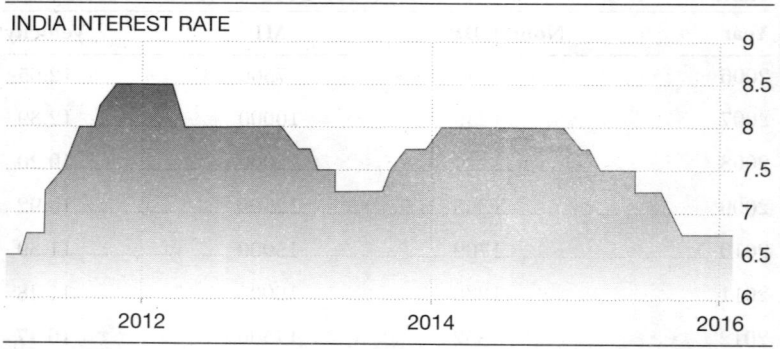

Source: Trading Economics, http://www.tradingeconomics.com/india/interest-rate, accessed September 22, 2016.

Figure 8.6   India: Ease of Doing Business: Rank

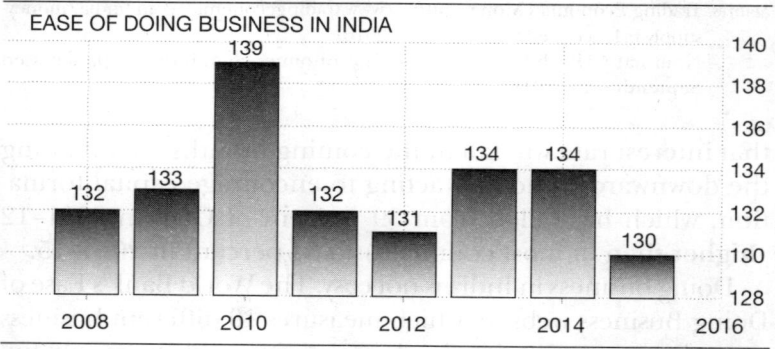

Source: Trading Economics, http://www.tradingeconomics.com/india/ease-of-doing-business, accessed September 22, 2016.
Note: Low ranking indicated by a higher bar.

A key factor that has helped India's exports, and restrained India's imports, is the rupee to dollar exchange rate. The rupee has undergone devaluation, from a high of about 40 rupees per dollar to around 68 per dollar in 2016 (see Figure 8.9). While this has caused some inflation, by raising the price of imports, it has also made the dollar price of Indian exports cheaper. According to the "Big Mac" PPP exchange rate, India's rupee

Figure 8.7 India: Global Competitiveness Ranking

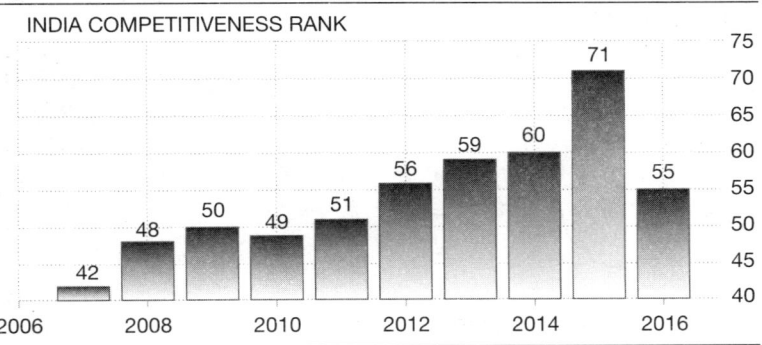

Source: Trading Economics, http://www.tradingeconomics.com/india/competitiveness-rank, accessed September 22, 2016.
Note: Low ranking indicated by a higher bar.

Figure 8.8 India: Corruption Perception Ranking

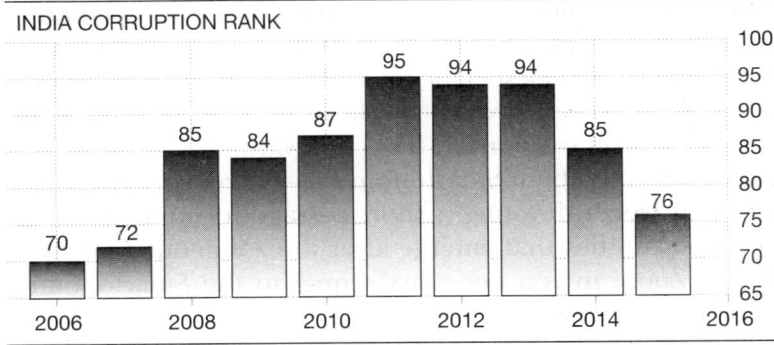

Source: Trading Economics, http://www.tradingeconomics.com/india/corruption-index, accessed September 22, 2016.
Note: Low ranking indicated by a higher bar.

is perhaps the most "undervalued" currency in the world. This is because a great many goods and services in India have very low domestic rupee prices, so that a dollar can buy a great deal. India is a great trading nation, with trade accounting for over half of India's GDP.

Figure 8.9 India: Rupees Per US Dollar: Official Exchange Rate

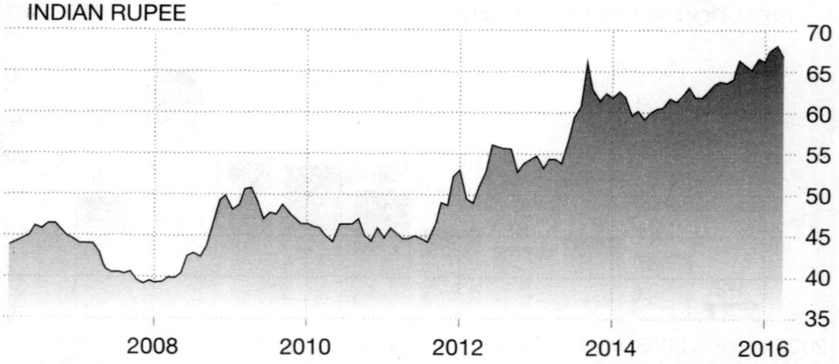

Source: Trading Economics, http://www.tradingeconomics.com/india/currency, accessed September 22, 2016.

ZOOM IN: FROM MACRO TO MACRO

Once we have built a clear picture of the macro economy, and visualized it with strategic, well-chosen graphs, it is time to zoom in and seek specific microeconomic opportunities—growth industries, growth markets, growth locations, and growth market segments. This is not within the realm of this book, which is about Smartonomics—macroeconomic tools. But it is worth devoting a short passage to some examples of opportunities that emerge after the zoom-out analysis of India. Zoom in is a necessary sequel to the Smartonomics zoom-out process.

Automobiles: This industry has grown rapidly, both in domestic sales and in exports.

Telecom: India has become the world's third largest smartphone market, after the US and China, displacing Japan.

Pharma: Biotechnology is growing rapidly in India, with high R&D spending and growing revenues. The Indian pharmaceutical market is predicted to reach $48.5 billion by 2020.

IT: India has some 3 million Information Technology professionals, whose value-added contributed some 8 percent of India's GDP and about a quarter of India's exports.

Healthcare: India's pharma industry is third in the world in volume of production, with most of the market comprising "branded generics" (India is the largest global provider of generic drugs). The industry is characterized by a large number of scientists and engineers.

BUILDING A NARRATIVE

Tell a story. This is the best way to think about Smartonomics' approach to independent thinking about how future events will unfold in global markets. Build a narrative—a coherent account of a series of causally related events, culminating in a clear conclusion regarding action. Chances are, to implement your vision, you will need to persuade other members of your team. To do this, you will need to build a coherent narrative, or story, connecting the teleology (causality) and weaving a plausible tale.

For example: "A perfect storm."

> ### A Perfect Storm
>
> Oil prices remain low and drop even further, as Iran emerges from international sanctions and adds another million or two barrels of oil a day to an already glutted supply. A wave of bankruptcies of energy companies, mainly smaller ones, occurs, especially in the US, as highly-leveraged companies fail to service loans and bonds. These bankruptcies rattle financial markets and bring down asset prices worldwide—bonds and equities. China's growth slows, removing a major source of global GDP growth. Brazil stumbles, Russia's economy

crumbles, and South Africa dips into recession. A "herd" mentality develops—greed turns into fear, and investors sell assets because they believe other investors may do so and for them it could well be too late. The mood of optimism during the global recovery turns quickly to pessimism, and pessimism is self-fulfilling.

The oil and gas sector globally is in debt to the tune of $3 trillion—an amount equal to nearly one-fifth of US annual GDP. Can the crisis in this sector "metastasize" to other sectors? "Over the last 45 years, the Standard & Poor 500 Index (of share prices) has lost more than 12.5 percent annually on 13 occasions. Six of these have led to a recession, providing a near 50 percent probability of a global downturn."[6]

The US economy, once the world's growth engine, is weak and GDP growth may well be less than 2 percent in 2016 and 2017.

A perfect storm, a term that derives from climate science, is defined as "a confluence of events that drastically aggravates a situation." Is what is described above a perfect storm?

Source: http://www.telegraph.co.uk/business/2016/03/25/a-perfect-storm-is-brewing-over-the-most-important-part-of-the-u/, accessed September 22, 2016.

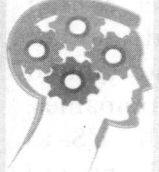

Action Learning: "Perfect Storm" Scenarios

What opportunities emerge from such a bleak "perfect storm" narrative? (For example: First, sell short. If you believe asset prices may fall, you can sell for forward delivery. Of course, this is risky. If asset prices rise rather than fall, you will lose substantially. Second, put options.

You can purchase options to sell assets at a future date, provided you know better than the option writer how future prices will unfold. Third, cash. Build reserves of cash, sell assets—and wait for the inevitable bargains that emerge as asset prices fall.)

Can you develop your own scenarios, including some extreme ones, evaluate their likelihood (probabilities), and then devise an action plan to profit from them?

Do you practice this exercise daily, as you read the news?

CONCLUSION

Smartonomics practitioners tell not one story but several. They build an optimistic narrative alongside a pessimistic one. They think about each story. They try them out on friends and listen to their reactions. They understand that perception drives reality and even wrong perceptions, if believed by enough people, will become reality when such perceptions drive actions.

And above all, Smartonomics adherents listen to their intuition—the inner voice that tells them what they really think, without the interference of their conscious mind, burdened with the myriad opinions of experts and the media. That inner voice is, in fact, the distillation of a long complex process in which our brains integrate our knowledge, wisdom, data, and hunches, let them ferment and bubble, and ultimately, generate a kind of consensus that manifests itself mysteriously—sometimes, as an "ah-hah!" moment; sometimes more quietly.

The eight tools of Smartonomics are instruments our brains can use to build insights and to foster independent bold thinking. In the end, Smartonomics adherents will master the simple tools of macroeconomics, while at the same time creatively shape their own unique thinking about global markets. The combination of mastery and rebellion is the essence of Smartonomics.

APPENDIX 8A: HELPFUL RESOURCES—WHERE TO FIND THE DATA YOU NEED

Where does one find the large amounts of up-to-date data needed to practice Smartonomics, exercise constant vigilance of volatile global markets, and recognize opportunities in markets that appear high risk? Here are a few tips.

Trading Economics: We have found the best single source of macroeconomic data to be a website known as Trading Economics.[7]

At this site, Smartonomics practitioners can find virtually every meaningful economic indicator, for a large number of countries in an extremely friendly format, one that facilitates graphs and enables a visual picture of the country in question and its economy. *The graphs for India are taken from this site.*

World Bank Indicators: The World Bank, located at 1818 H. Street, NW Washington DC, 20433, USA, provides its world development indicators database. It provides detailed annual data, starting in 1970, for some 500 different variables, and 209 countries and regions, for economic, social, and demographic categories. These data usually lag a year or two (for instance, the database available in August, 2015 included data up to 2013, starting in 1970). They include the main macroeconomic indicators, including detailed GDP figures, money supply, trade and capital flows, and prices. A major advantage of World Bank data: They are measured in consistent fashion, using standard definitions so that, in general, one can compare, say, GDP per capita for different countries.

A few key countries that are not World Bank members, like Taiwan, are missing. The countries for which detailed data are provided are: Albania, Algeria, Antigua and Barbuda, Argentina, Armenia, Australia, Austria, Azerbaijan, Bahamas, Bahrain, Bangladesh, Barbados, Belarus, Belgium, Belize, Benin, Bhutan, Bolivia, Botswana, Brazil, Bulgaria, Burkina Faso, Burundi, Cameroon, Canada, Cape Verde, Central

African Republic, Chad, Chile, China, Colombia, Comoros, Congo, Costa Rica, Cote d'Ivoire, Cyprus, Czech Republic, Denmark, Djibouti, Dominica, Dominican Republic, Ecuador, Egypt, El Salvador, Equatorial Guinea, Estonia, Ethiopia, Fiji, Finland, France, Gabon, Gambia, Georgia, Germany, Ghana, Greece, Grenada, Guatemala, Guinea, Guinea-Bissau, Guyana, Haiti, Honduras, Hong Kong, Hungary, Iceland, India, Indonesia, Iran, Ireland, Israel, Italy, Jamaica, Japan, Jordan, Kazakhstan, Kenya, South Korea, Kuwait, Kyrgyz Republic, Laos, Latvia, Lesotho, Liberia, Lithuania, Luxembourg, Madagascar, Malawi, Malaysia, Maldives, Mali, Malta, Mauritania, Mauritius, Mexico, Moldova, Mongolia, Morocco, Mozambique, Myanmar, Namibia, Nepal, Netherlands, New Zealand, Nicaragua, Niger, Nigeria, Norway, Oman, Pakistan, Panama, Papua-New Guinea, Paraguay, Peru, Philippines, Poland, Portugal, Qatar, Romania, Russia, Rwanda, Sao Tome and Principe, Saudi Arabia, Senegal, Seychelles, Sierra Leone, Singapore, Slovak Republic, Solomon Islands, Somalia, South Africa, Spain, Sri Lanka, St. Kitts and Nevis, St. Lucia, St. Vincent and the Grenadines, Sudan, Surinam, Swaziland, Sweden, Switzerland, Syria, Tajikistan, Tanzania, Thailand, Togo, Tonga, Trinidad and Tobago, Tunisia, turkey, Turkmenistan, Uganda, Ukraine, United Arab Emirates, United Kingdom, United States, Uruguay, Vanuatu, Venezuela, Vietnam, Western Samoa, Yemen, Zaire Zambia, Zimbabwe.

IMD World Competitiveness Yearbook: This database appears annually, and provides rankings of some 80 countries, along with underlying data for many hundreds of variables, across four competitiveness dimensions: Economic performance, business efficiency, government efficiency, and infrastructure (including education, science, and technology). It is published by the Swiss business school Lausanne.

Organization for Economic Cooperation and Development (OECD): This organization, which arose out of America's Marshall

Plan aid to Europe in 1947–48, comprises 27 countries, comprising over half the world's GDP.

The member countries are: Australia, Belgium, Canada, Czech Republic, Denmark, Finland, France, Germany, Greece, Hungary, Iceland, Ireland, Italy, Japan, Luxembourg, Mexico, Netherlands, New Zealand, Norway, Poland, Portugal, Spain, Sweden, Switzerland, Turkey, United Kingdom and United States.

A database provided as computer files exists for these countries.

OECD Better Life: This database, for 34 OECD countries, offers a comprehensive view of "the quality of life" across economic, social and financial indicators, shown visually.[8]

The Economist: This remarkable weekly magazine, published in London and available all over the world, offers weekly updates of key macroeconomic variables for both developed countries and emerging markets. The variables for which data are given include: GDP (including a GDP forecast from time to time), industrial production, retail sales, unemployment rate, inflation, producer prices, wages and earnings, money supply, interest rates, stock prices, trade balance, exchange rates, and foreign exchange reserves.

Financial Times, Wall Street Journal: These global publications have excellent online editions with search capabilities.

The CIA Website: It provides useful information on a wide range of countries: www. cia.gov.

Corruption Perception: Transparency International's website provides an ongoing annual index of corruption perception (CPI), measuring how global managers perceive the degree of corruption in a long list of countries.[9]

Freedom: The Heritage Foundation offers an annual index of freedom, which measures the degree to which "individuals are free to work, produce, consume, and invest in any way they please, with that freedom both protected by the state and unconstrained by the state."[10]

Ease of Doing Business: The World Bank sponsors a website that provides detailed information on ease of doing business, across a long list of business activities, including: land registration, starting a business, closing a business, firing an employee and suing or litigating.[11]

Global Competitiveness: How competitive is the country on which you are performing due diligence, in global markets? There are two databases that provide rankings and the detailed underlying data: IMD (Lausanne, Switzerland business school), World competitiveness yearbook;[12] and The World Economic Forum (Davos, Switzerland):[13]

E-Government: how advanced is the nation with regard to providing public services via the Internet?[14]

Cleantech: How does the country rank in the realm of "cleantech" (technology related to environmental protection, water quality, pollution, air quality, and so on).[15]

Innovation: How innovative is the country? Check out the global innovation index[16] and a similar index done by Bloomberg Business Week.[17]

Education: How does the country you are studying rank in terms of its secondary educational system, in science and math? Look up the Project for International School Assessment (PISA).[18]

NOTES

1 Carmine Gallo, *Talk Like TED: The 9 Public Speaking Secrets of the World's Top Minds* (New York: St. Martins Press, 2014).

2. Readers may want to read one of the best business books of all time: Andy Grove, *Only the Paranoid Survive*. Crown Business (New York: Doubleday, 1996, repr.1999).
3. A. Ruttenberg and S. Maital, *Cracking the Creativity Code: Zoom In, Zoom Out, Zoom In for More Creativity, Fun and Success* (SAGE Publications, 2014).
4. Martin Wolf, *Financial Times*, http://www.ft.com/intl/cms/s/0/1dc01f08-e90c-11e5-bb79-2303682345c8.html#axzz44Ir1LtHd, accessed September 22, 2016.
5. All the graphs in this section are taken from the Trading Economics website, www.tradingeconomics.com, accessed September 22, 2016.
6. UK Investor Show Magazine, March 2016, https://issuu.com/ukinvestormagazine/docs/ukim-mar_2016, accessed September 22, 2016.
7. www.tradingeconomics.com, accessed September 22, 2016.
8. http://www.oecdbetterlifeindex.org/countries/, accessed September 22, 2016.
9. www.transparency.org, accessed September 22, 2016.
10. http://www.heritage.org/index/, accessed September 22, 2016.
11. See www.doingbusiness.org. accessed September 22, 2016.
12. https://www.imd.org/wcc, accessed September 22, 2016.
13. http://reports.weforum.org/global-competitiveness-report-2015-2016/, accessed September 22, 2016.
14. https://publicadministration.un.org/egovkb/Portals/egovkb/Documents/un/2014-Survey/E-Gov_Complete_Survey-2014.pdf, accessed September 22, 2016.
15. http://www.cleantech.com/wp-content/uploads/2014/08/Global_Cleantech_Innov_Index_2014.pdf, accessed September 22, 2016.
16. https://www.globalinnovationindex.org/userfiles/file/reportpdf/gii-full-report-2015-v6.pdf, accessed September 22, 2016.
17. http://www.bloomberg.com/news/articles/2016-01-19/these-are-the-world-s-most-innovative-economies, accessed September 22, 2016.
18. http://www.oecd.org/pisa/keyfindings/pisa-2012-results.htm, accessed September 22, 2016. For higher education: http://www.shanghairanking.com, accessed September 22, 2016.

EPILOGUE

Dear Reader:

Having mastered the eight tools of "Smartonomics" in the preceding pages, you are now ready to read economic signals clearly and accurately as you prepare to assess the risks and opportunities of your organization's continued/potential engagement with various geographies/regions/countries across the world. However, as the book has repeatedly highlighted, the world is increasingly characterized by uncertainties like never before. This aspect is poignantly brought out in the subtitle of our book: *Smartonomics: Simple, Powerful Macroeconomic Tools for Success in an Uncertain World.*

While there are myriad sources of potential uncertainties in the world today, we will highlight a few that are fairly typical and cut across many countries. The idea behind presenting these is to sensitize you, global manager, to the fact that there are many factors outside the realm of rational economics that can derail the most well-intentioned plans. As a manager, you will have to keep your antennae well-tuned to catch these signals and factor them into your planning.

Environmental and ecological degradation: Nearly every part of the earth has been affected by the accelerating pace of deleterious effects of global warming, caused by the large-scale human economic activity and its consequences. Changing weather patterns and consequent non-predictability of weather, and the resulting frequent extremities of weather patterns are wreaking havoc across large swathes of populations, causing untold misery especially among the poorest of poor in country after country. This has raised fundamental questions about the sustainability of the current economic models and, in a broader context, of the world itself. While the inadequacies of current economic models such as capitalism in its current form is widely acknowledged, what the new alternate models should be are far from being clear.

Increasing crunch and pressure on natural resources: The rising aspirations of exploding populations among the developing countries are putting tremendous pressures on natural resources of all kinds. In many of these countries, forests and other natural habitats are vanishing at astonishing rates. Forests and river beds as well as lake beds are fast vanishing, as human settlements proliferate. This has put enormous pressure on natural ecosystems and drying up of water sources, in turn causing pressure on electric power generation. City after city, town after town, especially in the developing world, are fast becoming concrete jungles. The already scarce green cover is now becoming a distant memory. Once pristine lake beds are now flourishing urban sprawls. The massive human misery caused by intense and unprecedented rains during the last decade in Chennai, Mumbai, and Kedarnath, all in India, to name just a few of such incidents, with massive attendant loss of life and property, are ominous signals of a bleak future if urgent reversal of these trends is not initiated.

Man–animal conflict: Forests being cleared at an unprecedented rate, especially in developing countries, due to mining and related industrial activities, have resulted in wildlife, such as elephants, tigers, leopards, and so on., being driven out of their habitat. In search of food and water, they go on rampage, attacking proximate human settlements. The resulting mayhem destroys livelihoods of people and results in untold tragedies to both men and animals.

High level of intolerance and consequent violence: In a culture where "might is right," anyone who expresses anything against strong, vested interests is silenced brutally. As the pressures on various fronts build up in the country, the levels of intolerance for people to express alternate viewpoints have greatly increased, resulting in unleashing of violence on those who voice non-mainstream views. This trend makes a mockery of a democratic country.

Increasing aspirations among people, leading to widespread materialism and the "I, me, and myself" culture: With increased global communication, Internet, entertainment, and so on, the world is truly a global village. Consequently, people in the remotest parts of the world have raised their aspirations on possible lifestyles to emulate those of people in the developed world. While this has its positive connotations, it has also resulted in escalation of both aspiration and discontentment. With larger sections of the population seeking to greatly enhance their lifestyles, the question of the sustainability of the planet comes into stark prominence. One of the unintended consequences of this is the unleashing of greed and seeking of more and more material wealth as the key indicator of one's progress in life. As Mahatma Gandhi said, "The world has enough for everyone's needs, but not enough for everyone's greed."

Increasing economic inequality: As some sections of the society race ahead, large sections of the society continue to wallow in abject poverty, with little hope for improving their condition. The increasing importance of services in economies has made millions of people who are dependent on marginal farming and sundry unskilled labor practically irrelevant to the GDP of the country. This has resulted in increasing concentration of wealth in the hands of a privileged few, with large sections of humanity left to fend for themselves in a hopeless vicious circle of extreme poverty. As a consequence, incidence of suicides in these strata of society such as the notorious farmer suicides in India, which is a sickeningly recurrent phenomenon exacerbated by uncertain weather patterns and usury money lenders, has become everyday occurrence.

Terrorism: Terrorism is one of the biggest threats to the world. No part of the world is exempt from its deathly shadow. It is truly what can be classified as a "wicked" problem. There are clearly no solutions to it in sight and every country is grappling with this horror.

Breakdown of traditional cultures and consequent homogenization of cultures: Historically, most countries had their own very rich cultures that kept humanity in reasonable check on doing the right things and refraining from doing the wrong things. With the pervasiveness of the Internet, MTV, and much more, cultures have essentially become homogenized. While this phenomenon has its advantages, it has also left large parts of the world clueless on the way forward and led to widespread disenchantment. Such breakdown of culture is particularly visible in many "traditional" cultures. This has resulted in the lowering of empathy for fellow human beings, low levels of tolerance, inability to bear stress leading to unpredictable behavior including violence, breakdown of health and well-being of people, and many more aberrations of modern societies in many parts of the world.

Country-specific phenomena: Each country has its own peculiar undercurrents that have also to be factored in by the manager who wants to understand the economic landscape of particular geographies and markets. In the following, we explore some of them in the context of a specific country,

India, just to illustrate the need for understanding such country-specific phenomena.

- 24/7 Work culture: Work-life balance in many organizations in India has essentially collapsed, catalyzed by technology and aggressive competition to move ahead in life, as also the horrendous traffic situation in major cities that necessitates employees to spend long hours on the roads. It results in burnout among youngsters, high stress levels, road rage that requires very small triggers to explode, and lack of physical and mental well-being.
- Politics in the workplace: It is said that people do not leave organizations; they leave bosses. In a very heterogeneous society like India, divided on religious, regional, caste, and community lines, politics in organizations is a reality. Many high potential professionals end up leaving high paying jobs, simply because they feel disillusioned with the political maneuvering that is a reality in many organizations.
- Corruption: India ranks very poorly in the community of nations on corruption. While there are efforts at the central government level to improve transparency and reduce corruption, for a complex country like India with multiple levels of governance (central, state, regional, and local-level governments), it is a long journey to rid the country of this bane, with no easy solutions in sight.
- Lawlessness: The pervasive lawlessness that one experiences in India comes through vested interests and the noxious collusion of politics, bureaucracy, mafia, and business in varying proportions in different situations. Related to this are tax evasion, the feeling of "might is right," entitlement syndrome, perception that judiciary that can be purchased at a price, inordinate delays in getting legal redress, extensive deployment of black money resulting in a "parallel economy," and so on.

The perception among the rich, powerful, and mighty that anything in the country can be purchased at a price is perhaps a major driver for huge defaults of massive loans given to some of the major corporate houses by banks. For instance, the default of loans by the top about 50 corporates cumulatively is over ₹ 5 trillion (1 US dollar = about ₹ 70). The banks are left with no option but to write-off the loans and take a huge hit on their balance sheets. The defaulters essentially walk out scot free! The resulting threat to the financial health of the country is very grave. Once again solutions to this pervasive problem are evasive.

- Vote bank politics: This is a major factor in Indian politics. It results in the political party in power and those in the opposition working at cross purposes, resulting in policy paralysis. The country has been witnessing this strange spectacle over the last two years. While the ruling party has absolute majority in the lower house of the Parliament, consisting of elected representatives, the major opposition party which has the majority in the upper house of the Parliament, consisting of nominated representatives, has no intent on allowing any major proposals to pass, resulting in near paralysis in policy-making. The vote bank politics also results in political parties of totally different ideological hues coming together as strange bed-fellows, just to stymie the ruling party's functioning. In all this cross-fire, the interest of the country and the common people is relegated to last place.

- Inadequate world-class infrastructure: Although there are huge opportunities for growth of the Indian economy, this has been constrained for decades by inadequate infrastructure. This includes roads, power generation, industrial parks, ease of acquiring land, access to water for industrial use, and a host of other related issues. Over the last few years, the government has opened up this sector for private investment through the public–private partnership model. However, the payback period for such projects is typically very long and is plagued with many uncertainties, resulting in lukewarm response from the private sector to get into highly capital-intensive infrastructure development. The constrained infrastructure has attendant problems such as safety on roads, to take just one of many examples. Indian roads consequently have poor safety records on the highways and urban roads are choked resulting in long commute times and very high pollution levels.

- Pollution: Over 600,000 Indians die prematurely each year due to air pollution, which is now the fifth leading cause of death in the country. Six Indian cities including Delhi are more polluted than Beijing, China, which has traditionally had the dubious distinction as being among the most polluted big city in the world! In many cities in India, the pollution levels are off the chart. This puts tremendous burden on healthcare costs. The resulting compromise on the health and well-being of employees impacts their effectiveness.
- Skewed female-to-male ratio, leading to many shocking acts of crime against women: India's skewed gender ratio that is distorted by the practice of gender selection in favor of boys has been responsible for frequent and shocking acts of violence against women, with even young girls not being spared. The ratio of female-to-male population in the country is low at 940:1000, with some parts of the country having ratio as low as 800:1000. For organizations operating in the country, this puts additional pressure on ensuring safety of women employees at the work place as well as to ensure for their commute to/from work.

In the end, Smartonomics is about empowering bold and intelligent global managers to use a simple set of macroeconomic tools to help themselves and their organizations endure and in the end, prevail. It is our hope that Smartonomics creates value for our readers so that they too can go on to create significant value for their workers, shareholders, and customers.

The basic logic is very simple. In order to create value for the world, and find meaning for your lives, you need to understand the world in which you live. And the world is becoming both more complex and more unstable. This is why we have written Smartonomics. You, our readers, will determine whether we have succeeded.

INDEX

24/7 work culture, 225
Abe, Shinzo, 102
animal spirits, 123
ant countries, benchmarking, 37
Ariely, Dan, 192
austerity, 131, 145
automobiles, 212

Big Mac, 157, 170
biotechnology, 212
Bloomberg Business Week, 177
booms and busts, 202
    animal spirits, 123
    boom–bust cycle, 119
    business cycles, history of, 129
    complex mosaic of, 130
    consumer sentiment, 128
    credit cycles, 133
    economics, 120
    initial shocks, 131
    rational irrationality, 125
    real business cycles, 132
    twin deficit approach, 135
borrowers, country risk, 42
Boston Consulting Group, 185

burgernomics, 156
business cycles, 119, 129
business, 12

central banks, 33, 54, 92
China, 1, 43
Christakis, Nicholas, 125
CIA website, 218
cleantech, 219
cold turkey, 150
consequent homogenization, 224
consequent violence, 223
Consumer Price Index (CPI), 66
corruption, 225
cost-push inflation, 81
country risk, borrowers and lenders, 42
credit cards, 33
credit cycles, 133
credit default swaps, 177
crude oil prices, 150

Day, Peter, 121
deflation, 54, 58, 74
demand-pull inflation, 81

demand-side inflation, 68
depression, 119
dollars, 142
downturn, boom–bust cycle, 119
Draghi, Mario, 65
due diligence, 2, 7
   budget deficit, 206
   checklist, 200
   corruption perception ranking, 209
   government debt, 207

e-government, 219
ecological degradation, 222
economic inequality, 223
education, 219
environmental degradation, 222

European Central Bank (ECB), 65, 143, 148
European Union, 7365

Facebook, 189
fatal internal flaw, 163
Federal Reserve Open Market Committee (FOMC), 90, 91
Financial Times, 218
'flation, 58
   China, 64
   Consumer Price Index, 66
   demand-side inflation, 68
   European Union, 73
   global managers, 82
   India, 7, 164
   Japan, 7, 263
   Russia, 72
   South Africa, 62
   supply-side inflation, 68
   United States, 60
   Venezuela, 61
freedom, 218
Friedman, Milton, 98

gap, 203
   Bloomberg Business Week, 177
   income, cumulative distribution, 179
   Industrial Revolution, 188
   long-term wealth distribution, 180
   mysteries of capital and de Soto, 175
   Oxfam report, 174
   pyramid, bottom of, 182
   pyramid, top of, 185
   rich and poor, 50
Gladwell, Malcolm, 4
global competitiveness, 219
global due diligence, 2
global risk protocol, 125
global wealth, 49
Govindarajan, Vijay, 185
gratification, 31
gross capital formation, 25, 39
gross domestic product (GDP), 3, 25, 200–15
growth, 23
   United States, 16
growth world, 53

healthcare, 213
Heritage Foundation, 218
IMD World Competitiveness Yearbook, 217

inadequate world-class infrastructure, 226
index of corruption perception (CPI), 218
India, 7164
   due diligence,
      budget deficit, 206
      corruption perception ranking, 209
      government debt, 207
Industrial Revolution, 188

inflation, 54, 58, 73, 201
  consumer price, 85
  demand-side, 68
  forces, 85
  return of, 90
  supply-side, 68
information technology, 213
innovation, 219
interest, 201
International Monetary Fund
  (IMF), 19
Internet of Everything, 190
intolerance, 223
investment, comparing countries,
  36
Israel, 85

Japan, 72

Keynes, John Maynard, 131 123
Krugman, Paul, 145

lawlessness, 225
lenders, country risk, 42
Lucas, Robert, 120

man-animal conflict, 222
Marshall Plan, 218
Marx, Karl, 133, 177
money, 20 188
  addiction, 150
  central banks, creating, 92
  fatal flaw, 103
  mechanics of, 89
  momentum equals mass times
    velocity, 96
  mountain of, 99
  numbers, crunching, 103
  torrents of capital, 142
  velocity of, 107

Nestle, 185
net capital formation, 39

New Israeli Shekel (NIS), 85

oil prices, 150
optimism, 127
Organization for Economic
  Cooperation and
  Development (OECD),
  218
Ormerod, Paul, 121, 122

Peres, Shimon, 85
personal banks, 33
pessimism, 127
pharma, 212
Piketty, Thomas, 49
political cycle, 131
politics, 225
pollution, 227
Prahalad, C.K., 182
purchasing power parity (PPP),
  155
rational irrationality, 125

Rawls, John, 191
real business cycles, 132
recession, 119
Roosevelt, Franklin, 105
Russia, 72

Saft, James, 154
Samuelson, Paul, 131
Saudi Arabia, 151
saving, comparing countries, 36
seigniorage, 164
short-term interest rates, 146
Simon, Herbert, 122
skewed female-to-male ratio, 227
South Africa, 62
stagflation, 72
strategic inflection point (SIP), 110
supply-side inflation, 68
systematic systemic risk
  management, 3

Tata Nano, 185
telecom, 212
terrorism, 224
torrents of capital, 203
    austerity, 145
    buck passing, 160
    consequences of, 169
    fatal internal flaw, 163
    global trade stagnation, 153
    oilprices, 150
    short-term interest rates, 146
    speculation, 165
    world flooded with money, 142
Trading Economics, 216
traditional cultures, 224

twin deficit approach, 135

United States, 43, 60
University of Chicago, 118
US Congress, 100

Venezuela, 61, 69
vote bank politics, 226

Wall Street Journal, 218
World Bank, 216, 219
World Competitiveness Yearbook, 46

zoom out process, 212

ABOUT THE AUTHORS

Shlomo Maital is Senior Research Fellow at the Samuel Neaman Institute for Advanced Studies, Technion, and Professor (Emeritus) at Technion–Israel Institute of Technology, Haifa, Israel. He was the academic director of TIM–Technion Institute of Management, Israel's leading executive leadership development institute, and a pioneer in action-learning methods, from 1998 to 2009, working with over 200 high-tech companies and startups. He was summer visiting professor for 20 years at the MIT Sloan School of Management for Management of Technology MSc program, teaching over 1,000 research and development (R&D) engineers from 40 countries. He is the author, co-author, or editor of 12 books, including *Cracking the Creativity Code* (2014), *Technion Nation* (2012), *Global Risk/Global Opportunity* (SAGE, 2009), *Innovation Management* (SAGE, 2007; 2nd edition, 2012), and *Executive Economics* (1994), translated into seven languages. He was co-founder of SABE–Society for Advancement of Behavioral Economics.

D.V.R. Seshadri is Clinical Full Professor of Business at the Indian School of Business, Hyderabad. His areas of interest are business-to-business marketing, corporate entrepreneurship, and strategy. He holds a BTech (mechanical engineering) from Indian Institute of Technology (IIT), Madras, an MS (engineering sciences) from University of California, San Diego, and a fellow title (doctorate) from IIM Ahmedabad, with specialization in production and quantitative methods. He had over 15 years of industrial experience prior to joining academics since 2000. He teaches in the various programs at IIM, Bangalore, in his areas of interest and at IIM, Ahmedabad, in the one-year executive MBA program. He also teaches in various executive development programs at IIM, Bangalore. He works closely with several companies, providing them training/consulting services in his areas of expertise.

Over the last 10 years, he has developed a number of case studies and authored a number of research papers. He has co-authored three books: *Innovation Management* (2007) and *Global Risk/Global Opportunity* (2010) with Professor Shlomo Maital, and the Indian adaptation of the book *Business Market Management (B2B): Understanding, Creating and Delivering Value* (2010) with James Anderson, James Narus, and Das Narayandas.